TIME, EXPECTATIONS AND UNCERTAINTY IN ECONOMICS

G. L. S. Shackle by Oliver Thomas, 1983

Time, Expectations and Uncertainty in Economics

Selected Essays of G. L. S. Shackle

Edited by J. L. Ford
Emeritus Professor of Economics
University of Birmingham

Edward Elgar

Published by
Edward Elgar Publishing Limited
Gower House
Croft Road
Aldershot
Hants GU11 3HR
England

Edward Elgar Publishing Company
Old Post Road
Brookfield
Vermont 05036
USA

British Library Cataloguing in Publication Data

Shackle, G. L. S. (George Lennox Sherman)
    Time, expectations and uncertainty in economics: selected
    essays.
    1. Economics. Theories
    I. Title II. Ford, J. L. (James Lorne), *1939–*
    330.1

ISBN 1 85278 362 1

Printed in Great Britain by
Billing & Sons Ltd, Worcester

Contents

Preface

In April 1989, Edward Elgar asked me if I would be willing to edit an anthology of George Shackle's published papers. I agreed with alacrity because I feel that his substantial contributions to the literature should be more accessible, and also because some of those contributions, especially on the origins of the business cycle, have not been accorded the prominence they deserve, even by George Shackle himself.

In the Introduction, I briefly explain the background to the essays reprinted here, set in the context of the areas of economics in which George Shackle's interests have lain. In it I try to tread that careful line between descriptive content and critical assessment, for this is *not* a book about George Shackle and his work. However, it does seem sensible to provide some marginal comments of assessment, drawing upon the remarks of some of his peers, as well as to provide a comprehensive bibliography of his publications.

It will be noticed that the essays are facsimilies of the original journal articles. This was George Shackle's wish, and it does preserve the original pagination which is often helpful to researchers and commentators. I have been kindly assisted by the editors of the various journals whom I have formally acknowledged, but I have also received much help from George and Catherine Shackle in obtaining off-prints of key papers. I would like to extend my thanks to them for that particular assistance, and also for their general encouragement of this project. Finally, I would like to express my thanks to Mrs Maureen Hyde and to Ms Penny Willetts for preparing my share of this anthology with speed, efficiency and much-needed good humour.

J. L. Ford

Acknowledgements

I am grateful to several editors and to the publisher of the University of Liverpool Press for granting permission for articles originally appearing in their academic journals or other publications to be reproduced here. The full list of papers comprising this volume together with the original places of publication are recorded below, in their order of appearance.

'The Complex Nature of Time as a Concept in Economics', *Economia Internazionale*, Vol. 7, No. 4, November 1954, pp 743–757.

'Time and Thought', *British Journal for the Philosophy of Science*, Vol. 9, No. 36, 1959, pp 285–298.

'Time and Choice', Keynes Lecture in Economics, 1976, *Proceeding of the British Academy*, Vol. 62, pp 309–329.

'The Expectational Dynamics of the Individual', *Economica*, Vol. 10, No. 38, May 1943, pp 99–129.

'Expectation and Cardinality', *Economic Journal*, Vol. 66, No. 262, June 1956, pp 211–219.

'An Analysis of Speculative Choice', *Economica*, Vol. 12, No. 43, February 1945, pp 10–21.

'A Theory of Investment Decisions', *Oxford Economic Papers*, No. 6, April 1942, pp 77–94.

'Dynamics of the Crisis: A Suggestion', *Review of Economic Studies*, Vol. 4, No. 11, February 1937, pp 108–122.

'Some Notes on Monetary Theories of the Trade Cycle', *Review of Economic Studies*, Vol. 1, No. 1, October 1933, pp 27–38.

'The Multiplier in Closed and Open Systems', *Oxford Economic Papers*, No. 2, May 1939, pp 135–144.

'Interest-rates and the Pace of Investment', *Economic Journal*, Vol. 56, No. 2211, March 1946, pp 1–17.

'General Thought-Schemes and the Economist', Woolwich Economic Paper No. 2, 1963, pp 1–20.

'Economics and Sincerity', *Oxford Economic Papers*, Vol. 5, No. 1, March 1953, pp 1–12.

'Evolutions of Thought in Economics', *Banca Nazionale del Lavoro Quarterly Review*, No. 132, March 1980, pp 15–27.

What makes an Economist? Liverpool, Liverpool University Press, 1953.

Introduction

In one regard or another George Shackle's concern with what he has himself labelled his 'Pilgrimage in Economics' (Shackle 1983) has been with the concept of Time. One of the most succinct and pellucid summaries he has provided on the premise (or philosophy) underlying his insistent need for economics to be ever vigilant over the role of Time is given in his work of that same title, *Time in Economics* (1958, which contains *inter alia* his F. de Vries Lectures in Economic Theory delivered in Holland in 1957). By way of summary of his first lecture, 'The complex concept of economic time,' he writes:

> ... for the individual human consciousness time is not a mathematician's space nor a historian's panorama but a moment. In this solitary moment all the consequences that the decision-maker seeks or accepts must necessarily be contained. These consequences must therefore be experiences by imaginative anticipation. As the basis of these anticipations the individual cannot avail himself of a unique self-important picture free of doubts or counter-suggestions, but has in mind a set of rival diverse hypotheses. The word *uncertainty* however suggests an objectively-existing future about which we lack knowledge, rather than a void to be filled by new creation. Uncertainty thus comes to be looked on as a reasonable disadvantage rather than the essential freedom of the individual imagination to create afresh from moment to moment. Yet again, if this freedom were unbounded, if there were no discernible link between action and consequence, decision would be needless and useless. To afford enjoyment by anticipation, imagination must work within a sense of the possible, of the rules of the game, of the essential artistic constraint.
>
> In speaking of freedom, what do we imply? That decisions can be creative acts each injecting something essentially new into the world process: we imply the possibility of *inspiration*. In the universe, without inspiration decisions are empty; in the universe without order, without links between action and consequence, decisions are meaningless. Between these two extremes ... is there room for the world of inspiration and order, the world of continuing creation by the instrument of decisions made by men? (Shackle, 1958, pp 33–34 italics in original).

It is precisely that last kind of model which George Shackle assumes does exist, for it alone – the middle of his three world scenarios – entails that economic (or any) decision-making is 'non-empty', so rendering it logically valid to analyse decisions under uncertainty.

But that model is by definition one predicated or driven by inspiration. What interpretation does Professor Shackle give to that many-faceted world? In short-hand he defines it to be 'the birth of fundamentally unpredictable thoughts' (Shackle, 1958, p 23). In long-hand he describes this to be the consequences of his view that the human mind is creative; the individual will create imagined consequences which will follow from his own actions and not be limited in his choice by objectively given information. Decisions are founded on subjective data. There can be no such thing as a 'complete' list of items, predetermined, from which an individual can choose.

This notion of inspiration has a profound consequence in Shackle's scheme for the modelling of economic processes, whether of the micro or the macro (economy level) kind. It leads inexorably to the admission that economic dynamics, with its formal, natural linkage of economic variables through time, is impossible. For only if economic time has the same meaning as time does in the Natural Sciences can there be any validity in economic dynamics, set out either in the form of differential equations or of difference equations ('period analysis'). Such is Shackle's contention:

> In the classical dynamics of the physicist time is merely and purely a mathematical variable. The essence of his scheme of thought is the fully abstract idea of function, the idea of some working model or coded procedure which, applied to any particular and specified value or set of values of one or more independent variables, generates a value of a dependent variable. For the independent variable in a mental construction of this kind, *time* is a misnomer ... The solution of the differential equation, if it can be found, is complete in an instantaneous and timeless sense.
>
> This timelessness ... abolishes the distinction between past and future. The physicist has, within the stated limits of his problem, complete, perfect and indisputable *knowledge* of where his particle will be at any instant; the very nature of human consciousness ... depends ... upon *ignorance* of the future ... upon the necessity to live in one moment at a time (Shackle, 1959, pp 23–24; italics in original).

Shackle argues that the scientific concept of time has been very prominent in economic model-building, as explained in most of his writings on methodology, especially relating time to macroeconomics. This concept he greatly deprecates since in his view it produces empty-box economics. Models constituted on such a concept, linking sequences of moments, are essentially mechanical; they are engines purporting to describe growth or business cycles or both. There is no scope within their scheme of things for expectations, human decision and hence, in macromodels, for *invention* with its consequent impact on investment, output and employment. Invention necessarily requires inspiration. Also, the decision to invest in any machine which only incorporates the past 'state of the acts technology' is founded on expectations; it is not predetermined.

Furthermore, the models which have been formulated to consider a disaggregated economic system at any point in time cannot escape criticism. The neoclassical General Equilibrium Model is one which is totally devoid of uncertainty because it is timeless: it only functions because all information about markets (and so about the behaviour of market participants) is available to all economic agents. There is pre-reconciliation of all plans to sell/hire labour, sell/purchase commodities etc.

These themes which have emerged from an investigation of the concept and role of time in economic thought occur and recur throughout all of the journal articles, book reviews, monographs and textbooks which George Shackle has published since he was researching for his (first) Doctorate at the London School of Economics in the 1930s (he was later awarded a second D. Phil by Oxford in 1940). Whilst the recent questioning of some of the previously accepted fundamental laws of physics has reintroduced uncertainty as a major variable into that discipline and has led to a new perspective on the nature of time, the essential attributes of economic time *per se* as described by Shackle remain untouched. So too do the themes which he extracted from them.

It is those themes, centred around the twin concepts of Time and Uncertainty, which I have endeavoured to capture in this volume – a kind of quintessential Shackle. However, I have limited my selection of material to Shackle's published papers: I have not felt it proper to draw on any of the chapters of his several books, which all embrace issues covered in his papers. I have also deliberately refrained from reprinting any of the essays which appeared in the recent collection of Shackle's papers and review articles (1989) edited by Stephen Frowen. Shackle himself produced two anthologies of his own work for the period 1933–1954 and for 1955–1964, which appeared in 1955 and 1966 respectively. I have utilised four essays from the first volume, *Uncertainty in Economics and Other Reflections*. Two of these concern the multiplier and investment; the other two, to adopt George Shackle's own nomenclature, relate to the philosophy of economics. The first two appeared in 1939 and 1946; the several other major papers which he published from 1933 to 1950, Shackle has never reproduced. These papers are the original published versions of his seminal contributions to two major topics: the business cycle, and decision-making under uncertainty by firms and households.

The key theme which Shackle derives from his notion of time is the need for a theory of decision-making under *uncertainty*. His concepts of time and decision exclude any role for decision-making under risk, which was the paradigm in the literature in the 1930s and 1940s for analysing decision-making related to choices confronting the firm or the household, e.g. to invest in this or that machine; to produce this or that new product; to select this or that portfolio of financial claims ... He set about the task of providing what was a radical alternative to the risk-based probability, and (then) expected utility, approach to the analysis of decision-making. His alternative, predicated on the view that economic time was different from physical time, started from the premise that in economic decision-taking, an 'experiment' i.e. choice of action cannot be repeated infinitely. The act of choice will alter the circumstances surrounding the original choice itself; an individual could easily lose his fortune so that, for example, he could not keep on selecting a portfolio of financial assets in order to avail himself of the *knowledge* contained in a probability distribution for its monetary yields. Shackle proposed the concept of *potential surprise* as a replacement for that of probability; using that as a measure (indicator) of uncertainty, he constructed his own theory of expectation and of decision-making under uncertainty. This postulates that the decision-maker will ultimately focus on the 'best' and the 'worst' outcomes, rather than use some form of weighted average of all possible outcomes, in deciding upon his 'action-choice'.

Part II of this collection is devoted to that theory. It is preceded, as part of a natural order, by 'Time' in Part I where Professor Shackle's classification of time in economics and its implications on economic theory are set out. The first paper, 'The Complex Nature of Time as a Concept of Economics' (1954), in a sense provides background for his first lecture reprinted in *Time in Economics* (1958) from which we quoted at the outset. The other papers, 'Time and Thought' (1959) and 'Time and Choice' (1976), build on the first essay. There is an inevitable, unavoidable, overlap between Part II and 'Time and Choice' (incidentally declared by Shackle in the 1986 edition of *Who's Who in Economics* to be one of his outstanding papers).

Indeed, turning now to Part II, we note that in the essay 'The Expectational Dynamics of the Individual' (1943), Professor Shackle outlines his theory of expectation and of decision-making under uncertainty, using it to consider issues such as the 'change of own expectations'. Such a revision of expectations had had a key role to play in one of the theories Shackle previously formulated to explain the business cycle (in 1937 and 1938): but in that theory the revision of expectations was not founded upon the ideas in Part II since these were not yet developed. In the next paper, 'An Analysis of Speculative Choice' (1945), Shackle applies his theory to financial investment and to speculative choice. These two papers constituted the substantial part of the monograph which Shackle published in 1949 entitled *Expectation in Economics*, widely regarded not only as Shackle's, but also as one of *the*, most original contributions to economics. C. F. Carter (now Professor Sir Charles Carter) concluded his review of that monograph as follows:

All these solutions [to the investment-decision] are founded upon Mr Shackle's ideas, in that they involve *focus-values*; and here his contribution is fundamental. A final example will suggest the wide range of subjects which now require rethinking. The publication of Von Neumann and Morgenstern's *Theory of Games and Economic Behaviour* (1944, 1947) was an event in the economic world, since it opened up a new understanding of the nature of bargaining in small groups. But the keystone of that theory is the proof that the zero-sum two-person game is always strictly determined', and this proof depends upon the possibility that the players may vary their 'strategies' or schemes of play from game to game according to certain probabilities. In other words, the theory makes essential use of frequency-ratio probability. It does not follow that its applications to economics will be invalid, but clearly the whole theory will require careful reconsideration. (Carter, 1950, pp 104–105; italics in original.)

In Part II, the essay 'A Theory of Investment Decisions' (1942), besides providing a summary of Shackle's theory, demonstrates with great clarity how it could be used to explain investment in physical as opposed to financial assets. Interestingly, Professor Shackle himself considers this to be one of his five best journal articles (according to the 1986 *Who's Who in Economics*), even though he never reprinted it. The other essay in Part II, 'Expectation and Cardinality' (1956), provides a clear statement of the concept of potential surprise and of its measurement, whilst simultaneously giving a brief but lucid statement on the difference between potential surprise and probability. The paper was originally composed as an answer to critics of potential surprise and of his theory, especially Charles Carter in his review of the second edition of *Expectation in Economics* (1952) in the *Economic Journal* (1953). The proposition which Carter there advanced, that it would be impossible to obtain a unique ranking based upon two other rankings, became known as Carter's error; it was acknowledged as such by Carter himself and was later formally proved mistaken by M. W. M. Gorman (1957). In the paper reprinted here, Shackle provides his own refutation of the error, but of more importance is the lucid exposition he is forced to provide of some of his key concepts.

It did not seem appropriate to reprint the essays in Part II in chronological order. Instead, the paper describing his theory in detail comes first, followed by that on cardinality and thence by the two papers applying the theory to investment. The paper on investment in plant and machinery is placed last because it inevitably overlaps with Part III, providing a natural lead-in to it.

The main theme of Part III is the linkage between expectation and investment coupled with the linkage between investment and output (employment). The essays have a Keynesian complexion: emphasis is

placed on the relation between expectation and output, especially as a
vehicle for generating the business cycle via the multiplier process. Professor Shackle proposes a theory of the cycle which rests, first, upon the
over-pessimistic expectations of entrepreneurs, where their *ex ante* expectations regarding the profitability of investment in plant and machine are
below *ex post* results: expectations are revised upwards so activating a
boom; second, upon the over-optimistic expectations of entrepreneurs
which *mutatis mutandis* will provide a slump. In the paper, 'Dynamics of
the Crisis: A Suggestion' (1937), Professor Shackle outlines that theory,
though he emphasises those factors which cause the boom to end and the
crisis or slump to develop. Shackle's theory is rooted in his concept of
economic time; accordingly, it is in sharp contrast to the business cycle
engine as developed in the late 1930s, culminating in Hicks's 1950 trade
cycle theory.

Shackle's 1937 paper was incorporated in his Doctoral thesis, *Expectation, Investment and Income* (1938). In that monograph he also proposed
an alternative mechanism through which the business cycle could be
generated: the process of *invention*, hence its concomitant, innovation, as
the initiator of bursts of investment activity; booms and slumps economy-
wide could be caused by the *bunching* of innovations. Shackle never fully
described the process by which such a configuration of investment intentions by entrepreneurs could be set in motion. However, he does provide
an elegant, lucid, formal exposition of how, along general Schupeterian
lines, the business cycle can be explained, and how the 'expectations-
investment' cycle can be superimposed on the 'invention-investment' led
cycle. In his review of Shackle's 1938 monograph in the *Economic Journal*
of that year, Hugh Townshend wrote:

> If it is, as I think, not too much to say that the book makes some advance at
> almost every point it touches (even on the analysis of such a familiar concept as
> the 'multiplier'), this is due to the author's avoidance, practically throughout,
> of anything approaching the slipshod either in terminology or in reasoning. It is
> an unusual characteristic of the book that its most original parts are also the
> best parts (Townshend, 1938, p 521).

One criticism of Shackle's study of the business cycle raised by Professor
Townshend was that, even though he had given some consideration to
expectations and the long-term rate of interest, Shackle had largely neglected the potential role of monetary factors in the cycle. In fact, for
Shackle, ever since the publication of the *General Theory*, the fundamental
master-stroke of Keynes was to invent the theory of liquidity preference; it
is the desire for liquidity when expectations force net investment to decline
which is the manifestation of that theory. However, Shackle had given

some consideration pre-*General Theory* to the influence of monetary variables on the cause and course of the trade cycle. His main contribution in
this regard is reprinted here: 'Some Notes on Monetary Theories of the
Trade Cycle' (1933) which was prompted by the dispute between Hayek
and Keynes following the appearance of Hayek's *Prices and Production*
(1931) and Keynes's *A Treatise on Money* (1930). We might comment here
too that in the 1986 *Who's Who of Economics*, Professor Shackle cites this
as one of his major papers.

Part III also includes two essays on the multiplier and interest rates and
investment, both of which are concerned with the impact of investment on
the economy. The former, 'The Multiplier in Closed and Open Systems'
(1939), distils the ideas on expectations and the multiplier (differentiating
between those which are *ex ante* and *ex post*) which form the fulcrum of
Shackle's 'expectations-investment' theory of the business cycle. The
paper also extends the consideration of the multiplier to the open economy. This essay was reprinted in Shackle's first anthology (1956), as we
have noted previously; but even though literature on the multiplier is now
voluminous and embraces full-length works, it should not be regulated to
the archives. For Shackle's essay provides not only one of the clearest
expositions of the multiplier concept, but offers real insight into why the
multiplier mechanism can exist at all.

'Interest-rates and the Pace of Investment' (1953) implicitly considers
expectations and investment and also tacitly covers investment and the
macroeconomy. Its immediate focus, however, is the likely impact of the
rate of interest on the rate of net investment. The paper seeks to provide a
rigorous explanation as to the conditions relating to investment (e.g., that
it is long-term in nature) which must appertain if investment is to be
significantly sensitive to changes in the 'cost of capital'. The essay itself
was prompted as a means of rationalising the findings of the group of
Oxford economists who (whilst investigating in 1938 by a study of business practice, the relevance of a number of propositions in economic
theory) discovered little responsiveness of investment to alterations in the
rate of interest.

Professor Shackle has made several excursions into the philosophy of
economics, sometimes together with, occasionally separately from, his
discussion of Time. Part IV reproduces just four of his many contributions. While referring to his view of time, they convey his antithesis to
general equilibrium and to (mathematical) dynamic economics. However,
they also contain his valuable, lucid and erudite opinions on what economists should be doing, how economic thought-contents should be formulated, what the fundamental developments in economic theory have been
and how these have evolved. The essays have been reprinted in this

sequence: 'General Thought-Schemes and the Economist' (1963); 'Economics and Sincerity' (1953); 'Evolution of Thought in Economics' (1980), and 'What Makes an Economist' (1953).

The last-mentioned essay was the text of Professor Shackle's Inaugural Lecture at the University of Liverpool. Despite the many years that have elapsed since it was written, this essay is still full of wisdom and insight into the value of economics as well as the attributes, background training and interests required of a good economist. It is a cameo of a piece which will stand future tests of time not just because of its content but because of the style of its composition. As Charles Carter commented, when reviewing *Uncertainty in Economics and other Reflections* (1955):

> ... in expounding his own ideas he has the invaluable service of a command of the English language such as few economists since Marshall have possessed. He is a master of the homely but apposite example ...; he can lighten his argument by the sudden literary allusion, bringing in the Ancient Mariner or a clerihew with the deftness of Professor Robertson quoting Lewis Carroll. Like the psalmist, he is sometimes repetitive, driving home his point by the repeated light blows of a well-aimed hammer. The advantage of his style is nowhere better illustrated than in his final essay on 'What makes an economist?' which deserves long use as a tract for those aspiring to academic honours (Carter, 1955, p 701).

Of Shackle's clear and compelling style nothing more can be added to Carter's testimony. The general theme of Shackle's lifelong work as epitomised in these essays could be characterised by this tag from Aristole (*Ethica Nicomachea*, 1094b) which, given his training in classics, Professor Shackle might well have used himself:

> For an educated person should expect to obtain precision in each branch of study to the extent which its nature permits.

J. L Ford
University of Birmingham

References

M. Blaug (1986), *Who's Who in Economics*, Brighton, Wheatsheaf.

C. F. Carter (1950), 'Expectation in Economics,' *Economic Journal*, Vol. 60, December, pp. 92–105.

C. F. Carter (1953), 'A Revised Theory of Expectations,' *Economic Journal*, Vol 63, December, pp. 428–50.

C. F. Carter (1955), Review of *Uncertainty in Economics and other Reflections*, by G. L. S. Shackle (1955), *Economic Journal*, Vol 65, December, pp. 700–701.

W. M. Gorman (1957), 'A Note on "A Revised Theory of Expectations," ' *Economic Journal*, Vol. 67, September, pp. 549–551.

F. A. Hayek (1931), *Prices and Production*, London: Routledge and Kegan Paul.

J. R. Hicks (1950), *A Contribution to the Theory of the Trade Cycle*, Oxford: The Clarendon Press.

J. M. Keynes (1930), *A Treatise on Money*, London: Macmillan.

G. L. S. Shackle (1938), *Expectation, Investment and Income*, Oxford: Oxford University Press.

G. L. S. Shackle (1949), *Expectation in Economics*, Cambridge: Cambridge University Press.

G. L. S. Shackle (1955), *Uncertainty in Economics and Other Reflections*, Cambridge: Cambridge University Press.

G. L. S. Shackle (1958), *Time in Economics*, Amsterdam: North-Holland.

G. L. S. Shackle (1966), *The Nature of Economic Thought: Selected Papers 1955–1964*, Cambridge: Cambridge University Press.

G. L. S. Shackle (1983), 'A Student's Pilgrimage,' *Banca Nazionale del Lavoro Quarterly Review*, No. 145, pp. 108–116.

G. L. S. Shackle (1989), *Business, Time and Thought*, (Ed. S. Frowen), London: Macmillan.

H. Townshend (1938), Review of *Expectation, Investment and Income*, by G. L. S. Shackle, *Economic Journal*, Vol 48, September, pp. 520–523.

Part I

TIME

THE COMPLEX NATURE OF TIME AS A CONCEPT IN ECONOMICS

G. L. S. SHACKLE

The word time comprises for the economist a bundle of related but essentially distinct strands of thought. Whether in the abstract we can give any meaning to «the situation existing at a point of time» I do not know, but what we experience, in sensation, emotion, thought, and decision seems to me to have in its nature a sort of depth which corresponds to one meaning of the word time. Time in this sense gives room for things to happen, and is an inseparable part of conscious experience. The «present moment» seems to me not an instant or point of time but a brief span whose contents, however, the mind somehow grasps as a whole. Let us call such a span an element of time. The intuition which teaches that each such element of time is one of a set arranged as it were in linear sequence gives us several further ideas. There is first that of an ordered sequence of situations or events in which we may seek or think we see an inevitability, or perhaps several collateral strands of inevitability, or shall we say, of necessary pattern. Order or sequence by itself is here distinct from unity of the pattern, from *necessary* sequence. Next there is greater or less remoteness of situations or events, there is distance in time. And thirdly there is the sense of cumulation of time-elements, the sense of duration. But this is not all. Experiences can occur; they can also be re-enacted in memory; thirdly they can be created in imagination; and fourthly this imagination can be constrained into a harmony with current and remembered experience so as to approach them in validity and become able to generate emotion, so that it can be called expectation. I wish to consider these various aspects of time in relation, especially, to three other concepts : the idea of enjoyment and distress by anticipation, the idea of decision, and the idea of success.

Time as we experience it impresses on our human situation two overwhelmingly important features. First, every choice between mutually exclusive satisfactions, every decision amongst

3

possible courses of action, and every assessment of realised satisfaction or success, must be made at some one moment, but can
relate in general to events or situations distributed over much
of a human life span. Hence any one named, fixed calendar date
can be looked at by an individual from each of indefinitely many
distinct temporal viewpoints, and assessments and decisions can
be made at many of these viewpoints. How is the decision, or
the assessment of success, made at some one viewpoint to be
made consistent with those made at others? Is there any law in
the nature of things which guarantees that all evaluations which
an individual makes at different moments in his life will have
a common basis or frame of reference, will essentially belong to
one and the same scheme of tastes and ambitions? Is there even
any possibility that this kind of harmony will be achieved, is
there even, indeed, any meaning in the idea of such a harmony?
Is it meaningful to speak of comparing comparisons made at
different dates?

My suggestion is that it is not meaningful, that the judgments
and decisions made at distinct moments of a human life cannot
be said to be either consistent or inconsistent with each other,
since there is no viewpoint in time common to both. The essential
distinction here is between what I call dynamic time, on one
hand, and imaginary time, that is, expectational time and memory
time, on the other. Dynamic time is what allows events to happen, it is the locus of actual experiences involving bodily
sensation, and it is likewise the locus of acts of mind in themselves, the actual occurrence of thoughts and feelings. Memory
time is the freedom, or the power, of the mind to entertain
thoughts about events or situations associated with past moments,
and expectational time is its freedom to create images and associate them with future moments. By imagination, or if you
prefer, by expectation and memory, the whole range of time that
can directly concern the individual is in one sense brought within
reach of *each* of his moments of dynamic time. But this fact in
no way implies any means or possibility of bringing into comparison the separate moments of dynamic time themselves.

A past decision or choice, even though its visible consequences
have been just what, at the time of making it, was hoped for, may
now be regretted. But such regret can arise from at least two
quite distinct sources. One may believe that the decision ought
to have seemed foolish even when the circumstances surrounding
it were looked at from the viewpoint of their own date, and that

the choice must have resulted from a momentary lapse of rationality. Or one may be reflecting that the satisfactions or enjoyments which flowed from the decision have already been experienced and are now past, only the associated pains and sacrifices still remaining in prospect. In this latter case, was the decision rational or not? At one date it was elected, at another it was regretted. At which of the two dates was the individual's judgment just?

Such a dilemma leads us, it seems to me, to ask what do we mean or what various things can we mean by a *successful* life? At what stage of my life is it meaningful or reasonable for me to decide that it has been successful or unsuccessful? « Call no man happy till he is dead » said the Greeks. But what, in old age, am I to say if, having enjoyed each moment of my life by spending it on ephemeral pleasures, I am now assailed with regret for the wasted years which have left me nothing to show? Are we driven to the conclusion that *subjective* success has meaning only in regard to the individual moment of time, so that I *can* meaningfully say « This present moment or brief temporal element of experience has the character that I call success, a character depending indeed on existing mental traces of past events, on actual current contemplation of the situation they have led up to, and on imagination of future situations and events capable of following from this present situation », but that I *cannot* meaningfully say : « The result of adding together the feelings I actually experienced in each past moment up to now represents a successful life », because it is logically impossible for me to bring to a focus at one moment of time the feelings I *actually* experienced. Any such « summation », however generously interpreted, would have to be a summation of objectively recordable and therefore *public* aspects of past events. Life, I find myself driven to maintain, can be *subjectively* successful in each moment but not « as a whole ». But from this it follows, as I now maintain, that a man will make at each moment those plans and decisions which contribute more than any other plans or decisions he can think of to the enjoyment, the happiness and subjective success, of this present moment in which the plans and decisions are made. For it is surely reasonable to say that each person seeks subjective or private, not objective or public, success, he seeks his own satisfaction as assessed by himself, even though his privately estimated subjective success may depend very much on what he deems to be the degree of his public suc-

cess. Now if subjective success has meaning only in reference to
the moment, and not to any extended period of time as a whole,
it follows that each of the rival possible courses of action that
at this moment seem open to him will have merit in his eyes only
in so far as it seems able to contribute to his enjoyment of and
satisfaction with this moment; and a plan will be embarked on,
not directly because of its «objective» characteristics as giving
any calculable guarantee of future public success, but directly
on account of the enjoyment by anticipation, or by imagination,
which the contemplation of it affords him when he has in fact
or in deliberate and experimental imagination committed himself
to it.

Let me at once insist that this proposition has nothing to
do with any idea that men pursue only the sensational and bodily
pleasures of the moment, or that they are content, for the rest,
with day-dreams that they recognise as such. I am at the opposite
pole from saying that men neglect and dismiss the future; on
the contrary, a great part (with some men, much the greater
part) of their enjoyment in the present is derived from their
imaginative contemplation of the future, an imagination constrained however into at least a credible harmony with the present.
The future matters to us, I am saying, because by appropriate
choice of present action it can be made to yield this or that
combination of enjoyment by anticipation and distress by anticipation; its importance is an essentially subjective and imaginative one.

This conclusion, if you can accept it for the sake of argument,
makes a fundamental difference to the answer we must give when
we ask how men deal with the second of the two conditions which
time imposes on us, that is, our ignorance of the future. If in the
nature of things (as I hold) a man cannot know, but only conjecture within wide bounds, what consequences for himself a given
present action of his own will have, how can he choose rationally
amongst the variety of actions open to him? Only by choosing
that course which, in his «present moment» of deciding, affords
him a preferred combination of enjoyment by anticipation (by
imagination) and of distress by anticipation. For if I am right
in maintaining that subjective success refers only to the moment
and not to whole stretches of time, these intensities of imaginative
or expectational experience are the only relevant attributes of
present actions. Between the best hope that a man can seriously
associate with any action, and the worst fear he need seriously

attach to it, there will in general, I think, be a wide interval, wide in relation to his resources at his moment of deciding for or against the action; to say that there is such an interval is the same thing as to say that there is uncertainty and that knowledge of the future is lacking; but it is not to say that present action and the expected sequel are regarded as independent of each other, for this would be to abolish the distinction between expectation and phantasy, and would also of course abolish any possibility of using expectation as a basis of choice between possible actions.

Now I have brought you a certain distance along this particular path and we find ourselves looking over the hedge at a part of the garden which, as some of you may remember, I have elsewhere tried to cultivate. I do not wish to take up your time in traversing again that ground, which you may be already weary of. Let me turn instead to another aspect of the separateness and isolation of each moment of the time that each of us experiences.

Two possible meanings of the term « an economic dynamics » ought I think to be explicitly distinguished from each other. There is, on one hand, the objective aggregative mechanical predictive dynamics sought by the econometricians, and on the other the subjective private descriptive dynamics of an individual. One reason for making this distinction is that economics, being part of a study of human conduct, is faced with the question of free will or determinism. Another way of expressing this latter problem is perhaps to say that determinism assumes a single initial act of creation while free will supposes continuing creation. Now if we suppose that in some sense creation via the decisions of «free-willed» individuals is all the time going on, we cannot have a dynamics which embraces within a single theory several successive moments of time, but we are logically confined to the study of each moment singly; we must have in a strict sense what the dramatists call «unity of time and action». Nevertheless the «free-willed» originative acts of individuals, which must by their nature be unpredictable, may be supposed to require some time to have an appreciable effect on the apparent course of the economy as a whole as seen in the behaviour of large economic aggregates. Thus it may be permissible and convenient to have a short-term predictive dynamics of the economy as a whole even when, by assuming individual free will, we preclude ourselves from a predictive dynamics of the individual. For the individual we have then to be content, in the nature of our view of life, with

a descriptive, single moment, dynamics which purports only to
tell us what, with *given expectations,* he will at that moment
decide to do. We cannot proceed to his next moment by arguing
deterministically from this first moment, for we cannot know what
his next inspiration will be. You will notice that I am giving to
the term « free will » a rather different content from that of
ordinary discourse, where we tend, perhaps rather vaguely, to
treat the free willed individual as an individual who acts or is
capable of acting *arbitrarily* in face of a *given* situation. I am
proposing instead to say that it is his *situation,* his vista of
expectations, that he is in some sense free to create, or derive
from some unexplained inspiration, but that his conduct in face
of any *given* expectational situation will be non-arbitrary; if you
like, that it will be rational.

In constructing his predictive macro-dynamics the econometrician naturally and properly treats the economy as a machine
whose future behaviour, in the absence of shocks from outside
itself, is fully determined by its history over some stretch of the
past, so that this future behaviour is in principle predictable. The
individual in so far as he looks upon himself as a free originative
decision-maker cannot logically admit that his own actions can
be predicted with certainty by another person. Thus our distinction
between the two attitudes is a multiple one : one kind of dynamic
theory is constructed by a theoretician who (in so far as he deems
himself to have any originative power or freedom of decision) does
not think of himself as even potentially part of the thing which
his theory is about. The theory can thus be called « objective ».
This theory concerns the total results of what is done by large
numbers of people all taken together, and is thus « aggregative ».
It treats this mass of people as though they constituted a machine
with a stable, knowable structure whose manifested result is
capable of being described by differential equations or at any rate
by integro-differential equations. Thus the theory can be called
« mechanical ». The theory allows a step-by-step argument from the
situation of one moment to the situation of the next and the next
and so on indefinitely. Thus it is predictive. In contrast with
such a theory we have one which purports only to describe the
events of a single moment inside a single person's mind. Into that
moment may be packed thoughts, feelings, imaginations and decisions; but amongst these, something which has not arisen as a
necessary consequence of the events of preceding moments but has
been newly inspired or created in this moment. If the moment can

be thus essentially novel there can be no predictive inference from one moment to another but only description of the kind of brief system of events that can happen in the individual's mind in each separate moment. So this second kind of dynamics is descriptive and not predictive. Finally a theory constructed by someone who looks upon himself as a free-willed element of the thing his theory is about is plainly private and subjective and not public and objective.

I should like now to pick up afresh one of the threads of my skein that I have already made some play with. I want to discuss an aspect of enjoyment or distress by anticipation which, although I have never seen or heard any reference to it, (1) seems to me to require at least some study before we can dismiss it as unimportant. I myself believe the « pyramiding » of enjoyments or distresses by anticipation to play some real part in affairs.

The point is that if, on Saturday, I am able to make and embark on a plan which allows me to imagine with some plausibility that some particular agreeable thing will happen on Sunday, I can on Saturday experience some enjoyment by anticipation. This makes Saturday an enjoyable day. But if on Friday I imagine Saturday as an enjoyable day, I can on Friday look forward with enjoyment not only to Sunday but also to Saturday; on Thursday if I have already in mind the plan referring to Sunday I can experience enjoyment by anticipation of the enjoyments to be experienced on Friday and on Saturday as well as those of Sunday itself; and so on. Economists have usually assumed that an imagined future agreeable event (2) would afford less intense anticipatory enjoyment the more distant its supposed future date, but it is not clear what combination of three possible influences or mechanisms they were taking into account. There is first what we might call the « pure » effect of remoteness in time, analogous perhaps to the effect of perspective in reducing the apparent size of physical objects as their distance increases. However such metaphors really explain nothing; and for my own part I feel that the onus

---

(1) My own earlier suggestions concerning it are in *The expectational dynamics of the individual*, « Economica », May 1943, and in *Expectation in Economics*, Cambridge, 1949, pp. 70-72.

(2) They have not spoken of *imagined* events, nor have they, however, explained what existence future events can have, within mortal ken, except in imagination.

of proving the existence of this « pure » effect rests on those who believe in it. Secondly there is the hypothesis that the longer the time over which one looks forward to an event, the more room there is, so to speak, for intervening mischances to thwart one's hopes. Thus increasing remoteness will be accompanied by increasing doubtfulness, and this is surely an easily accepted cause of the dimming of anticipatory enjoyment. Thirdly we have the pyramiding effect which I have just suggested, which works however in the opposite sense and must tend, in itself, to increase the *total* intensity of enjoyment by anticipation as the distance in time of the event, forming the apex of the pyramid, increase. If, as we suppose a greater and greater remoteness of the event, this third effect is sufficiently powerful, over some range of such distances, but not over an indefinitely great range (and human mortality if nothing else must assure this ultimate limitation), to outweigh the second or the combined first and second effect, then there will be for a particular individual, looking forward in particular circumstances to a specified kind of event, some particular time-distance into the future which will make the total enjoyment by anticipation a maximum. All this amounts to saying that an expected event can be *too near* in time to afford the maximum enjoyment or distress by anticipation. And this surely agrees with common experience. An intended visit to the dentist is a more powerfully depressing influence on the preceding day than on the day itself, when « it will soon be over ». Why do we like to plan our holidays far ahead? It is not solely because better accomodation and travel facilities can be secured by the first comers, surely it is also because we enjoy looking forward. Yes, you may say, the pleasure of looking forward will be greater in total the longer it goes on, without the need to suppose any complex pyramiding effect. I hope that what I said in the first part of this paper will have made it clear why I cannot accept that argument. Enjoyment must be measured or assessed as an intensity at a moment of time, cumulation over time does not make sense except in so far as it can be resolved into a factor contributing to momentary intensities.

One concept on which I think the idea of the pyramiding effect may have a bearing is that of the so-called «horizon». This word is usually taken to mean the length of future time from the present which the individual deems it worth while to take into account in forming his expectations and plans. It seems possible, for example, that for the typical consumer, the person whose anticipations of enjoyment bulk much larger in his mind than any associated anticipations of distress (in which respect, I would say, the consumer stands in contrast to the investor), the pyramiding effect will tend to push the horizon to a greater futurity than it might otherwise have. Those income-receivers who nowadays make deliberate and systematic private provision for their years of retirement or for the education of their children are a small minority; many who formerly attempted this must surely nowadays have a nearer income-disposal horizon than before the coming of the Welfare State, and I would conjecture that its distance is often no more than a week or two or a month or two, except in regard to those things where « looking forward » is the main part of the whole pleasure, such things as the annual holiday and the Christmas present-giving and festivity. But having suggested the pyramiding effect I do not want at this time to try to push its analysis further. I should like now to turn instead to a different kind of horizon, what we may call the *decision interval.*

A difficulty which seems to me to arise in bringing face to face with each other different theories of the determination of the interest-rate, is that some of these theories work with « stocks » and some with «flows». The distinction between «stock» concepts and « flow » concepts is itself, of course, one of the very first distinctions connected with time on which we as economists insist in our exposition and carefully attend to in building our arguments, and it would certainly be out of place for me to discuss so familiar a matter here. But a flow, of course, yields a stock as soon as we name a time-period during which the flow is to go on. Now one way of studying the factors which affect the interest-rate is to consider them as emerging from the administration by individuals of the stocks of wealth which they respectively control. One kind of decision which has continually to be taken about such a stock is how fast it shall be allowed to grow or diminish through the owner's spending less or more than the whole of his income on consumption. Let us call the utility obtained from prospective consumption of wealth, during some time-interval measured forward from the present, *consumer-satisfaction,* and the utility derived from prospective possession of wealth, during the same interval, *possessor-satisfaction.* In this same forthcoming interval the individual counts, let us suppose, upon receiving a definite number, say N, of money units as disposable income. A decision to spend in the interval C units on consumption and to add N—C units to his stock of wealth would afford him a certain

consumer-satisfaction and a certain increment of possessor-satisfaction. To decide instead upon C+1 and N—C—1, or again upon
C+2 and N—C—2, would increase his consumer satisfaction but
by diminishing marginal differences, and would reduce his
prospective increment of possessor satisfaction by *increasing*
marginal differences. It is plain on the most familiar lines that
some particular choice of C would maximise his total satisfaction
from the two sources together, that is, from consuming some
newly-accruing wealth and from adding some to his stock. The
question now arises, whether the choice of the time-interval is
perfectly free or whether it must satisfy some conditions.

To possess something, in the full sense, is to be free to dispose
of it. If a decision has been taken to part with it at some future
date, even an unstated date, the feeling of possession will have
been partly destroyed by this mental commitment which infringes
the full freedom of disposal; for power to dispose of a thing of
course includes power to retain it as well as power to let it go.
To possess a thing, in a complete sense such that full possessor-
satisfaction can be derived, must surely mean the intention to
retain the thing indefinitely, or it must at least mean the absence
of any commitment, even a private and unspoken one, to part
with it. However, it seems to me questionable whether it is psy-
chologically possible for a person to commit himself mentally to
actions of more than some limited futurity. There is surely in
any given context a tendency for the degree of commitment, of
private irrevocability and reluctance to change one's mind, to
diminish as the futurity of the contemplated action increases, and
this diminution may I think be steep enough to constitute a
« horizon » in a sense analogous to the economist's ordinary use
of this word. The length of such a decision-interval would no
doubt vary according to the nature of the decision. If for each
person there is some length appropriate to decisions to part with
things possessed, this is the relevant interval for my argument
about the balancing of consumer and possessor-satisfactions at
the margin.

May I, in conclusion of these reflections, try to bring to a
sharp focus the contrast between the view of the relation between
time and the individual human being that I have here tried to
suggest, and the view which would emerge from a study of the
literature of economics. The orthodox view has, in my opinion,
overlooked and ignored the difficulty of giving a meaning to the

summation or integration of subjective experience over time. The very word « uncertainty » suggests an objectively existing future which it would be to our advantage to know exactly, comprehensively, and for certain. Uncertainty thus comes to be looked on as an inadequacy of our own powers, or a disadvantage of our situation, which are in principle to some degree remediable. I am suggesting instead that the future is created afresh from moment to moment by the individual imagination. What we speak of as «uncertainty» is the essential freedom of this imagination, bounded by the consciousness of law in nature but not paralysed and killed by a knowledge of something objective. If we believe in a fully determinate universe, a universe engaged in working out a destiny irrevocably fixed in the beginning, then the individual imagination is merely a link in the mechanism. But if we believe in a nondeterministic universe where creation of something essentially new can happen from moment to moment, then the individual imagination seems to be the locus, so far as human beings are concerned, of this continual projection of essential novelty into the world process.

I am not suggesting that introspection will tell us whether the ideas that come to being in our minds are or are not the mere necessary consequence of what has gone before. I am not suggesting that it will tell us whether each of our thoughts follows necessarily as a determinate, inevitable outcome of our previous thoughts and sensations. But neither can it assure us that pure inspiration is excluded. To believe in the possible essential novelty of thoughts is not to confuse hopes with phantasies. Expectation is *constrained* imagination. We can believe that the exact detail or form of the constraint can be changed by some means not discernible by any scrutiny of past events, and still hold that at each moment some constraint will exist. Enjoyment by anticipation is not to be derived from mere day-dreams, but from imagining a future course of events which the nature of things as we have come to see it makes plausible or credible in some degree as a sequel to some present action amongst those which are open to us, an action to which we have committed ourselves. There is a sort of artistic conscience which makes expectation work within the « rules of the game » that seem to be imposed on us. The freedom to imagine a good outcome is necessarily associated with a freedom to imagine a bad outcome; human rationality is the drive which impels us to use both these freedoms and treat fears as the cost of hopes.

TIME AND THOUGHT *

G. L. S. SHACKLE

1 Two Views of Time

ARE there, I would first of all ask, two utterly different views of time, the outside view and the inside view ? What I mean by the outside view is illustrated especially by the ways of thought of academic people in their academic capacity. The mathematician and the historian are the examples I have particularly in mind. The mathematician treats time as a space, or as one dimension of a space, in which all points have an equal status or importance or validity *together*, within one and the same prospect of the world; they have, as I would paradoxically say, a *simultaneous* validity, each of them means the same to him when he thinks about them all in one thought. This attitude of the mathematician is brought to a focus when we consider what is implied by his writing down a differential equation to express, say, the motion of the 'particle' of classical dynamics. In this equation, which, at each moment when he contemplates it, he regards as valid, he has implicitly

* Received 27. viii. 58

[1] This paper stands as it was written in the winter of 1957-58, as one more result of the kindness and encouragement of Professor Burton Keirstead. Since completing it, I have had the marvellous intellectual experience of reading Professor Michael Polanyi's *Personal Knowledge*. This book, whose passages of luminous beauty give it rank as literature no less than as science, provides an epistemic setting within which, perhaps, the difficulties that I have tried in this paper to define might find solutions and lead to constructive development. To Professor Karl Popper I owe an early impulse to attack these questions. The excitement and ferment of thought that I carried away from a lecture of his in 1936 live with me still. He has now with very great kindness written out a detailed criticism of the views here expressed, and some radical differences between us will act as a fresh incentive to thought. Professor Keirstead himself takes issue with me in a forthcoming article in *Metroeconomica*, with delicacy and subtlety that are, perhaps, too kind. Amongst such relevant work as I have read in earlier years Professor W. B. Gallie's masterly book on Charles Peirce is outstanding. Mr J. W. N. Watkins by his perfect understanding of what I was driving at in earlier work, and now Professor Johan Åkerman in a just-published article of searching insight in *Kyklos*, have greatly improved my grasp of my own ideas. To each of them I am very deeply grateful. All my efforts for eight or nine years past have drawn strength from Professor C. F. Carter's critical support.

G. L. S. SHACKLE

stated the position which the particle will, or did, or would, occupy at each instant during some stretch of time. The equation cannot exist and have meaning, therefore, unless all those instants can be looked on as having an equal validity *together*. In the mathematician's act of writing down his equation, all the instants and the corresponding positions of the particle are folded up into one indivisible statement. At which of these instants does he place himself, at which does he take his stand ? At none of them, he is an *outside observer*, not part of the system he is describing, and for him all the instants are, in the instantaneous logic of his own thought, equally and simultaneously valid and meaningful.

Consider the historian who is thinking, say, about the constitutional changes produced in England by the war between king and parliament in the seventeenth century. Can he at that moment help looking back, half unconsciously perhaps, at the beginnings of political freedom in England, at Magna Carta, at Simon de Montfort; and looking ' forward ' to the great reforms of the nineteenth century, and on to the beginnings of the Welfare State in Asquith's government of 1911 ? All this long process presents itself to him in one panorama, as a unity, every part of it as real as every other part; he is an outside observer, not himself part of what he describes.

With this outside, detached, sophisticated view of time, I want to contrast the *inside* view which each of us has in the very act of living, the time *in* which we sense-perceive, feel, think, imagine, and decide. From this inside view, the time of our actual psychic experience is but a moment, utterly solitary in its isolation from all other moments. It is what I would like to call the *solitary present* or the *moment-in-being*. The experienced moment, the moment-in-being, is for the individual person the only thing there is, the only actuality. I do not mean that it is the only *real* thing: he may believe in the reality of things outside his own sense perceptions and psychic processes. Let me put the contrast, as I see it, between the outside and the inside view of time in another way. Time from the inside is the time *in* which we think, time from the outside is the time about which we think. Thus I want to attach a rather special meaning to the word *actual*, the meaning of presence and pressure upon the mind, the fleshly existence of events, as distinct from the content of those events that pass upon the mental screen of memory and imagination. I would say, then, that for any one person, no two distinct moments can be actual together, the actuality of one denies and excludes the actuality of any other.

TIME AND THOUGHT

In what sense, then, can the *actual* experiences of two distinct moments be compared ? In no sense at all, such comparison is meaningless and impossible, for there is no ' common ground ', no meeting place for two mutually destructive actualities. Within the actual present, of course, different elements of the picture can be compared. These elements include, on the one hand, the sense-impressions of what is going on ' now ' and also, I would say, that sort of neurological expectation, that forward-feeling of our nervous system which links one moment to the next; and on the other hand, those things which the mind creates, as it were, unaided: memories and *experiences by imagination*. Memory and imagination are both of them part of a person's present experience, they belong to the essence of the moment-in-being, they are in it and of it. The content or subject-matter of their images does, indeed, bear a label with a date other than that of the moment-in-being, but this fact no more allows us to treat these images as effective *substitutes* for the actuality of other moments than the presence in a painting of the images of other places enables us to treat the painting as a full substitute for those other places.

2 *Dynamic and Imaginary Movement in Time*

The moment-in-being must surely be looked on as something which exists only by changing. It is a unity, a self-interlocking whole, yet I suggest we can better use the analogy of a wave rather than that of a particle. Can a wave be identified ? There is, presumably, a certain balance and mutual dependence between the parts of a wave, the crest and the trough, which entitle and require it to be thought of as a unity, yet we can ' cut off' the segment at any two suitably related points, at the bottoms of two troughs or at the tops of two crests. Any such analogy is crude in the extreme, perhaps scarcely worth invoking. Yet it seems vital to distinguish between two ways in which the moment-in-being, time from the inside, is related to the calendar axis, time from the outside.

By the phrase *dynamic movement in time* I refer to the notion, first, that the moment-in-being, even from the outside view, is not a bead upon a string but rather a colour of a spectrum, distinguishable as something in itself yet overlapping and growing out of and into other colours, so that while it is possible to name a particular wave-length of light, say 0.0000 metres, yet such a wave-length is not the whole of a discernible colour but rather corresponds to an *instant* or point of time

G. L. S. SHACKLE

than a moment; and secondly, that the moment is the locus of events, that is, of sensations, thoughts and acts, which 'take time' and whose very nature, intimately bound up with that of the moment, is such that by merely taking place they carry us into a different moment. Thus by dynamic movement in time I mean the translation of the moment-in-being along the calendar axis; that is the outside view. Or I mean the transformation of one moment into another; that is the inside view. There is, however, another thing that we might call 'movement in time', and this other thing is indeed my central theme. It consists in the mind's power to create images unaided by outside stimulus, and to label them with dates other than the actual date at which such images are created.

Imagination, I would say, is of three kinds. It can be, firstly, the free unlimited fantasy of day-dreams. Regarding this it is irrelevant to ask whether what is imagined could come true. Secondly, there is the imagination which constrains its images in two ways, making them in the first place compatible with the individual's beliefs about the nature of things and about human nature, so that they represent something that seems to him possible in the abstract, and in the second place attaching them to named future dates and restricting them to such transformations of his existing situation as seem to him possible in the time-span between 'now' and 'then'. Such images are thus subjectively possible consequences of action-schemes open to the individual, and I shall call them *expectations*. Thirdly when, amongst all the courses of action open to him, the individual has chosen one and mentally committed himself to it, constrained imagination becomes *anticipation*, an experiencing beforehand of some supposed outcome of a decision.

Imagination in the two latter of these senses might seem to provide a substitute for the actuality of moments other than the individual's moment in being. Yet surely this is a delusion. Actuality is unique, expectation is multiple and uncertain. As the individual's viewpoint advances, as his moment-in-being transforms itself, the relative vividness of the rival expectational pictures which he forms of the outcome of any one action-scheme shifts repeatedly with the impact of news and the continuous process of interpreting it. How can this be a substitute for the uniquely certain actuality of a moment-in-being? If we are still tempted to think that two actualities can exist together and be brought face to face in the same moment of thought let us suppose that the action-scheme which a man has decided on affords

288

TIME AND THOUGHT

him by anticipation both pleasures and pains. The pleasures are associated in his mind with a calendar label t_1 and the pains with a later calendar label t_3. As he did decide on this action-scheme there was plainly some date, t_0, when the good anticipations outweighed the bad. But what are his feelings at a date t_2, part-way between t_1 and t_3? There is now nothing pleasurable, we are assuming, for him to look forward to amongst the consequences of the action-scheme but only its pains that are the price, still unpaid, of the pleasures which now belong to memory. Is it not possible that in this moment he will regret his decision? It is not certain he will, for memory has pleasures of its own. But if, as outside observers, we see him regretting at t_2 the action-course that, at t_0, had seemed preferable to all others, we may want to ask: Which of these two views, taken at different dates by the same man about the same act, is just? I contend that this question is meaningless. There is no co-existence of these two moments, t_0 which contains as part of itself the decision to adopt the action-scheme, and t_2 which contains as part of itself the regret for that course. These two moments cannot, for the individual to whom alone the question could matter, be ' in being ' together, the actuality of one denies and excludes the actuality of the other, and it is only by assuming ourselves to be observers standing *outside* of the system under discussion, the thought-system of this individual, and outside of the time, the moment, in which his thoughts take place, that we can make the question even seem to mean something.

If it be true that the *actualities* of two distinct dates cannot co-exist, it follows that choice between rival action-schemes must surely be based on comparison of their expected consequences. It is accordingly experiences by imagination, subjective entities, which guide decision. We cannot look upon decision as depending on a subjective evaluation of objective realities: it is subjective from the start. If the act of deciding is the act of maximising something, that something must be a feeling belonging to the same moment as the act of decision itself. The purpose, the desired effect, of decision will be experience by *anticipation*, that is, by imagination limited to the seemingly possible, and this act of imagination will be part of the moment of decision.

What is left of the distinction between rational and irrational conduct? Conduct is judged, by an outside observer, to have been rational when it has brought consequences which, at the moment of experiencing them, the individual finds superior to any others which he now judges he could have secured. Does this mean that, in any

G. L. S. SHACKLE

other case, his conduct at some earlier date was ' mistaken ' ? By what right does the later moment claim jurisdiction over the earlier ? The earlier had its own enjoyments by anticipation towards which, in their actuality at the moment of decision, the later moment can contribute nothing and from which its conflicting evaluation has the right to detract nothing. The two moments are eternally exclusive of each other and wholly incomparable. Rationality means something only for the outside observer. Those who claim that, in choosing an action-scheme in face of a not-to-be-repeated set of circumstances, a decision-maker would do himself most good by applying a calculus of ' objective ' probabilities to the rival claims of various imagined outcomes of each action, are looking at time from the outside and making all the dates ' co-actual '. Would do himself most good, *when* ?

3   *The Nature of Decision*

Either of two suppositions would destroy the meaning with which our habits of thought and speech seem to invest the word *decision*. If the transformation of the moment-in-being as it reaches point after point of the calendar axis is no more than the rolling of a wheel along a road which constantly and fixedly exists in its entirety wherever the wheel is located, so that the human consciousness merely comes across situations, or the events which carry one situation into another, as in-evitably as the traveller comes across the mountains and oceans that lie in his path, then human decisions are mere acts of recognition of the compulsion of circumstance. If we regard the history of the world and of each person in it as the unrolling of an initially complete design, as determinate and pre-destinate, then ' decisions ' can play no more vital and spontaneous role in this process than the shapes of the pieces of a jig-saw puzzle play in the fitting together of the puzzle. The final picture takes its character from the necessity of fitting the pieces together in just the one possible way; yet the profile of each piece was cut before ever the fitting together began to be attempted; the character of the ultimate picture was pre-determined, and it would be against all sense to ascribe what gradually emerges as being created by the profiles. Yet we speak and think as though decisions were *creative*. Our spontaneous and intuitive habits of mind treat a decision as introducing a new strand into the tapestry as it is woven, as injecting into the dance and play of events something *essentially* new, something not implicit in what had gone before. The two conceptions are totally opposed. Either decision is nothing or it is everything.

A supposition virtually equivalent to that of determinism is perfect knowledge. If a person felt himself to have in mind a complete specification of the entire set or range of action-schemes open to him, and for each of these action-schemes, a complete and certain knowledge of its entire consequences as far as these were of interest to himself, and if also he could order these outcomes, one for each action-scheme, according to his preferences; then his selection of one action-scheme out of all those open would, we should surely have to say, be mechanical and inevitable, and would have no content of the kind which makes our *working* ideas about decision interesting. Decision would be *empty*, the mere registering of a formal solution to a purely formal problem.

Exact, complete, and certain knowledge of what would follow from any possible act, utterly remote as this notion is from experienced life, is the tacit basis of much of economic theory. Yet when this strand is relinquished, it is exchanged only for the most worthless substitute, the assumption that, even if the individual cannot pick a unique train of consequence for each possible act, he can make a list, complete and, somehow, known to him to be complete, of all the possible trains, and attach to each of them a proper fraction giving the proportion of times, in an infinitely long lifetime of repetitive experiment, that this outcome would prove the true one. I do not want at this moment to consider the second half of this assumption, the invoking of notions of relative frequency. That is a separate matter. The true basis of the disaster wrought upon economic theory by the *games of chance* universe of ideas is the notion of the existence and the attainability of a list, complete and known to be complete, of all the possible outcomes of an action. In games of chance this possibility, of listing completely all the contingencies, is assured by the very nature of these games, their inherent and essential dependence upon a set of explicit rules. It is the completeness of this list which makes it logically possible to distribute relative frequencies over the contingencies. Once we abandon the notion of rules of an artificial game and the ‘objective’ list of its possible states, and mean by ‘possible’ outcome of an act anything that the individual thinks to be possible, we find that outcomes are not *given to* the individual but imaginatively *created by* him. And who is to predict, and how, what outcomes will be imagined by the individual for each possible one of

G. L. S. SHACKLE

his acts ? Who is to say when he has finished his work of creating his list of possible outcomes ? In what sense can such a list, even in the individual's own reckoning, ever be complete ?

The word *decision* surely epitomises part of our intuitive, spontaneous attitude to life, and an attitude which appears more surprising the more attentively it is compared with that other attitude which has been conditioned into us by education, our scientific attitude to life. That spontaneous and natural attitude is, I suppose, common to all of us, so our habits of speech suggest; and it is surprising only when we look at it against the background of the characteristic scientific attitude. Between man in his spontaneous naturalness, and man in his superior scientific wisdom, there is a deep divorce and alienation. Natural man believes, without thought or question, in his own creativity, in his power to conjure from the air a new strand in the texture of affairs, by merely saying *I decide*. . . . Scientific man says that he can predict the course of events. Give him an adequate description of what has been up to now, and he will tell you what will be after this. Now these two decisions are utterly at variance. One cannot suppose that the man who claims to predict allows to himself, but to no-one else, the inceptive power of genuine decision, the capacity to inject something *essentially* new into the whirlpool of events; and one cannot suppose that he believes it logically possible to foresee his own decisions while still looking upon them as decisions, as future events which will be creative in the full sense. Yet if he does not make these claims, how does he suppose himself able to predict ? Someone else's decision, or even his own, could blow his prediction to the winds.

4 *The World of Order and Inspiration*

If a man felt that he knew completely and for certain all the consequences, of any practical or emotional concern to him, that would flow from each given act in the range of acts open to him; and if he felt that he could rank these various trains of consequences, one for each act, according to his preference; then for him the act of choosing between these acts would be purely formal and automatic, his ' decision ' would be empty. If we opt for this assumption there is nothing in the idea of decision worthy of being discussed. All we need is an analysis of ' economic forces ', a theory of the economic system fully as independent of any specific psychic or humane elements as the theory of the solar system is.

TIME AND THOUGHT

But if not, what must we mean by decision ? If it must not be choice under perfect foresight, it must be choice in face of doubt and ignorance. Yet it cannot be choice in face of chaos and anarchy; for a man who thought that any act could have any sequel whatever, and that there was no possibility of excluding *anything* as incapable of following from any stated course of action, would believe any one act to be just as eligible, just as wise and efficient, as any other, and decision would be pointless. Decision can only mean what we ordinarily do mean by it, it can only be non-empty and non-futile, in a world of bounded uncertainty. Let me then state my definition: Decision is choice in face of bounded uncertainty.

The world of pure determinism where ' decisions ' are the mere clicking of the machine as it works, the world of perfect foresight where everything is actual at once and all possible experiences are in effect pre-experienced in one comprehensive explosion of events, and the world of anarchy where nothing that happens is constrained in any degree by what went before nor itself constrains what will come after, are alike fatal to that content of the word that our whole attitude to life assumes, the implicit belief that a decision is in some strict and full sense a beginning, something constrained indeed but not determined. In order to study decision in this sense, we must assume a world which satisfies two conditions. First, it must be a world where natural law operates, where a man feels that if his immediate act were different the sequel would be in some respects different, where, in fact, the course of the game can be influenced and affected, but not determined, by the individual player: in short, a world of order. But within this order, secondly, there must be room for the creative process to be still at work. For we have, it seems, the choice between two assumptions. Either creation was a single act and all that comes after was thereby settled and fixed forever; or creation is a continuing process and the shape of events can still arise from the void through men's inspired decisions. We have to suppose that into each moment in each man's mind there can be injected something *essentially* new, something not arising, in its completeness and its essence, merely as the one inevitable response to the impact of a given stimulus on the existing stock of his mind, nor as the only possible upshot of the inner working of that existing stock of thoughts, ideas, and knowledge.

In short, whether or not there is such a thing as *decision* in the full sense that our spontaneous working habits of mind give to this word,

G. L. S. SHACKLE

such decision if it does exist belongs only to a certain scheme of thought about the world, that which supposes in it *order and inspiration*.

5 Prediction

If, as the basis of our thinking, we opt for a world of non-empty decisions, we are denying the possibility of exact, unlimited prediction of human affairs. For a decision, we are saying, is a cut in the logical connectedness of past and future. We are saying that part of what enters into a decision is uncaused. Are decisions creative or predictable ? They cannot be both, for the meanings of the two words are mutually exclusive. Thus prediction will have to mean, for us, something other than exact calculation. But the idea that, in principle, the entire conduct of every individual, and of all individuals together, could be predicted, if we knew all there is to know about what has happened up to ' the present ', conflicts both with our experience of time from the ' inside ', as an evolving, solitary moment, and with our view of time from the ' outside ', as an extension, an axis on which a plurality, indeed an infinity, of separated points can be distinguished. For to have perfect foreknowledge of the future would surely be to pre-experience the future, to telescope all of life into a moment. It is hard to regard this even as an idea, so plainly does it conflict with the nature of consciousness itself. But perfect foresight appears even to involve logical self-contradictions. What could be meant by perfect foresight of an invention or discovery ? This is a contradiction in terms. We might say the same of the idea of perfect foresight of a decision of one's own, were it not that the concept of non-empty decision is in any case not meaningful in a deterministic world. The logical absurdity involved in supposing two people both to have perfect foresight of each other's free actions was happily shown by Oskar Morgenstern with the help of Sherlock Holmes. If the escaping criminal, Professor Moriarty, had perfectly foreseen the course of Holmes's pursuit, he could have evaded it; but if Holmes had perfectly foreseen this evasive action, he would have defeated it. The self-contradiction of the idea that several people can all use perfect foresight in pursuit of rival ends closely parallels the dilemma pointed out by Popper, that some predictions, if made public and believed, would induce action tending to falsify them. We could suppose the predictor to use his power of foreknowledge merely to choose for himself whatever course of action would most benefit him, keeping this knowledge and his own

-TIME AND THOUGHT

intentions secret from others. But why should we suppose that the system contained just one and only one person with this power ? It could not contain several, for their respective powers of foresight would mutually cancel each other. The only possible predictor whom we could suppose to escape any danger of causing the falsification of his own predictions would be an observer entirely outside and detached from the system. And it is, indeed, only for such a person that the idea of an economic dynamics in the orthodox sense, a scheme of thought embracing a stretch of historic time and treating it as all actual at once, could have any meaning.

6 *Can We have an Economic Dynamics ?*

Economic dynamics can be comprehensively defined only as everything that is not the analysis of a system abstracted from every meaning of time. The pure static system is one where either there are no changes, or where all changes take place instantaneously, so that all *connected* changes take place simultaneously. Nothing short of this will really do. The stationary state is a mere concession to intellectual weakness. What can an infinite repetition of moments, all identical with each other, and each perfectly self-contained in the sense that all that happens within it exhausts its effect within the self-same moment, teach us, that a single one of these moments cannot teach ? You may object that in the stationary state we can suppose today's work to produce tomorrow's saleable goods, so that there is a certain temporal interlocking without change. But what is the good of such a supposition ? So long as there is no change, we might just as well suppose every moment to be self-contained. The stationary state is at best as artificial as the static system, since while the latter abolishes expectation altogether, the former constrains it to such beliefs about the future as can be entertained without giving rise to change. The static system is clear-cut and goes the whole way to exclude time, the stationary state only pretends to admit it.

It would be natural now to ask whether our departure from the static system, in order to obtain an economic dynamics, should lead us to the inside or the outside view of time. I would answer that there are two conceivable classes of economic dynamics, one corresponding to each of the two views of time. It is plainly the outside view which gives us an economic dynamics in the accepted and orthodox sense. For in that sense we consider a sequence of moments to belong to one

G. L. S. SHACKLE

and the same actuality, and that actuality must therefore be that which is seen from the outside by the eye of an observer who is himself no part of the system; were he to include himself in his view of it, all moments except the solitary present would lose their actuality. This *exterior* dynamics falls further into three kinds. In its strict and *calculable* form the current values of all variables are made to depend on some set of their previous values, so that, if over some sufficient interval or series of dates the values of a self-contained set of variables are known, all subsequent values can be calculated. In such a dynamics there can of course be decision only in the empty sense. Inspired decision, true decision in our sense, is, precisely, an unpredictable initiative. But there is an inertia in affairs. However far a decision may depart from being an obvious reflection of obvious circumstance, its effect will take time to work through the economy, which mean-while will swing along a path at first largely shaped by its antecedent states. It is, perhaps, only a relatively few key individuals at any time whose decisions can singly contribute to this course anything that can ever be imputed to them by our outside observer, though we must suppose, perhaps, that any man's decision can set off a chain reaction that will amount to a great effect. Nevertheless we are supposing each man to make his decisions in a world of subjectively bounded uncertainty; for each action open to him he discerns a great range of possible ultimate consequences, but a range which, within any finite horizon, is not utterly unlimited. All this may give to the sequence of states seen by our detached observer a sort of continuity of texture which will enable him without absurdity to make short-range guesses. The basis of such guesses is the second kind of exterior dynamics. Thirdly we can in a certain manner combine the first two kinds into what I would call a *ceteris paribus* dynamics. We assume like the Swedish period analysis, that at a particular instant a number of eco-nomic agents all take decisions simultaneously, and that thereafter during a certain interval everything that happens is the direct or indirect consequence of these initial decisions. By a direct consequence I mean here an act which precisely executes the initial stages of a decision, and by an indirect consequence I mean an act which is the 'automatic' response merely to events which themselves spring directly from the initial decisions, or from the interplay of acts directly arising from those decisions, without any new decisions in the non-empty sense. In this manner we can at one and the same time bring fully into our analysis the inseverable structure of expectations

TIME AND THOUGHT

and decisions and yet allow ourselves to trace consequences from antecedents on the supposition that no *essentially* new initiative interferes.

Let me turn to the *interior dynamics* of the individual's solitary moment-in-being. It can be constructed only by each person for himself, since he alone can have insight into his own mind. For this reason many will reject the notion of an interior dynamics as unscientific. Extraspection is scientific, introspection is not; senseperception is respectable, self-perception is delusory. Why? Descartes at any rate did not agree. He based his belief in his own reality on the fact of his own thoughts: *Cogito, ergo sum.*

The psychic solitary moment I would suppose to consist in the creation and use of expectations; to consist in imaginative creation of the set of possible action-schemes and, for each action-scheme, a bounded range of its possible outcomes; in the focusing of attention on certain *expectation-elements* of each such bounded range; and the selection of one action-scheme out of all those open, whose focuselements of expectation will serve as the basis of anticipatory experience. I must apologise here for having had to bring in a reference to arguments and ideas which there is no space to develop in this paper.

Between an exterior and an interior dynamics there are plainly many essential differences of nature. An exterior dynamics is *public* and *objective:* the thing studied by one outside observer can be studied by another, since it exists in some sense independently of the existence of any observer. It is *mechanical,* for it looks upon each momentary state of the system as a phase in the determinate behaviour of a *machine of limited design,* a machine whose whole potentialities we can in principle know, so as to be able to tell, from information about what has happened up to now, what will happen next. And an exterior dynamics will be *aggregative,* for it deals with the totality of the actions of many individuals to each of whom the observer's own relation is the same: that of aloof and detached study. And above all, the exterior dynamics will claim to be *predictive.* In its calculable form an exterior dynamics is in a certain sense, paradoxically, timeless. The time which it considers is denatured, its vital principle of creative uncertainty, which belongs only to interior time, has been wrung out of it, so that all its infinity of distinct points along the calendar-axis are, to the outside observer, all equally actual and their ' content ' or events all equally known. Exterior dynamics of our second kind, which I would like to call inertial dynamics, is by its whole purpose predictive,

G. L. S. SHACKLE

though in a tentative and undogmatic way. The writer of 'inertial' dynamics invites his readers to watch for departures from the inertial course of events, he continually suggests what could happen if this and if that unpredictable impulse should strike the system from outside its defined boundaries of internal interdependence. In this use of the word *if*, he is moving away already from the role of prophet towards the task of scientific *description*. To describe the orderliness of nature: this is all that it lies within the power of the scientist, as such, to do. In this light, economic statics and economic dynamics of any and every kind are one: a means of description merely.

Department of Economics
The University
Liverpool

TIME AND CHOICE

By G. L. S. SHACKLE

1. *Choice: the formal essentials*

CHOICE, as the name of something that men do, seems to involve three formal essentials: a set of elements distinct from each other; a standing which can be conferred on any one, but only one, of these elements; and an origin and mode of this conferment. In relation to that standing, the elements amongst which there is choice are thus mutually exclusive. I shall call them *rival choosables*. Then, what essential nature does the human condition, the Scheme of Things, prescribe for the rival choosables? What incentive does it offer for making choices? And what is the essential nature of the part played in choice by human capacities? This third question implies a quite fundamental choice which we ourselves, inquirers into choice, must make at the very outset by taste or temperament, but with decisive suggestion from the logic of things.

2. *Determinism incompatible with originative choice*

Determinism is the view that history in every particular from eternity to eternity exists independently of human knowledge or initiative. If so, choice is the empty name of an illusion. If so, the choices which are said to be made are themselves mere details of a fixed eventless picture, all of it co-existing and co-valid in some world uncognisant of time. Time itself is then a deception of the human consciousness, a blindness ordained for humanity requiring them to grope through an invisible field filled, none the less, with objects, objects vaguely guessable from their earlier encounters. If so, choices are not made. They exist. If they are not made, nothing can influence their making, their making can influence nothing. Nothing, indeed, is capable of being influenced. If such is the truth, what claim has choice upon our interest and intellectual exertion? As the receptacle of an interesting concept of choice, determinism will not do. What, then, instead?

3. *Non-determinism. The new. The void. The solitary present*

What notions are annihilated, what words are made meaningless, when we embrace the eternal stillness of determinism? They are the contradictories of stillness. In determinism, history is independent of thought. Determinism makes thought otiose. A negation of determinism makes thought the condition *sine qua non* of history, the thing without which human history would have no existence. In a non-determinist view, history is *the news*. In determinism nothing is new. In the negation of determinism, only that *is*, which is new. To be, is to be new, to be is to come into being, to take place. To be new is to take place in thought. To be new is to be in essence thought itself. In the view that negates determinism, to exist is to be new. It is thus to be cut off, both from those things whose newness, in an unseizable transience, has ceased and vanished, and from that void out of which, alone, new things can come, that void which, in conceiving the notion of the new, we are obliged also to conceive in the same thought, as part of the essence of the notion of newness. We have a name for this double cut-off, this isolation and solitariness of the sole existent, the new. We call it *the present*. The void indispensable to the possibility of newness, the notion of the void inseparable from the notion of newness? If all that takes place were the mere elaboration and implication of something else, of antecedents, we should be back in determinism. Non-determinism is obliged to envisage an origin and genesis *ex nihilo* for some elements or characters of what takes place. Whether we can go beyond these expressions, 'the void', 'ex nihilo', we shall briefly consider below.

4. *The contrast of time as a space and time as the transient present*

The contrast which in these foregoing sentences I am seeking to suggest is that of two incompatibles, two meanings of the word *being*. Determinism is history without humanity. Men and their roles appear in the still and complete (though perhaps infinite) picture as mere details on the same footing as all else. In such a view, time is the mere canvas on which the picture is painted. Time in this view is a space, a set of distinct but ordered locations where the pigments in their variety of form and colour are deposited. In this view, man must not cast himself as the painter even in the role of employed agent, even with the most limited discretion. He is a mere part of the painting, his very existence is his mere fixture in it. He has no *choice*. In absolute contrast, there is the notion of being as thought, and of thought as a *transient*. Only that *is*, which is vanishing before our eyes in giving place to something new. Instead of saying that *being* means a wholly different thing, we can say that *time* does so. For in this contrasting view, time is the present, the ever-elusive moment within which there must, none the less for its unseizable brevity of passage, be 'room and time enough' for all thoughts of every kind in the most inclusive Cartesian or Russellian sense: all sensation, intellection, emotion, imagination, and decision. Determinism invokes infinity, eternity. Non-determinism looks at the moment, the present. But the present is not merely a small portion, an infinitesimal particle of something indefinitely more extensive. The essence of the present, the essential effect of our rejection of the view of history as something timelessly complete and indifferent to human postures, is to make possible the notion of transience.

5. *Transience, succession, the calendar-axis*

Transience, that existence consisting in arrival and departure, where arrival and departure are one and indivisible, by its nature would leave a void, were that void not continuously filled by a new transient present. Time as transience suggests continuity, yet by force of native intuition or grammatical expediency we make it in our discourse particulate. We speak of the *present moment*. The inquirer into time is bound to conform to that usage, if he is to be understood. And after all, the difficulty of verbalizing these gossamers of conception is so intense as to sanction any resource of language. The present moment is something which of its nature will have a successor. No one will expect me to say what is meant by *successor*. This term names a primitive notion not subject to analysis in other terms, an elemental building-block of discourse. Yet it has for all of us an indispensable and chiselled meaning, protean in circumstance yet constant in essence. Transience as the nature and essence of the present implies a successor of the present, will not that successor have a successor in its own kind, and so on unendingly? How are these successors to be accommodated in thought? In what work of formal imagination can they take their place? Transience has suggested succession, and succession has suggested the calendar-axis where the inferred, supposed, imagined succession of moments is conceived as a metric space and represented, in a million applications, as a straight line in a Cartesian system of co-ordinates. The human direct intuition of time is the transient present. Is not all else an invention, an artefact, a convenient scheme for the arrangement of thoughts and a basis for a theory of Nature?

6. *Choice and the origination of history*

If we elect the non-determinist view, we cannot leave the matter there. If history is not the mere enactment of a stage-play whose every detail exists independently of our being shown its scenes and episodes in sequence, how does history come to pass, what gives it rise and form, what originates the course of things in step with their appearing to our senses and our minds? For the non-determinist view is that the origin of the stream of transformations which we perceive is immanent in that stream itself. Non-determinism is the view that the present shows us a process of creation. How do we suppose that such a process works? Evidently if our aim is to find a meaning for the word choice, a nature and essence for the notion we thus name, the generative process of history must be its locus. If choice means more than an illusion, it means the origination of history, an origination which is seeded in men's thoughts and germinates in their inter-active deeds. If so, what kind of thing are the entities amongst which choice can be made? Why is it made? What is the source of the rival choosables, what presents them to the mind of the chooser, or how does he come to envisage them? What is implied by the two suppositions taken together, that choice *originates the new* and that it has effects and consequences visible and know-able to other minds? What is implied by the supposition that choice is effective? If choice is a source or origin in some funda-mental sense, what is thus implied for men's power to know what will be the sequel of any specific chosen step of theirs? In a world of effective choice, what is the role of the notion of cause? These seven questions are my intended theme.

7. *Choice and cause*

If my experience has been that some specifiable difference between two sets of circumstances was always accompanied by some other specifiable difference, provided all the rest of the circumstances, other than these two, included in either set was matched in the other, I may be inclined to call one of these two differences the cause of the other. If one alteration of circum-stance precedes the other in time-sequence, I shall regard that one as the cause. I may have other reasons for naming one difference the cause and the other the effect. Now if I assume that such an account of things could be given concerning every

transformation that I have observed or may observe, so that not
only those circumstances which in any particular case are seen
to change, but also those which form the background of the
change, are deemed to be locked in a universal and all-pervasive
system of causality, am I not back in a determinist world? To
assume the universal determinate and precise operation of cause
and effect, so that everything which takes place is the only thing
which can take place, is to allow no meaning to the expression
rival choosables, except that of a delusion. If all that takes place
is implicit in what has taken place, there can be no rival possibilities in any context. Thus there can be no choice. Let us then
consider the opposite of universal rigid and exact causation. If
all bonds were dissolved and non-existent, so that any state of
affairs which the world can be conceived to assume could be
assumed by it no matter what had gone before, there might then
be choosing on the part of individuals, but their choosing would
be powerless and ineffective. We may go further, and say that in
a world of the anarchy of Nature no publicly visible expression
or physical embodiment of the act of choice could take place.
Thought would be not only powerless but dumb. Causation
deemed to be rigid and universal, causation deemed to be
entirely absent, seem alike fatal to any interesting notion of
choice.

If when a man elects one out of several rival steps of action
which were present to his thought, we claim that this choosing
is a source from which some aspects of subsequent history will
flow, we are claiming that the history would have been different
had his choice of action been different. We are thus claiming
that his choice is a cause and some aspects of history an effect,
within the meaning of cause and effect which we have adopted in
the foregoing. If we do not recognize the notion of cause and
effect, in some such interpretation as I have sought to express,
how can we claim that choice is effective, that it is an origin of
history? Yet, if we claim that cause and effect operate universally, we are saying that thoughts also are caused, and that
choice is a mere link in a chain of causation. We are then saying
that choice is not spontaneous, is not a manifestation of human
freedom, has no part in the *creation* of history, and lacks all the
character which our unexamined habits of thought and speech,
by which we live from hour to hour, implicitly assign to it.
The pursuit of a notion of choice which satisfies men's sense of
their own dignity; which puts upon them a not delusive respon-
sibility; which allows them to feel that the burdens of anxious

decision are not placed upon them for nothing, that does not make a mockery of self-discipline, of effort, of seemingly creative endeavour; this pursuit confronts us with dilemmas and with the need for audacities of thought, even for what may seem perversities of thought, which go against the grain of much that is inculcated into us in the scientific and technological environment. If we subscribe to the uniformity of Nature, can we accept the operation of causes in one part of it and deny it in another? And yet, if we cannot, what of choice?

8. *Origin and uncause*

Whatever view we take of the nature of history and of the universe which enacts, suffers, or embodies it, there will remain a question which eludes thought, let alone verbal formulation, let alone the finding of an answer. In cosmology the alternative hypotheses are offered of the big bang or the steady state. In the steady state we are obliged to contemplate the continual creation of hydrogen atoms *ex nihilo* to make good the continual evacuation of space by the mutual retreat of the galaxies. But in the big bang hypothesis, how are we better off? Is there not still the question, what was the origin of the primeval atom? The ultimate question of *origin* is surely beyond reach. Determinism suggests an origin 'before history', outside of history. But what obliges us to deem the origin to be so dissociated from what is originated? Can we not conceive of a continuous origination? If a conception of the origin is denied to human capacities, are we not thereby permitted to suppose that human thoughts can arise in some part, in some degree, *ex nihilo?* That they are, if you wish, part of a continuing creation? Such a supposition is compatible with a large and indispensable role of suggestion. The role of suggestion in the engenderment of history has, I think, been much neglected. There are many masks which a hypothesis of continuing creation can wear. We may speak of randomness, of inspiration. These phrases name, they do not explain. What they name, however, would free us from the fetters of complete determinate causation of thoughts, would free us from the abolition of inceptive choice, of choice in the sense of an *origin of the new*. For that is not new, which is wholly implicit in the antecedents. What is wholly implicit in the combination of natural principles with the particular existent circumstances is, in principle, calculable, foreknowable. By the new I mean the *unforeknowable*. I do not think an argument is condemned by its resort to the notion of an *origin not explainable*.

Men's pride in reason is reflected in their imprisonment in reason. Reason is analysis, the breaking down of everything into something else. If this proceeding is deemed to be an infinite regress, there must be some practical limit to its useful pursuit. If it is deemed to have a limit in the nature of the human condition, then again it must end. In either case I think we are defended against those who deny to the notion of the *uncaused* any place in scholarly discourse. Let them acknowledge that the gates of my argument are wide open to the large, unforeknowable role of suggestion. If thoughts are in some degree liberated from cause, choice is rescued from being empty illusion. But this mode of rescue has fundamental consequences.

9. *Two rubrics: news of what is, imagination of the possible*

My business is to infer the nature of choice from postulates which make it the continuous creator of history. The question at the heart of that business is the nature and origin of the rival choosables.

Descartes distinguished between *res cogitans* and *res extensa*. Let us mean by these expressions that which has thoughts and that which supplies the field of those thoughts, which offers elemental suggestions from which those thoughts can be composed. These elements are put together under two rubrics. There are the compositions which purport to describe the circumstances of the present, which report what is taking place, which are *the news;* and there are those which abstract formal elements from the field as the means for work of imagination, which describe circumstances of the field as, in some sense, they *might be*. 'They might be'. In what sense? If the individual mind, the chooser, knows of nothing in the nature or the posture of things, nothing of principle or circumstance, which fatally obstructs some imagined set of circumstances from becoming a description of some present, that set is for him possible. Let us call the two rubrics, that is to say, the purported description of the present and the imagination of the possible, respectively, *present fact* and *possible history-to-come*. Can present fact offer rival choosables? Can any components into which we may resolve it be mutually exclusive? Or can there be for any individual more than one description of the present as a whole? Despite some profound speculations, such as those of Gödel, which allow us to question the one-ness and self-consistency of the field, we in practice deem the reports of present fact to refer to a unique and self-consistent whole. Any parts into which we conceptually divide this whole are compatible and co-valid co-existents, they are not rivals, they cannot offer choice. Things which are *news* are already beyond the reach of choice, in our terms they are fact. Fact is that which has already chosen itself. The choosables are not presented by the field direct and ready-made, they are not components of *what is*, they do not exist independently of the chooser, they are the poems of his own imagination, poems in a very literal sense, things made by himself. In some essential sense the chooser must *originate* the choosables. It is in this origination that we find, I think, a possible conception of non-determinism.

10. *Imagined histories-to-come: an infinitely extensible plurality*

The history which we are deeming to be created by *choice* is the history of *res extensa*, the history of the field which we suppose to be the common source of suggestions variously coming to individuals as reports of *what is*, as *the news*. That history, we are supposing, is created by *res cogitans*, and originates in the thoughts men have under our second rubric, the rubric of imaginative composition. What, then, is the link between the work of imagination, the work of originative thought, and the things that take place in the field? That link presents itself, as soon as we think about it, as a matter of the most extreme elusive subtlety and complexity. The task of the individual imagination at all moments is to fill the void of time-to-come. Can the history-to-come which it conceives be an unique, self-coherent, unified processional image? Can a man find in his knowledge of general principles or of prevailing circumstances a fatal obstacle to every imaginable course of history in time-to-come, except one? The question answers itself by the merest glance at our universal experience, let alone the consideration of the overwhelming depth of detail in a fathomless universe of affairs which, at the very least, would evidently be required even if calculation were basically possible. But we need not appeal to experience or to the absurdities of the practical task. We have already excluded it in logic. If men's choices are inceptive this means that they are not wholly grounded and implicit in their antecedents, they are not implied in the present and what can be known of it, they are not implicit in its summation and suggestion of what is already the past. Inceptive choice brings in essential novelty, the unforeknowable. But unknowable choices to come will help to create circumstance-to-come, and that circumstance will influence the sequel of choices made in the present. The imaginable histories-to-come are necessarily a skein of many rivals. Will the business of composing such histories enjoy a boundless freedom? Of course it will not. The business is not undertaken for nothing. What is choice for? What can choice do? It can produce a *good state of mind*, the enjoyment of realizable ambitions by anticipation. But if those ambitions are to be realizable in thought (they cannot, at the moment of composition, be realized in fact, for they are the imaginative content of time-to-come) they must conform to the world as the chooser sees it, they must pass a test imposed by *practical conscience* for compatibility with the principles of Nature and of human nature, and with these principles in their application to the circumstances of the chooser's present, the posture of things present to his thought. That posture, however, involves the thinking being as well as his field of contemplation. For an element in that posture is the moves that he himself envisages that he will make. What must we mean by the delicately chosen word *envisages*?

11. *Moves and effects*

Any history-to-come which the chooser composes will, if it is to be of concern and interest to him, include moves of his own. These moves will, in the grammatical sense, be transitive, in them he will move *something*. He will move resources from one line of activity to another, he will transform the orientation of his capital equipment, of his armies or his fleets, of the minds and spirits of his congregation, the thoughts of his hearers or his readers. To envisage such action he must suppose, for each imagined path of history, that the things to be moved will be within his reach. To bring them within reach, the history in question must be suitably designed, its course must be an organic march from one move to another, each move contributing to provide the 'movables' of subsequent moves. The plurality of such rival histories will multiply at innumerable stages. But is not this conception a thing of immeasurable and ineffable complexity? Can we give it any intelligible form?

The thoughts of the chooser when he deems himself an originator of history, even on that small scale to which his capacities, his resources, and his suggestive reach confine his imagination and his practical conscience, will not be directed to particulars and precise proper-named details. His thoughts must engage with a hierarchy and a classificatory system of formal and symbolic notions of action. What sort of thing can he put to the test? What can he, as it were, put his money on? If for a moment we pursue the horse-racing metaphor, what he can put his money on is not an exact discription of every movement and momentary location of the horse's limbs, from its arrival at the race-course to its passing the final post, every endeavour of the jockey and exhortation by the crowd, every gust of wind or squall of rain. Such descriptions are not the items which appear in the card of runners, or even in the tipster's analysis. What carries the punter's money, within the punter's thoughts, is a symbol, a general, formal notion of a horse and of his jockey's and his trainer's skills and of the pedigree which has provided them with the physical means of exploiting those skills. This formal scheme, only identified by the proper name of the horse and of the two or three human beings, the race-course, and the date, is what carries the punter's money in his thoughts. The enterprise which a business man conceives, the almost physiological organism of land, plant, technological systems, men of every kind and degree of knowledge and capacity, the environment of fashion, politics, and seething technological advance in which its powers must be tested, is different only in complexity and the stretch of time involved, from the race-horse and his endeavour. Such complexity and the necessity to encapsulate it in symbolic forms and phrases imports into the very scheme of inceptive action itself, which is the immediately operative part of the choosable, that plural rivalry of ideas which we have described as an inherent character of the *sequels* of choice. In truth, the vessel of hopes, the race-horse or the business enterprise, the political campaign, the programme of research in natural science, the writing of a play or of a poem, the tide of musical excitement which launches the composition of a symphony, is joined by a continuous transition with imagination of the testing of these hopes, the histories-to-come which they bring into the field of the possible. The *choosable*, the imagined thing and thought-construct which contends in rivalry in the chooser's mind with others of its kind, encompasses both means and ends. The skein of rival strands, however infinitely its potential proliferation multiplies with contemplation of more-and-more distant epochs-to-come, extends from the very threshold of that time and is the texture of its content even in the most immediate impending moments. A contemplated step of action in our sense is a *class* of actions, a scheme of such steps is a *class* of configurations of classes of actions. Throughout the imagined thing, the choosable, from the chooser's present moment to every stage of the infinitely time-extensible history to come, there is plurality, rivalry, and uncertainty. Plurality would be irrelevant without possibility: histories-to-come deemed impossible are of no concern to the chooser. Without rivalry, mutual exclusiveness, there is no need of choice. Where there are rival acknowledged possibilities there is uncertainty, unknowledge. *Possibility* is here the master-thread which binds all else together. Choice in my sense pre-supposes the endless origination of possibilities, and it is exposure to this or that member of a potentially limitless set of mutually rival skeins each composed of endless rival possibilities that in principle choice offers us. What the choosing of an action-scheme can do, is to make some desired imagined paths of history possible, in my subjective sense, at the cost of making some counter-desired imagined paths also possible. Choice can place defences against misfortune, but ultimately such defences are also obstructions against success. A different choice will remove the defence in removing the obstruction. This is the practical bearing and essence of uncertainty, which I claim belongs essentially and fundamentally to the nature of choice.

A choosable, I have been suggesting, even in those parts of it concerned with immediate time-to-come, will comprise plural rival imagined strands of history, each strand including some formalized and symbolic notions of actions of the chooser's own. Some such actions will seem to him unquestionably within his power, provided they are conceived to be taken immediately or nearly so. I have been calling these actions *steps*. The steps belonging to any one choosable's immediate foreground of time-to-come will compose a coherent scheme, even though that scheme may comprise plural rival variants. Thus I shall refer to that part of a choosable, which forms in some sense a bridge between the act of imagination and the unfolding of its first effects, as an action-scheme. So long as a choosable is still a choosable, so long as it is still able to be *rejected*, the action-scheme which forms its first stage is imagined only. Choice of 'what to do', choice of an action-scheme, thus stands in utter contrast to the notion of an election amongst a set of elements given to the chooser independently of his own thought, presented complete in fixed, exact, and fully known character and implications. The business of gathering suggestions from the field, of composing in their light histories-to-come as rival paths multiplying themselves, in principle, indefinitely with increasing remoteness of time, stretching indefinitely along the calendar-axis, is I think poorly represented by the word choice. I am obliged to put an extraordinary burden on this word, but I wish to retain the link it offers with more conventional ideas.

12. *Possibility, desiredness, and influence of hypotheses upon choice*

I have sought to infer from the inescapable condition of men, that is to say, the necessity they are under to create the history-to-come by continual choice of steps of action in face of a void of knowledge concerning the circumstances-to-come which will shape the sequel of any such choice, the essential nature of the rival choosable entities. Each such choosable, I am led to suppose, must be a skein of rival figmental histories-to-come, each such history having two characters which govern its influence on the choice. Each imagined history must in the first place, as a condition of its entering at all into the business of choice, be deemed in some degree possible, that is to say, it must be deemed not fatally obstructed by anything in the chooser's thought. Each imagined history deemed possible will, secondly, be in some degree desired or counter-desired by the chooser. All that his act of choice can immediately do for him is to expose him to one or other of the mutually rival skeins of rival possibilities which, up to this point in an endless business of imaginative creation, he has faced himself with. In one such skein, the worst of the imagined histories-to-come will be worse than the worst in some other skein, but its best may be better than the best in that other skein. Neither of the two skeins is then prima facie superior to the other in the chooser's esteem. Such situations will inevitably emerge from a process of elimination of those skeins which are inferior on all counts. Into the business of arriving at this stage of the comparisons there has entered both of the characters of each individual imagined history, its *desiredness* and its *possibility*. Both, let me insist or admit once more, are characters of the thought of the chooser, they are in this sense subjective, personal feelings or judgements. How, otherwise, could we claim that they help to create the history-to-come in a manner not wholly implicit in the history which is past? But if both desiredness and adjudged possibility contribute to the influential force of each figment, how do these two characters bear upon each other, what is the claim of each to contribute to that force, what conceptual frame will display to us the system which all these influences compose?

13. *A formal frame*

In taking for my title two words, Time and Choice, of such

boundless suggestion and fundamental presence in all discussion
of human affairs, I have felt it necessary until now to use the
most general and capacious frame of terms and ideas that I
could compass. But now we approach a task which I may call
technical. The inexpressible elusiveness of thought must be
abstracted from by means of a manipulable set of ideas and
symbols, to each of which we can give distinct and rather simple
properties. 'Force of influence' must be represented by a variable
in the mathematical sense, and it must be treated in that sense
as a function of other variables. Despite the continuous grada-
tion of plurality and uncertainty throughout the time-stretch of
each choosable, which I have suggested, I shall for simplicity
speak of each choosable as composed of an action-scheme and
its imagined sequels. I shall at first deem the chooser to be able
to construct a private scale on which the desiredness of any
specified sequel can be located by him. Thus 'desiredness' will
for us at first be a *measurable* represented by an (arbitrary)
numerical scale. It will be evident, I think, that any interval on
this scale, stated as to length and position, can be occupied by an
unlimited number of distinct sequels. In other words, any degree
of desiredness can seem to correspond to, or be conceivably
attainable by, any number of different sequels or histories to
come. In saying that it can be, I mean that there is no formal
and general obstacle in logic why this cannot be the case. If all
the sequels which the chooser has imagined for some one action-
scheme are looked on by him as perfectly possible, I say that
his concern will be only with the questions: How desirable is the
most desirable of these sequels, how counter-desirable is the most
counter-desirable of these sequels? Let us remind ourselves that
the direct incentive for his undertaking the business of choice
is a state of mind, the *enjoyment by anticipation* of imagined histories-to-come. If all the sequels which he entertains, at some
moment of choice, for some one choosable are for him equally
possible, will not the state of mind engendered by this choosable
depend solely on what it offers, at best and at worst? The issue
is an essential and crucial one.

14. *Possibilities not combinable*

   Can the chooser's esteem for any choosable action-system be
increased by the presence in his thought of a larger number of
sequels all affording like high degrees of desiredness? If a specific
degree of enjoyment by anticipation is *made possible* by one
sequel, will it be made *more possible* by the presence of other *rival*

sequels? I say that it will not. Possibility, in my sense, is the absence of obstacles. An obstacle cannot be absent twice, or several times, over. It requires only one sequel to remove the obstacles to a given degree of enjoyment by anticipation. To suppose that many rival sequels can render *more possible* the anticipation of a given degree of desiredness, whose anticipation is made *perfectly possible* by any one of these sequels, seems to me fallacious. It is an illicit transfer, to the question of *possibility*, of a mode of thought (itself questionable) derived from the frequency interpretation of *probability*. This vital matter I will touch on below.

15. *Focus points*

From the foregoing argument it follows that, under our present supposition that the sequels imagined for some one choosable system are all of equal possiblity, the degree of desiredness offered at best by the system is simply that of the most desired of these sequels. The desiredness of this best sequel represents the utmost degree of desiredness which the system and its skein of imagined sequels as a whole can offer. What of its sequels of lesser desiredness than this one? One of them is as essential to the matter of choice as that sequel whose desiredness is greatest. This other relevant sequel is that of greatest counter-desiredness. If that choosable system which the chooser is assessing is to claim the desiredness of its most desired attributed sequel, it must equally assume the burden of its most counter-desired sequel. Have we not here an incoherence, an assertion that a choosable, an action-system, is to be evaluated by reference to both of two mutually conflicting and contradictory suppositions? Indeed we have, and this is the direct, necessary, and essential reflection of that *uncertainty* which flows, in the nature of things, from inceptive, non-implicit choice. Those two imagined sequels, the best and the worst among the possible sequels, on our present supposition of equal possibility of all sequels will be the only ones relevent to choice. We have already argued that no piling-up of supernumerary sequels of given desiredness and all of equal possibility can increase the possibility of that degree of desiredness. Let me now argue that no sequels of lesser desiredness than the most desired, but of equal possibility with it, can be of concern to the chooser. The argument is the same as that concerning sequels of equal desiredness with the best. Even if the inferior sequels were not inferior, they would do nothing to alter the situation constituted by a given greatest degree of desiredness associated with, sanctioned by, a given degree of assigned possibility. A parallel argument shows that only the most counter-desired of a set of counter-desired sequels all of equal possibility is of concern to the chooser. This, the most counter-desired sequel, is the one which determines the degree of counter-desiredness of the worst threat which seems to be offered by the choosable system in question.

In order to suggest that these two points on the desiredness scale: that of the most-desired of the possible sequels and that of the most counter-desired, were the two on which the chooser's concern and attention would be exclusively concentrated, I have usually called them *focus-points*. I have now to extend the argument to include those cases where the chooser, in contemplating some one choosable system, entertains for it imagined sequels of various degrees of assigned possibility. For this we need a second axis of co-ordinates, orthogonal to the axis of desiredness, on which we can represent degrees of possibility. However, it is convenient to express those degrees by means of a variable which increases in the opposite sense of the axis to possibility itself, in order that perfect possibility may be represented by a zero numerical value of this variable.

16. *An inverted measure of possibility*

Perfect possibility is something utterly different from certainty. The chooser, in assigning perfect possibility to any hypothesized sequel, does not mean that he has positive belief in its eventual actuality, he means that he *does not disbelieve* in this eventual actualizing. Perfect possibility is zero disbelief. I am therefore led to express possibility by a variable whose content is disbelief. This variable may be taken to range from zero up to an absolute maximum representing total disbelief, that is to say, entire adjudged impossibility. Will not an imagined sequel which is assigned a lesser possibility than another of equal desiredness have less interest for the chooser than that other? If so, our frame of reference can be completed by a third axis representing the power of any sequel, in virtue of its desiredness and its possibility, to claim the chooser's interest when considered by itself. Let me call this power *ascendancy*. The ascendancy of any sequel will be an increasing function of that sequel's desiredness and a decreasing function of its assigned disbelief, its obstructedness. Likewise it will, in a different range of the desiredness-counter-desiredness axis, be an increasing function of the counter-desiredness of a sequel which is counter-desired, and again a decreasing function of its assigned disbelief. It may now seem appropriate to re-interpret the term focus-points to mean two points, associated with some one choosable system, whose ascendancy is greater than that of other desired or, respectively, counter-desired sequels.

17. *Endlessness of potential origination of sequels, and the nature of epistemic standing*

Let us now return to the matter of the number of sequels, that is, paths of history-to-come, which can be conceived by the chooser as flowing from some one choosable system of action and accorded by him some greater-than-zero possibility. I suggested that because any one such path must incorporate at countless points the choices-to-come to be made by others, and because the character of what will be chosen cannot, in the nature of choice as we are understanding that term, be foreknown by anyone, the number of variant imaginable and possible paths is in principle unlimited. The number of such paths that the chooser will have envisaged, at any moment when choice has to be made, will be finite. But this does not entitle him to treat the list of those he has already envisaged in some degree of specificness as *complete* nor as *completeable*. Is he not thus debarred from assigning to the members of the list, values of any variable whose assigned values all taken together must by their meaning sum to a definite total? This difficulty is one of the two which we principally avoid when we resort to possibility, rather than prob-ability, as the expression of epistemic standing accorded by the chooser to imagined sequels of any choosable action-system. For perfect possibility, that is, complete epistemic unobstructedness allowing *zero disbelief*, can be assigned to any number of rivals at the same time. Probability by contrast must be regarded as *distributed* over the members of some list which, to make sense of such distribution, must not be treated as indefinitely extensible.

18. *Characters of probability*

In its most general and inclusive meaning, probability names a class of interpretations of epistemic standing (in the sense we have sought to suggest for that term) which have one very important character in common. These interpretations all in-dicate the degree of that standing, if such indication is possible, by means of a variable which increases in degree or numerical value with any improvement in the epistemic standing of the proposition in question. This is not a merely formal matter. For while freedom from recognized obstacles is something which can be enjoyed in common by any number of rival hypotheses or propositions, and for which, therefore, they are not in formal competition with each other, this cannot be true of a variable whose increasing numerical values indicate, for any proposition to which they are assigned, an approach towards *certainty*. Whether higher probabilities are held to mean higher relative frequencies of occurrence, a higher degree of rational belief, a stronger confirmation, or any source or sign of positive confidence, the increase of this kind of standing for one proposition must imply its decrease for some of the rivals of that proposition. In the extreme, a proposition which is held to be *certain* necessarily excludes any degree of acceptance, other than zero, for propositions which are its rivals; that is to say, propositions whose truth would deny the truth of the one in question. A proposition, a hypothesis, a suggested answer to some questions, which is deemed to be perfectly possible, may stand alone in that adjudgement, or may be one of many mutually exclusive propositions, or one of a list of such mutual exclusives which seems in principle to be capable of endless extension. But a proposition which is deemed to be certainly true, cannot allow any truth to propositions which contradict it. Certainty, whatever nature we assign to it, must be in some sense, on some principle, by some procedure, *shared* amongst rivals if these present themselves and cannot be excluded. Probability, whatever basis we adopt for it, is a *distributional* measure or indicator of epistemic standing. It seems to me inappropriate and inapplicable to a situation where rival propositions (for example, the rival sequels imagined for some system of action) are in the nature of things an infinitely extensible list. Let me consider a question which may here suggest itself. Choice must be made at the moment which circumstances propose. There is a deadline. There will not be time (how could there ever be?) for the chooser to compose, for each rival choosable action-scheme which he has envisaged, an infinite list of rival sequels. The notion of an infinite list contradicts the notion of the *completion* of such a list. Will it not then be appropriate and permissible for the chooser to treat the list so far as he has gone with it *as if* it were complete? To do so will, I think, be plainly fallacious. If I know the names of only some of the horses entered for a race, it will not do to treat the sub-set whose names I do know as though the winner were bound to be found amongst them.

The association of the various notions of probability with the notion of *lack of knowledge*, with the notion of *unknowledge*, is a strange one in origin and nature. We are asked to believe that by some juggling, the insufficiency of an available body of knowledge to establish a one-one correspondence between choosable actions and their sequels can be abolished or disregarded. Broadly it may be said that there are two proposed methods for this. One is to treat that *knowledge* which statistical probability provides concerning some *class of instances taken as one whole*, as applicable to single instances each taken on its own. The other method, proposed, for example, by Leibniz and by Maynard Keynes, is to suppose that reason, though insufficiently provided with evidence for the construction of a demonstrative proof of some proposition, can none the less inform us that that proposition has a better or a poorer claim on our belief. Are we not obliged to ask: If a body of knowledge is, for some purpose, insufficient, if it exhibits a *gap*, what means or justification have we for ignoring that gap, for declaring the contents which, if we were better informed, might fill that gap and make the body of knowledge complete for the purpose in hand, to be unimportant in some degree? There seems here to be a contradiction. Either the needed knowledge is partly not there, not available, or else the knowledge which is present is only superficially incomplete, and can be made visibly complete by reasoning from what is explicitly known. How can we have it both ways? At the head of his first chapter, Keynes quotes a sentence from Leibniz in his support. Leibniz was a philosopher of boundless audacity and intellectual ambition. Keynes also was a mind of untrammelled daring. Can it not perhaps be, that in this matter of probability they over-reached themselves? Keynes denies that his conception of probability involves anything subjective except the specification of that body of evidence which is to be deemed relevant. I would venture to say that the notion of degree of rational belief can be salvaged only by invoking an act of creative invention and subjective, non-demonstrable judgement. The assessor can ask himself: What additional postulates or evidence would render my existing body of knowledge sufficient for demonstrative proof of the proposition I am considering? and: How difficult, in some sense, how lacking in intellectual respectability, how much against the grain of practical conscience, is the invention, the figmentation, of such suppositional extra 'evidence'?

Degree of rational belief, in the sense which Leibniz adumbrated and Keynes tried to establish, when considered as a means of expression of epistemic standing where that standing cannot amount to certainty, has one great virtue. Its applicability is not confined to the assessment of classes, each class treated indivisibly as one whole, of numerous instances all arising in a specified set of conditions of bounded variability. By contrast, it applies to a single proposition. When a frequency-ratio is assumed to throw light on the question: What will be the result of the single, indivisible, identified, 'proper-named' instance of some sort of trial which I am about to make, such as the throwing of two dice at one go, are we not obliged to ask what our attitude will be when we can compare *ex post facto* the actual result with any particular hypothetical result on which our attention had been fixed beforehand? Suppose that before making such an identified, proper-named trial, say the throwing of two dice together at 8 a.m. on 29 September 1975, I have before me a table showing how many ways, out of the thirty-six different ways in which the two dice can fall in regard to the faces which lie uppermost, will show a total of two dots, three dots, and so on up to twelve dots. If, when the trial has been made, I see a total, say, of five dots, what relation can I claim to find between the table and this result? Does the result confirm the table? Does the result dis-confirm the table? Plainly it does neither. Did the table tell me beforehand what the result would be? Plainly it did not. What the table did purport to tell me was that if I were to make say, three thousand six hundred throws of the two dice, a table of the realized results would bear some recognizable resemblance to the frequency-table arrived at in advance. Statistical frequencies (whether obtained by inspection of structure or by experiment) are *knowledge*. They are knowledge which cannot claim to be exact. What knowledge can claim to be exact? Perhaps only that of the positional astronomer. But we are not now seeking a means of knowledge, but a means of *expressing attitudes to unknowledge*. The means I have been for many years suggesting, the notion of possibility treated as the absence, complete or in some degree imperfect, of any obstacle within the assessor's knowledge, can evidently apply to single propositions or to single instances. If we take one further step we can make a further claim of some interest.

19. *Epistemic standing as a variable of feeling*

Above I proposed a system of three co-ordinate axes, one of which would represent possibility. How are degrees of possibility to be assessed or expressed so as to be locatable on a scale? If we turn for this purpose to the nature of the obstacles which are the source or basis of judgements of imperfect possibility, we shall find of course that they show an unlimited diversity which seems to offer no hope of any common measure. However, the variables measured on the other two axes are *variables of feeling*. They are *desiredness* and *ascendancy*, the latter being the power of some kinds of ideas to gain the individual's attention and perhaps thus influence his choice. It may well seem that our third axis ought likewise to be occupied by a variable of feeling, and there is in universal experience a feeling which exhibits degrees of greater or less intensity, and which arises solely from cognitive situations, namely, from the comparison of what was imagined *ex ante* with what has appeared *ex post*. The feeling of *surprise* expresses by its degrees the degree to which possibility has been misjudged. If something presents itself in 'the news', the reports of *what is*, despite having been hitherto dismissed as impossible, that even will cause a high degree of surprise. The falsifying of lesser supposed obstacles will engender less surprise. The potential surprise to which the chooser exposes himself by an adjudgement of possibility may serve as a variable of feeling to represent possibility on our third axis.

20. *Choosables as originated vectors of non-coherent possibilities*

At the outset of my lecture I proposed that in face of the perennial question of determinism or non-determinism we should feel free to make an election between the two hypotheses on grounds of the fertility of each in leading to interesting argument and further speculation. On this ground, or with this defence, I rejected determinism for the purpose of my enquiry into the fibre and fabric of the concept of choice. The economist often pretends to discuss choice, but his meaning for this word is the determinate response of men with given desires to their assumedly fully-known circumstances. Choice would then be the mere clicking of the machine as it works, or a mere fleck of pigment in the still picture of eternity. The theme which has flowed (if I may so dignify my thoughts) from that rejection has led to a view of human affairs which some of you will dismiss as an extreme subjectivism entirely abhorrent to the scientific outlook. Science searches for cause and effect. Cause and effect are indispensable to my argument, but only subject to the exemption of thought itself from entire governance by influences outside itself. Let the statistician interpret me as meaning that thought can be random, let the poet understand me as saying that thought can be inspired.

I have suggested to you a meaning for the word choice which may seem to discard entirely the content that either conversational usage or rigorous discourse has given it. The fundamental difference between my conception and the orthodox notions is my insistence that choice is a business conducted in face of a void of knowledge, that void which simply expresses the non-existence of what the knowledge would be knowledge of. Choice cannot have knowledge of the pre-existing contents of its field, because those contents are the very thing which it is the business of choice to create, to originate. Nor can the chooser foreknow what the sequel of his present choice will be, for if his own choices are inceptive, if his own choices are non-implicit, in some degree, in their antecedents, so are the choices of others and so are all the choices-to-come of himself as well as others. But these choices-to-come, unknown though their sequels will essentially be to those who will make them, will supply in part the circumstances shaping the sequel of choices made now. Inceptive choice is choice made (because of the nature of *other* inceptive choices-to-come) without knowledge of a precisely described, uniquely possible sequel, for *there is no such uniqueness*. Inceptive choice at best can only expose the chooser to a skein of rival possibilities, a skein with which he represents to himself as well as he can the real indeterminacy of the history-to-come which will affect him. With a different choice, this skein would be a different one. Choice makes a difference, but this difference, for the chooser when he makes his choice, is between one set of permissible imaginations and another. If each choosable offers rival sequels, some desired and some counter-desired, how can comparison of the choosables be made? Can such a question be evaded? It cannot, for in the essential nature of choice we discern uncertainty, and uncertainty is the entertaining of rival, mutually incompatible answers to one and the same question. Can rival action-schemes be compared on such a basis? A mundane illustration offers itself. When a man makes a bet, he deliberately exposes himself to the possibility of a loss, a loss which he could have excluded. He does so for the sake of exposing himself by the same act to the possibility of gain. The two hypotheses, that he will lose and that he will win, are mutually contradictory, yet he must weigh against each other the two mutually incompatible anticipations, and he must weigh against each other *different* available wagers, different pairs of incompatibles. Can it be denied that he does so?

Part II

UNCERTAINTY AND DECISION-MAKING

The Expectational Dynamics of the Individual

By G. L. SHACKLE

I

THAT new part of economic theory which seeks to explain the level of employment and the rate of flow of output as a whole had its historical origin in the theory of money. Thus it was held that the quantity of money existing at a given moment determined in some way the general level of prices, and that this level, or its changes, determined whether enterprisers would make profits or losses, and thus whether they would extend or reduce the scale on which they engaged in the making and selling of goods, and the quantity of employment they offered. It was possible to develop a self-consistent theory on these lines without any reference whatever to the process of thought, the motives, and the temperament of the *individual enterpriser*. He was assumed to react in an almost mechanical way to a change in *current* prices or profits. Thus while in the theory of value the individual was king, and his preferences and reactions were the fundamental theme, in the theory of money he found no place at all. The theory of money has developed into and been absorbed by what is now sometimes known as macro-dynamic economics, and this term itself implies that we are concerned with phenomena " in the large " and can neglect the individual. Yet the most modern forms of economic dynamics admit that it is, after all, the decisions of *individuals* which determine what will happen. Professor Hayek, for example, has defined equilibrium as that state of affairs where the plans of *individuals* are mutually compatible. And the need to study what goes on in the mind of the individual is also tacitly admitted by modern dynamic theories in the importance they assign to *expectations*.

Judgment of what is implied for the future by what we know of the present situation, summarising past history within itself, and above all, the choice of what *assumptions* to make, what produc ts of almost pure artistic imagination to introduce, in order to supply the deficiencies of this knowledge and complete in some rough sense the data for logical inference as to the future course of events, will vary at least as much between different individuals as their preferences. Yet there has been no open recognition so far in economics of the need to study the psychology of expectation as a process of the individual mind. It would be hard to exaggerate the difficulty of the field thus

99

IOO   ECONOMICA   ⌈MAY

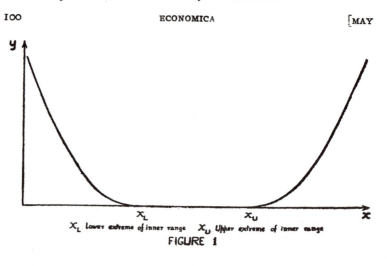

X_L Lower extreme of inner range X_U Upper extreme of inner range

FIGURE 1

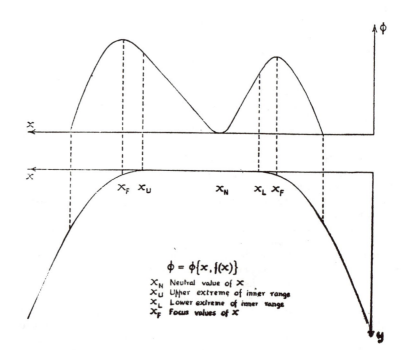

$$\phi = \phi\{x, f(x)\}$$

X_N Neutral value of X
X_U Upper extreme of inner range
X_L Lower extreme of inner range
X_F Focus values of X

FIGURE 2

opened up. The central problem of all is the nature of the mental process by which a man considers, first, the entire set of all rival courses of action open to himself, and second, the entire set of all the different paths which the future course of events could follow, and decides which members, that is, what sub-set, of the second set correspond to each member of the first set. In what follows,[1] I have done no more than indicate some of the limitations of our power to establish this correspondence, and traced some consequences which follow from this limitation ; and have then tried to indicate, in a very tentative way, what seems to me a possible line of attack on the core-problem of this subject, the mode of formation of expectations. Many of the suggestions advanced in this article are, I believe, possible constituents of a *general* theory of expectation, and are not confined to the economic field by means of which they are here illustrated.

II

Between a feeling of certainty that a given event will happen (or some particular answer to a given question turn out to be the truth), and a feeling of certainty that it will not, there seems to be a continuous range of different levels at which our degree of belief can stand. By what operation can a person compare his own respective degrees of belief in two different outcomes of some course of action or two different answers to a question ? I think he can do this by taking each of these outcomes or answers in turn and asking himself what intensity of shock or surprise he would feel if, without there having been any change in the knowledge available to him on which he based his belief in it, he were to learn that this belief is mistaken. That is to say, the operation by which he measures his degree of belief, corresponding for example to the application of a column of mercury in measuring temperature, is the act of imagining himself to learn that this belief is false. The measure so obtained is what we may call the *potential surprise* associated with the falsity of the particular answer or the non-occurrence of the particular hypothetical outcome. In some circumstances it will be appropriate to ask ourselves what degree of potential surprise we attach to the fulfilment rather than the non-fulfilment of a given hypothesis. For suppose we are not concerned simply with the question whether one single particular hypothesis is true or untrue, but rather with the question *which* out of a set of rival hypotheses is the true one. In this case there may be a sub-set of several hypotheses, each member of which is superior, as regards our degree of belief in it, to any hypothesis outside the sub-set, but of which no one member is

[1] The exposition in Sections II and III of this article will be found to follow closely the lines adopted in my article " A Theory of Investment Decisions " (*Oxford Economic Papers*, No. 6), though the argument is more explicitly stated on some important points. Sections IV to VIII of the present article contain an entirely fresh formulation of two of the main themes of the former article, and in addition open a new theme by considering the logical structure of enjoyment by anticipation and a consequence which flows from it. Section IX opens a discussion of the problem of how expectations are generated.

superior to any other member. In this case it will be impossible for us to attach any non-zero degree of potential surprise to the non-fulfilment of any particular member of the sub-set: for to do so would *ipso facto* mark it off as claiming a higher degree of our belief than the other members. The most we can do is to attach *nil* potential surprise to the *fulfilment* of any member of the sub-set. But we *can* attach some positive degree of potential surprise to every hypothesis *outside* the sub-set, and by doing so we shall express its inferiority in the matter of the degree of our belief in it, to every member of the sub-set. And further, we can attach different degrees of potential surprise to different hypotheses outside the sub-set, thus assigning to them positions on a scale of belief. If the sub-set has only one single member, and if for *every conceivable* non-member the degree of potential surprise attached to the fulfilment of this non-member is indefinitely high, this will mean that we feel completely certain that the one member will turn out to be the truth.

By the *outcome* of a given course of action we shall mean the entire set of advantages and disadvantages which the adoption of this course, rather than some other which is being compared with it, will bring to the individual concerned. Experience teaches us that he will virtually never be able to specify for each of these courses a unique outcome which he can feel completely certain will turn out to be the true one. For any one course of action he will have in mind many different hypothetical outcomes, and out of these there will be a large number any one of which would cause him some degree of surprise if it were to turn out to be the actual one without there having been, in the meantime, any change in the knowledge on which he is now basing his expectations. The degree of this potential surprise will differ between different hypotheses. Some will seem to involve assumptions which conflict with elements in the present situation, and therefore to involve the further assumption that special factors will arise, of which there is no evidence at present, capable of cancelling these adverse elements. The potential surprise attached to these hypotheses may be extreme. Other hypotheses will seem potentially less surprising, and others less still, in descending steps which will lead ultimately to the other group of hypotheses, those, namely, for each of which the potential surprise is *nil*. Now it is clear that this " inner " group must comprise at least one hypothesis : but our knowledge of the present intentions and of the capacities of other people, and of what will be their reactions in the further future to each other's more immediately future acts, is so extremely slight and insecure that, in reality, the inner group will always consist of a large number of hypotheses whose mutually most dissimilar members will differ from each other very widely. This conclusion brings us to our central problem : How will an individual choose between different courses of action when the outcome of each cannot be known in advance, but is only represented in his mind by a whole set of differing hypotheses ?

The real incentive for embarking on some given course of action, whose objective results will not develop and their character become known until some date in the future, is the *immediate* mental experience which the decision to embark on this course will give us, namely, the *enjoyment by anticipation* of a high level of success. I do not believe that the impossibility of feeling *certain* that a particular unique result will be attained by the contemplated course of action implies that the individual will not desire a unique focus for his imagination, that is to say, that he will not centre his hopes on *one particular* level of success. He will, it seems to me, desire a single clear-cut mental image concerning the outcome to provide the *content* of his hope, and this will need to be given, as it were, an extra dimension, by association with a sufficiently low degree of potential surprise, to render it a motive force behind his decision. There is a phrase of common speech which seems to throw much light on this matter (such phrases, moulded unconsciously by the actual modes of working of our minds, of many minds over many centuries, should surely be a safe and fruitful source of instruction): we speak of having " a *lively* expectation " of something. This must surely mean a *life-like, vivid and active* expectation, one which carries conviction by the realism and insistent presence, as it were " in the flesh ", of the imagined thing. A lively expectation, something which seems a living projection of the future into the present, is what is needed to induce us to take action now to attain the reality. This " liveliness ", this realism, cannot conceivably be possessed by a bundle of divergent hypotheses or conceptions: it must require uniqueness in the mental image on which we finally focus our attention, even if there is no such uniqueness in the contingencies we pass in review in our minds. The question that we have to answer, if this view be accepted, is, how will the particular level of success upon which he will settle his hopes be determined from amongst the whole range of hypothetical outcomes which in varying degree he entertains?

The enjoyment by anticipation of a favourable result will not be experienced unalloyed, except in the rare case where the outcome is felt to be uniquely certain. In most cases there will be some positively hurtful outcomes which will be not less insistently present to our imagination than the favourable ones. Here again the individual will tend, I think, to concentrate his fears at some specific point, selecting *one particular* degree of misfortune to represent what he " stands to lose ".

Now the intensity of enjoyment of a given hypothetical outcome from imagining it in advance is a function of more than one variable, but it is surely a *decreasing* function of the degree of potential surprise attached to this outcome. It is also evidently an *increasing* function of the desirability of the outcome. In the same way the distress the individual will feel at the thought of a positively hurtful outcome will be a decreasing function of the potential surprise and an increasing function of the hurtfulness. Out of the whole assembly of hypotheses as to the outcome of any one course of action, those hypotheses the thought of which causes him the most enjoyment or the most distress will mainly focus his attention and influence him in assessing the attractiveness of this course of action in comparison with others. Thus, in general, there are two possible reasons for the individual to pay more attention to one of a pair of hypotheses than to the other : first, there may be a difference in the respective degrees of potential surprise he associates with them, and second, when both outcomes are advantageous one may be more advantageous than the other, and when both are hurtful one may be more hurtful than the other.   But among all the outcomes for which his potential surprise is *nil*, there will be only one reason for him to concentrate his attention on some rather than others, namely, that some are more desirable or more undesirable.   I suggest, therefore, that when he contemplates this inner group of outcomes each of which carries no potential surprise, the individual concentrates his attention on the *best* and the *worst* hypotheses in this range.   Evidently he need not confine himself to considering only the inner group ; outside it there may be outcomes even more desirable or hurtful than any of those inside it.   But it will usually be true that outside the inner group, the greater the desirability or hurtfulness of a given outcome the higher the degree of potential surprise it will carry ;   and since, for some outcomes, the potential surprise is indefinitely great, amounting to absolute disbelief in the possibility of these outcomes, and since in such a case there can be no enjoyment of these outcomes by anticipation, there will be a point beyond which no outcome offers a sufficient extra advantage (or extra detriment) over the next most desirable (or hurtful) to compensate for the extra potential surprise which it carries.   At such a point the total differential of the degree of enjoyment by anticipation, or distress by anticipation, will be zero, and the degree of enjoyment or distress a maximum.   At these two points will be found that particular pair of hypotheses which will mainly capture the individual's attention and will represent for him the attractiveness of the particular course of action in question.

The set of hypotheses in an individual's mind regarding the outcome of a given course of action, in the sense of the net advantage or disadvantage that will result from it, can consist of all the possible values of a continuously variable quantity x.   Let y stand for the degree of potential surprise associated with x.   Then we have seen that there will usually be a range of values of x for all of which $y = 0$, this range being what we have called the " inner " group of hypotheses.   We shall call it the " inner range ".   For all values of x above the upper extreme of the inner range, y will be an increasing function of x, and for all values of x below the lower extreme of the inner range, y will be a decreasing function of x.   Thus the shape of the function $y = f(x)$ will usually be of the general type illustrated in Figure 1.   It is reasonable to suppose that the segment of y corresponding to the inner range of x will merge smoothly into the decreasing and increasing segments of y, so that $\frac{dy}{dx}$ will be everywhere continuous. We shall call the function $y = f(x)$ the potential surprise function.

The intensity of enjoyment or distress caused by the thought of any hypothetical outcome will be a function, first, of the degree of success or advantage represented by this hypothesis, and second, of the degree of potential surprise associated with it. For this intensity of feeling, whether it be of enjoyment or distress, let us write ϕ. Then ϕ will depend on x in two ways, first directly, and second through its dependence on y, which itself depends on x. Thus we can write $\phi = \phi\{x, f(x)\}$. Now let us suppose that at some value *within* the inner range x is such that the thought of it causes neither enjoyment nor distress ; and for simplicity let us assume that this neutral value of x happens to be $x = 0$. Over the interval of x between zero and the upper extreme of the inner range $\frac{dy}{dx} = 0$ and therefore $\frac{\partial \phi}{\partial y}\frac{dy}{dx} = 0$, while $\frac{\partial \phi}{\partial x}$ is positive. Over this interval, therefore, ϕ will increase as x increases. Beyond the upper extreme of the inner range, $\frac{dy}{dx}$ is positive, and therefore, since $\frac{\partial \phi}{\partial y}$ is everywhere negative, $\frac{\partial \phi}{\partial y}\frac{dy}{dx}$ is here negative, while $\frac{\partial \phi}{\partial x}$ is, of course, still positive. Now when y approaches a value amounting to a feeling of complete certainty that the hypothesis will not be realised, ϕ will be reduced to zero whatever the value of x. But clearly in most concrete cases there are finite values of x for which y will be indefinitely great. There will therefore be some value of x at which $\frac{\partial \phi}{\partial x} = -\frac{\partial \phi}{\partial y}\frac{dy}{dx}$ and at this point ϕ will be a maximum. Turning to the negative values of x let us put $z = -x$, so that increasing values of z stand for increasing degrees of hurtfulness or disadvantage in the outcome. Then an argument similar to the one above shows that there will be a point where $\frac{\partial \phi}{\partial z} = -\frac{\partial \phi}{\partial y}\frac{dy}{dz}$ and here ϕ will again have a maximum value. These two values of x, we suggest, where ϕ is a maximum, will attract to themselves the greater part of the individual's attention, and we shall call them the *focus-values* of x. His basis for comparing the attractiveness of the course of action in question with that of another course will consist in these two values.

The function $\phi = \phi\{x, f(x)\}$ will resemble in shape the one shown in Figure 2. This figure ought, of course, to be a three-dimensional model with the x, y plane and the ϕ, x plane perpendicular to each other. In Figure 2, however, the x, y plane is considered to have been rotated about the x axis through one right angle, so that both planes lie flat on the page. Thus in the upper half of the diagram we see the projection of the ϕ curve on the ϕ, x plane, while in the lower half we see the y curve placed so that each point on it lies in a position on the page exactly beneath that point on the ϕ curve which corresponds to it. In the true three-dimensional model, $\phi = \phi\{x, f(x)\}$ would, of course, be a twisted curve whose projection on the x, y plane would coincide exactly with the y-curve.

III

By the earnings of a piece of equipment in any year we mean the difference between the receipts in that year from selling its product and the outlay in that year for the materials and the services needed to operate it. If the assumed earnings of each future year of its useful life are discounted to the present at the rate of interest now obtainable on a riskless loan repayable at the same date, and the results for all these years added together, we get a " present value " for the plant. The difference between the present value of a proposed new plant and what this would cost to construct is what we mean by the gain or loss from constructing such a plant. This gain or loss is a specially clear-cut example of an outcome to which the conception of focus-values described above is appropriate. Even the construction-cost, though it refers to proposed operations in the immediate future, cannot always be exactly known in advance. The *value* of a new plant to an owner who intends to retain possession of it during the whole of its working life clearly depends on the circumstances of a long series of years stretching into the future. If instead he hopes to sell the plant, once he has brought it to concert pitch as a going concern, then its value to him depends on what he thinks will be the opinion concerning those future years held by the most sanguine potential purchaser ; or on what that purchaser himself thinks will be the opinion of some subsequent purchaser ; and so on indefinitely.[1] Clearly in either case, whether the potential constructor intends to hold or to sell the plant, the present value to be assigned to it, while it still exists only in his mind, is open to extremely divergent conjectures. Thus the outcome of constructing the plant will present itself as a wide range of hypotheses varying from a gain of several times the amount laid out on construction to the loss of the whole of it, and a considerable inner range of these hypotheses will carry *nil* potential surprise. The choice which faces the holder of a large sum of cash, between putting into execution one or other of a large number of projects for constructing equipment of widely differing characters, or retaining the cash or lending it at fixed interest, will be resolved according to our theory by comparing, in the manner suggested in the next paragraph, the pairs of focus-values assigned to the different courses of action.

---

[1] The dependence, e.g., of Stock Exchange values on what people think other people are going to think is going to happen, and so forth, was first pointed out by Lord Keynes in *The General Theory of Employment, Interest and Money*, Chapter 12.

Let us use the term " blueprint " to mean a project, existing only in a person's mind or on paper, for constructing a block of equipment of a specific character. One of the focus-values which the individual assigns to the outcome of each blueprint will usually represent a gain and the other a loss, and we shall call these the " focus gain " and the " focus loss " of the blueprint. If we write v for the value and c for the construction cost of a plant, and put $x = v - c$, then positive values of x will represent a gain and negative values a loss, and we could speak of a *numerical* increase of the loss $c - v$ as a decrease of x. But for simplicity of statement we shall say that the loss increases when we mean that it increases *numerically*, passing to an algebraically smaller value of x. We shall sometimes speak of the focus-values of x as the " focus-outcomes " of a given course of action. Suppose that for a blueprint A the focus gain is g_A times the construction-cost and the focus loss a proportion h_A of the construction cost, while for a blueprint B the ratios are g_B and h_B. For each ratio $\dfrac{h_B}{h_A}$ there will be some critical ratio $\dfrac{g_B}{g_A}$ which would make blueprint B neither more nor less attractive than blueprint A. If $\dfrac{g_B}{g_A}$ exceeds this critical level, the investor will decide, so far as the choice between A and B is concerned, in favour of B. All other pairs of uses for his cash can be compared in the same way and his course thus decided on.

IV

A blueprint has amongst its attributes not only the nature of its product and its own technical design and its location, but also the specific period of future time in which it is intended to be operated. An investor who has in mind at a particular date a given type of plant, will assign to it different pairs of focus-outcomes according as he considers constructing it now or at various distances in future time. For not only will he expect the circumstances of two different specific periods to differ, but the more distant the period considered, the less light his present knowledge will seem to throw on it, and the wider will be the range of values of each important variable[1] in the period which he must regard as non-surprising. Thus if we designate different physical types of plant by letters A, B, etc., we must also attach to each letter a subscript indicating the particular fixed date[2] at which we are supposing that the plant will be completed and begin its operating life.

Let each of the symbols $A_{[1]}$, $A_{[2]}$, $- - A_{[r]} - -$ represent the idea of

---

[1] Such as prices, total value of backlogs of orders, size of inventories in various hands, rates o taxation, relative numerical strength of parties in Congress or Parliament, etc., etc.

[2] i.e., specified date such as January 1st, 1944.

constructing a plant of given technical design on some fixed, specified date, denoted by the subscript, the design of the plant being the same for all the dates. When the present moment is located at date [1] the investor will have in mind for each of these blueprints its own schedule assigning to each hypothetical outcome of this blueprint its particular degree of potential surprise. That is to say, at date [1] he will have in mind for any blueprint $A_{[r]}$ a unique specific form of the potential surprise function, such functions differing from each other in general for blueprints of different construction dates. But this form which he can specify *now* is not the only form of the potential surprise function for $A_{[r]}$ which he must take into account. He can foresee that when the present moment will have arrived at date [2], and again at date [3], and so on, up to date [r] itself, he will construct a fresh potential surprise function for $A_{[r]}$ which, since at each of those dates he will have in mind knowledge and ideas which will have come to him in the interval, can differ from the form he assigns now. He cannot, of course, specify exactly *now* the form of function that he will assign to $A_{[r]}$ *at date* [r]; but we shall see that he can sometimes form some judgments about it which are as important, for deciding on his present action, as the form which he assigns now. For convenient reference we must have a notation distinguishing from each other the ideas, present in his mind at date [1], of constructing potential surprise functions for $A_{[r]}$ at different future dates. For this purpose, let us attach to the letter y, standing for some form of potential surprise function, two subscripts, of which the first will specify the *viewpoint* or moment at which the investor is actually doing his thinking, and the second will specify a date, which may be the same as the viewpoint or may be still in the future, at which he will be assigning a particular form to $y(x)$. Thus $y_{[1][3]}, A_{[3]}$ is the identity-disc, as it were, which the investor attaches, at date [1], to that particular form of the potential surprise function which he will assign to $A_{[3]}$ at date [3]. By its nature $y_{[1][3]}, A_{[3]}$, if it is other than identical with $y_{[1][1]}, A_{[3]}$, clearly cannot be a unique form, but must consist in two or more hypotheses. When the investor's viewpoint or present moment arrives at date [3] then $y_{[3][3]}, A_{[3]}$ will come into existence and will be a unique form, and any differences between this form and $y_{[1][1]}, A_{[3]}$ will have been due to fresh news or inferences which came into the investor's mind between dates [1] and [3]. Thus so far as he can make, at date [1], any judgments as to what questions will be answered by the fresh news or knowledge which will come to him before date [3], he can give to the symbol[1] $y_{[1][3]}, A_{[3]}$ a content consisting of a number of hypotheses, each of which will be a different specific form of potential surprise function, and will correspond to one particular set of answers to the questions; and *to each of these hypotheses he can attach its*

---

[1] For clearness of presentation, we will continue throughout this section to use an actual numeral [3] to represent a future date. It will be understood that the use of the particular numeral [3] for this purpose has no significance : any other numeral would have done. In later sections we shall represent future dates by [n].

particular degree of potential surprise. If any of these hypotheses assigns to $y(x)$ a *lower* value than is assigned to it, for the same value of x, by $y_{[1]\,[1]}$, $A_{[3]}$, then the investor will attach to this hypothesis an indefinitely large potential surprise : for a value of x which he thinks, at date [1], will be potentially surprising to him at date [3] cannot be less potentially surprising to him now : any other state of mind involves him in a logical contradiction.   But there is no logical hindrance to his attaching *nil* potential surprise to any of the hypotheses constituting $y_{[1]\,[3]}$, $A_{[3]}$ which assigns to $y(x)$ a higher value than is assigned to the latter, for the same value of x, by $y_{[1]\,[1]}$, $A_{[3]}$.   Thus it is in the nature of focus-outcomes that the investor will attach indefinitely high potential surprise to the idea that the focus-gain or the focus-loss of a blueprint of distant construction date might increase as the present moment advances towards that date.   But he can, so far as logical consistency is concerned, and in some circumstances will, attach *nil* potential surprise to the idea that either of them may decrease.

The possibility that the focus-gain or the focus-loss of a blueprint of distant construction date may get smaller as that date approaches will usually arise in the individual's mind in a special form : he may have in mind one or more particular questions, such as what will be the result of some election, the provisions of some new statute, the character of a Budget, or the outcome of a mineralogical survey, whose answers if they are of one kind will curtail the inner range at its upper end or steepen the slope of the increasing segment, or both, and will leave the rest of the curve unchanged ; and if they are of an opposite kind, will curtail the inner range at its lower end or steepen the negative slope of the decreasing segment, or both, and leave the rest of the curve unchanged.   We shall refer to a change of form involving only some part of the curve above the lower extreme of the inner range, whether this change involves a curtailment of the inner range or a steepening of the increasing segment, or both, as a shift of the *upper branch* of the curve ; and we define correspondingly, *mutatis mutandis*, a shift of the lower branch.

If the investor attaches some positive degree of potential surprise to the two equivalent ideas :

(1) that the questions will not be answered before date [3] ;

(2) that $y_{[1]\,[3]}$, $A_{[3]}$ can be considered unique and identical with $y_{[1]\,[1]}$, $A_{[3]}$;

then he cannot at the same time discriminate, by attaching some positive potential surprise to one of them and *nil* to the other, between a shift of the upper branch of the curve, implying a decrease of the focus gain, and a shift of the lower branch, implying a decrease of the focus loss.   For if he did thus discriminate, this would mean that *both* the non-answering of the questions, *and* the shift of one of the two branches, would carry some positive potential surprise ; and since these are the only two alternatives to a shift of the *other* branch of the curve, *the non-occurrence of this latter shift* would carry some positive potential surprise ; but in this case it would no longer be something which might occur in the future, but would be already embodied in the form he assigns *now* to $y(x)$, namely $y_{[1][1]}$, $A_{[3]}$. On the other hand, if he attaches *nil* potential surprise to the *non*-answering of the questions, he can then attach some positive potential surprise to a shift of one branch of the curve and *nil* to a shift of the other.

The special questions may sometimes, of course, have not merely two but any number of different possible answers : for example, the different answers can consist in different values of a continuous variable. In this case, some of the possible answers may imply an inward shift of *both* branches of the curve. But here again, provided that the investor attaches some positive degree of potential surprise to the non-answering of the questions on or before the future date he has in mind, then there must be amongst all the others two sets of answers, both carrying *nil* potential surprise, of which one set implies no shift of the upper branch of the curve specified by $y_{[1][1]}$, $A_{[3]}$, and the other implies no shift of the lower branch.

The main conclusion to which this section has led us is the following : In regard to some particular blueprint, which can be either a blueprint for deferred construction or one for immediate construction, the investor can sometimes feel that he will be very surprised if *neither* the focus-loss *nor* the focus-gain decreases at some specific future date. In the following two sections we shall see two ways in which this feeling may induce him to refrain from immediate construction of a blueprint which he would otherwise find attractive. If for either reason he does so refrain, the aggregate national investment-flow will be lower, over some period of the immediate future, than it would otherwise have been.

V

Let us suppose that the investor has in mind a blueprint for immediate construction $A_{[1]}$, which he would embark on, rather than retain his cash or lend it at fixed interest, if he had no other blueprint in mind. And let us suppose that he has in mind a blueprint for deferred construction $B_{[n]}$ to which $y_{[1][1]}$, $B_{[n]}$ assigns an extremely high focus gain, but also assigns a focus loss so large that, if the blueprint's attractiveness depended on this pair of focus-outcomes alone, the investor would dismiss it from consideration. And further, let us suppose that $y_{[1][n]}$, $B_{[n]}$ comprises a number of different hypotheses as to the form of the potential surprise function which the investor will assign to $B_{[u]}$ when date [n] is reached, and that amongst these there is one, carrying *nil* potential surprise, which would imply the same focus gain as $y_{[1][1]}$, $B_{[n]}$, but a focus loss so small as to render $B_{[n]}$, in view of its high focus gain, an extremely attractive investment-opportunity. If the opportunity which would thus be created were actually and immediately open to him, the investor would construct it in preference to $A_{[1]}$. But the creation of this opportunity is in fact only a contingency, and both the occurrence *and the non-occurrence* of this contingency carry *nil* potential surprise. Accordingly, he must consider what alternative investment-opportunity would be open to him at date [n] should the focus-loss of $B_{[n]}$ fail to decrease. If this alternative is not less attractive than $A_{[1]}$, then a decision to retain his cash until date [n], in order to be assured of the power to venture on $B_{[n]}$ should he then wish to, will imply at worst a postponement and not the losing altogether of an investment-opportunity of the quality of $A_{[1]}$. In such a case, provided the date [n] is not too remote from the present, it seems clear that the investor will decide to retain his cash. But this will imply, of course, that the national aggregate investment-flow will be lower, over some period of the immediate future, than it would have been in the absence of any blueprint such as $B_{[n]}$.

Even if it seems to the investor that the best alternative to $B_{[n]}$ which will be open to him at date [n], should the answers to the special questions turn out unfavourable to $B_{[n]}$, will be less attractive than $A_{[1]}$ now is, he may yet decide to retain his cash : for the contingency of a deterioration in his position, such that he will be offered at date [n] a worse instead of a better opportunity than $A_{[1]}$, may be out-weighed in his mind by the contingency of a great improvement. On the other hand it is possible than even if the best alternative to $B_{[n]}$ is actually *better* than $A_{[1]}$, he may yet decide to construct $A_{[1]}$; for the length of the period from date [1] to date [n] is also, as we shall see, a factor in his decision. If this period is short in comparison with the useful lives of plants such as A and B, and if, for example, as will frequently be the case, he expects $A_{[n]}$ to be not less attractive than $A_{[1]}$, then the existence in his mind of a blueprint for deferred construction which is *contingently* very much more attractive than $A_{[1]}$ will cause him to retain his cash.

Why should a decision to invest now in $A_{[1]}$ preclude the investor from investing a little later on in $B_{[n]}$, if by then he has come to prefer the latter, even supposing his cash resources, owned and borrowed together, are only sufficient to pay for one or other of the blueprints at a time ? Could he not sell plant A when it is complete, or obtain a loan secured on it ? This is the heart of the problem of *liquidity*, which consists essentially in the fact that a man can hold with perfect sincerity (and often, as it turns out afterwards, with justice), expectations which imply a far higher value for the plant than he can persuade others to believe in. The focus gain which he himself assigns to A may be larger, and the focus loss smaller, than the corresponding ones in the mind of any potential buyer of plant A. If in such a case he yet insists on selling A, he will make, according to his own expectations and corresponding valuation of A, a loss, and this may well offset the superior attractiveness which $B_{[n]}$ may by then have acquired. Thus, if **having constructed** A **he finds when date [n] is reached that** $B_{[n]}$

has become a very attractive proposition, it may seem better none the less to hold on to A : *but he will regret not having retained his cash.* If at date [1] he foresees that this position may arise at date [n], he will decide to retain his cash.

The mere existence in the investor's mind of a blueprint for deferred construction whose focus gain and loss are both very high in relation to its construction cost will not by itself constitute an inducement to him to retain his cash.   For in regard to many such blueprints he will attach high potential surprise to the occurrence of any considerable decrease of the focus-loss at or before the construction date.   He may often feel sure that no extra light will be thrown on the prospects of a given blueprint except in the actual course of using the plant after it has been constructed.   He may have hypothetical future events in mind which could occur without surprising him, and which would reduce the focus loss, but by an amount insufficient to render the blueprint attractive.   In the nature of things, events must be rare which can seem so comprehensively to block up all paths by which misfortune might strike the enterprise in the course of its career, that they reduce the focus loss to nothing.   But there are certain classes of " experiment ", such as elections, parliamentary voting on particular pieces of legislation, lawsuits, and harvests, the date of whose occurrence can be known in advance, and whose outcome can, if it is of the right kind, defend the enterprise against some of the hazards whose impact would be most disastrous and would otherwise carry no potential surprise.   If the question, the answer to which is expected to throw light on the prospects of a blueprint, is one whose answer will be some value of a continuous variable, then $y_{[1][n]}$, $B_{[n]}$ may contain not merely a finite set of different hypotheses as to the form of potential surprise function which will be assigned to $B_{[n]}$ at date [n], but an infinite set, each member of which will, of course, imply a different focus loss or gain, and in this case the *amount of the decrease* of either of these latter which can be imagined to occur at date [n] will itself have to be looked on as a continuous variable associated with a varying degree of potential surprise.   The idea of a large decrease of the focus loss will, of course, be more interesting to the investor than that of a small decrease ; but beyond a certain size each larger hypothetical decrease will carry a higher degree of potential surprise.   Thus in such cases we can identify and speak of the *focus decrease of the focus loss.*   When the investor is deciding whether the prospect of a decrease of the focus loss of a particular blueprint for deferred construction is a sufficient inducement to him to retain his cash, the particular amount of decrease which concerns him is this focus decrease.   We shall refer to that one of the hypotheses contained in $y_{[1][n]}$, $B_{[n]}$ which corresponds to the focus decrease as the focus-hypothesis of $y_{[1][n]}$, $B_{[n]}$.   It will be seen that if the investor is to attach low potential surprise to the occurrenc e of a given decrease of the focus loss of $B_{[n]}$ at date [n], this requires him to attach low potential surprise to *two* hypotheses : (1) that a suitable question bearing on the prospects of the blueprint will be answered at date [n], and (2) that the answer will be such as to effect this amount of decrease in the focus loss. Now, as we have seen in Section IV, if the investor attaches some positive degree of potential surprise to the *non-answering* of such a question on the date [n], it is not logically possible for him to attach any positive degree of potential surprise to the idea that the question, if answered, will *not* effect a decrease of the amount in question, since he is bound to attach *nil* potential surprise to the hypothesis that *no* decrease of the focus loss will occur, as otherwise the lower branch of $y_{[1]\,[1]}$, $B_{[n]}$ would not have the form which it has. From this it follows that, although frequently in practice, as in the case of a Budget or election, he may attach some positive degree of potential surprise to the *non-answering* of the question on the date [n], this will not make the inducement to retain cash any stronger than it would be if he merely attached *nil* potential surprise to the *answering* of the question at that date ; for when some given result depends on the fulfilment of several conditions, then the non-attainment of the result can only carry positive potential surprise if the non-fulfilment of *all* the conditions carries positive potential surprise. It may be worth while to enlarge on this point for a moment. In general, it will be seen, if we attach positive potential surprise to the *non*-occurrence of some particular result, this implies, of course, that the *occurrence of all alternative results* carries positive potential surprise : in the case of a continuous variable x, for example, $y(x)$ might have the form shown in Figure 3_A or 3_B, amongst an infinite variety of others :

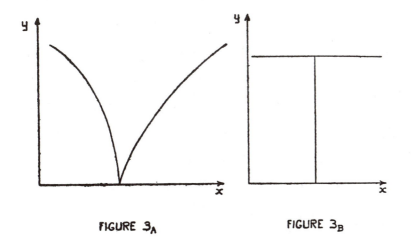

FIGURE 3_A FIGURE 3_B

The degree of potential surprise attached to the non-occurrence of any given result is evidently identical with the least degree of potential surprise attached to any alternative result.

The strength of the inducement to retain cash, arising in the way we have described in this section, will depend on four sets of factors :

(a) The focus gain and loss of $A_{[1]}$; the focus gain and loss of $B_{[n]}$ according to the focus-hypothesis of $y_{[1]\,[n]}$, $B_{[n]}$; and the focus gain and loss of that blueprint, say $C_{[n]}$, which would become the most attractive one in the investor's mind for construction at date [n] if the questions should be answered in a sense *unfavourable* to $B_{[n]}$.

(β) The length of the interval between date [1] and date [n].

(γ) The degree of potential surprise attached to the hypothesis that the questions will be answered not later than date [n].

(∂) The amount by which the value we attribute to $A_{[1]}$ if we assume that its focus gain will be realised exceeds the price for which plant A could be readily sold at date [n].

Regarding (a), the investor may have in mind as an alternative to $B_{[n]}$, in case the latter's focus loss fails to decrease at date [n], a blue-print $C_{[n]}$ whose focus loss would be greatly reduced, and $C_{[n]}$ thus rendered extremely attractive, by that same set of answers to the special questions which would reduce the focus *gain*, instead of the focus loss, of $B_{[n]}$.   This circumstance would, of.course, tend greatly to strengthen the inducement to retain cash.   Next it is clear that the *length of time* he must wait in order to know the answers to the special questions is an influence on the inducement to wait.   For, by assumption, there is something he would prefer to do with his cash rather than lend it at fixed interest.   To wait therefore involves an item on the debit side, a cost, and the longer the prospective time which it will be necessary to wait, the stronger the temptation to choose the other alternative, the immediate construction of $A_{[1]}$.   Regarding (γ), we have seen that the investor cannot attach any positive degree of potential surprise to the *non*-occurrence at date [n] of a decrease in the focus loss of $B_{[n]}$: at best, he can attach *nil* potential surprise to the *occurrence* of a decrease. This requires him to attach *nil* potential surprise to the hypothesis that the questions will be answered on date [n].   But there may still be some degree of inducement to retain cash, even when this hypothesis carries some positive potential surprise.   We can say, therefore, that the inducement to retain cash will be stronger, the more nearly the potential surprise attached to the idea that the questions will be answered not later than date [n] approaches zero.

Clearly we cannot explore all the possible combinations of circum-stances which can face the investor in making a choice between con-structing a certain blueprint now and retaining his cash in view of the contingency that some other much more attractive opportunity may present itself a short time hence.   What we have done in this section is to isolate the essentials of such a situation.   It will be understood that throughout this discussion the word " attractive " is used in a purely subjective sense.   An investment-opportunity, or blueprint, is something which exists in the investor's mind.   Its characteristics and qualities are thoughts, and not something which can be observed without reference to the individual.

VI

We have now to consider how a particular blueprint for immediate construction, say $A_{[1]}$, whose focus outcomes according to $y_{[1][1]}$, $A_{[1]}$ are in themselves highly attractive, may be rendered unattractive by the fact that one of the hypotheses contained in $y_{[1][3]}$, $A_{[1]}$, and carrying *nil* potential surprise, implies a much lower focus gain than $y_{[1][1]}$, $A_{[1]}$. To explain this proposition we must consider the inherent structure of enjoyment by anticipation.

If we attach low potential surprise to the future occurrence of an event which, when it occurs, will give us pleasure, we can take pleasure in *imagining* this event in advance. To do this is to get *enjoyment by anticipation*. Since to enjoy by anticipation is itself a pleasurable act, and can itself be imagined in advance, it can give rise to a secondary enjoyment by anticipation, in which we enjoy the prospect of enjoying the prospect of a pleasure-giving event. And there can evidently be a tertiary, etc., enjoyment by anticipation. To make matters precise, let us consider an arbitrary short period called a " day ", and let us call the day on which the event itself is due to occur day n, let the preceding day be day n – 1, and so forth. Then on day n – 1 the individual will enjoy the direct anticipation of the event itself. On day n – 2 he will enjoy, first, a direct anticipation of the event itself, though at a greater distance in the future, and therefore less vivid and intense, than that which will be felt on day n – 1 ; and second, he will enjoy looking forward to the pleasurable feelings which he is going to experience on day n – 1. On day n – 3 this two-fold enjoyment which is going to be experienced on day n – 2 can itself be looked forward to, as well as the feelings which are going to be experienced on day n – 1, and the event itself ; and so on. Each day added to the intervening period has two distinct and opposite effects on the total degree of enjoyment by anticipation felt by the individual at the moment from which he is looking forward : first,[1] it will remove the event itself, and also day n – 1, day n – 2, etc., one day further off from the present moment, and hence the intensity of enjoyment from looking forward to each of these days will be reduced. Secondly, it will add an extra day to those future days on which pleasurable feelings are going to be experienced, and which can therefore themselves be looked forward to with pleasure. This second effect has not, so far as I know, been anywhere discussed heretofore ; but the first effect is a familiar idea in economic theory,

[1] We shall refer to these as the first and the second effects. These " effects " merely describe the comparison of what a person would feel when looking forward to a given event *n* days ahead with what he would feel when looking forward to the same event *n* + 1 days ahead. The " cause " of these " effects " is merely the shift of our attention from one idea to another, and the " effects " are therefore, of course, simultaneous.

since it has no doubt been in the minds of all those who have used the concept of "impatience" in discussing the rate of interest, and this first effect will be generally admitted to be often strong and important. Hence if we can show that the second effect is sometimes powerful enough to overcome the first effect, the importance for theory of the second effect will have been established. Now it may be that the first of these effects is always stronger than the second, so that *any* lengthening of the intervening period, however short that period was, causes a net reduction of the intensity of present enjoyment by anticipation. But there seems to be strong evidence that this is not so. Introspection and the testimony of others indicate that a prospective enjoyable event can be *too near* in time for the intensity of enjoyment by anticipation due to it to be a maximum. Suppose we know that a holiday is due to us at some unspecified time in the coming twelve months. Then if we are suddenly informed that it is to begin to-morrow, we shall feel that we have lost something by the shortness of the notice, even supposing that all our plans and preparations have been made. In greater matters I believe this factor is correspondingly more important. For example, a man who might be prepared to venture a quarter of his fortune on an expedition to prospect for gold, whose outcome will not be known, perhaps, for years, might decline to risk it on the turn of a card, though the focus gain and loss were the same in both cases. However, the question whether the first of the two effects is or is not stronger for all lengths, however short, of the period which separates the present moment from the date of the anticipated event, is irrelevant for our present purpose. What we can say, on the basis of pure logic, is that an investor will feel that a blueprint for immediate construction, of given focus gain and focus loss, whose outcome will be known at a specific future date, say T, will be rendered less attractive by the presence in his mind of some question, due to be answered at a much nearer date than T, which question if answered in one particular way would greatly reduce the focus gain of the blueprint while leaving its focus loss unchanged. For the possibility, carrying low potential surprise, that the question might be answered in that way, will cause him to fear the loss of part of the period during which he could otherwise hope to enjoy by anticipation a favourable outcome of the venture. When he begins construction of the blueprint, he looks forward to being in " enjoyable doubt " (less enjoyable, of course, than certainty of a gain equal to the focus gain, but more enjoyable than certainty of a very small gain) as to its outcome during the whole of a period of years. It will be a serious impairment of the attractiveness of the blueprint if he feels that he would not be surprised to learn something one month hence which will greatly reduce the focus gain : for this contingency would transform his prospective state of mind, for the rest of the period up to date T, into one of " disagreeable doubt ".

VII

If the argument of the preceding sections is accepted, it is clear that the approach of some event, such as a Presidential election or an international conference, some conceivable outcomes of which are widely different from each other and would have extremely different effects on the valuation of a specific investment blueprint, will tend to make the aggregate investment flow less than it would otherwise have been. There will be a *general* tendency amongst investors to wait and see. At a date when such an event is still remote, most of the investors who are then making such comparisons as that between $A_{[1]}$ and $B_{[n]}$, which we described above, will feel that the waiting time would be too long, and will each decide to construct at once the plant representing his $A_{[1]}$. But at a date nearer to the event, most of them will feel it worth while to wait and see. Thus the strength of the tendency for investment to be discouraged will continually increase as the event draws nearer, and then jump discontinuously to zero at the moment when the event has just occurred.

It follows that such an event when it actually occurs may release a large number of investment-decisions, *even though it has not lessened the focus-loss nor raised the focus-gain of any blueprint in the mind of any investor.* Blueprints for immediate construction will no longer have to compete in the investor's mind with the contingency that opportunities of still higher promise may arise at a near future date ; and their attractiveness will not be decreased by the fear that a near future date may bring an abrupt reduction of their focus gain. Thus many blueprints such as the one which in Section V we labelled $A_{[1]}$ may begin to be constructed.

VIII

An actual occurrence which causes surprise proves that the individual's structure of expectations[1] either contained a misjudgment or was incomplete. Either the event was included amongst his hypotheses but excluded from the inner group, where clearly it ought to have been, or else it formed no part of any hypothesis.[2] If his exclusion of this event from the inner group was wrong, so may be that of other hypotheses still to be tested, and he must consider again his other judgments of this kind. If the event was something entirely

---

[1] i.e., the whole assemblage of sets of variants in his mind.

[2] I believe the distinction may be important between these two types of surprising events, which I propose to call *counter-expected events* and *unexpected* events :

Counter-expected event :	an hypothesis which has been considered and to which as a consequence of this examination a high degree of potential surprise has been assigned.
Unexpected event :	a contingency which has entirely escaped attention, which has never entered the individual's mind, and has formed no part of any hypothesis.

A person's structure of expectations may be more completely demolished by an unexpected event than by a counter-expected event : the former reveals not merely a misjudgment but the fact that the individual has been unaware both of the essential features of the situation and of the existence and extent of his ignorance.

unthought of he must consider a mass of new ideas which it will generate concerning the future course of events. Thus an important surprising event will require him more or less to create afresh his structure of expectations. Such an event will cause his whole existing set of judgments, by which he has assigned to each hypothesis its particular degree of potential surprise, to become a dead letter.[1] He cannot instantly substitute for this old set of judgments a new set emerging from a thorough examination of the surprising event in all its bearings and implications, for this examination will take time. But in the nature of things it must be possible for him at any moment to answer the question whether the actual realisation of such and such an hypothesis would surprise him. It follows that he will have in mind, during the interregnum between the abandonment of one set of fully considered judgments and the establishment of a new one, some set of provisional judgments. This must, in the nature of the case, admit of a wide allowance for events, and values of variables, which formerly he would have labelled as potentially surprising, but which he cannot now condemn offhand. Thus the impact effect in his mind of a major surprising event[2] will include a great precautionary increase in the focus gain and focus loss of each one of the blueprints he has in mind. But at the moment when he makes these increases, he will be able to look forward to a moment, that moment namely when he will have completed the examination of the significance of the surprising event, when many or all of these focus gains and focus losses will again have been reduced; not, of course, in general back to their original positions, but to new levels higher or lower than their original levels but lower than their provisional levels. He will, at least, attach very high potential surprise to the supposition that most of them will *not* by then have been thus reduced.[3] Thus, if at the moment when a surprising event has just occurred, he looks ahead to the moment when his examination of this event will have been completed, he is looking ahead to a future date at which the answers to special questions, in the sense we have given to this phrase above, will become known to him. Thus the occurrence of a surprising event will give him the same incentive to " wait and see " as the approach of a date when the outcome of special " experiments ", such as elections or harvests, will be known. He will be tempted to hold off from embarking immediately on the construction of any blueprint $A_{[1]}$ for two reasons :

    (1) in case some other blueprint may emerge from his process of examination with a more attractive pair of focus outcomes

---

[1] These existing judgments will not necessarily be altered as a consequence of his studying the implications of the surprising event, but until this examination has shown whether or not any change is called for, their authority will be suspended.

[2] By a major surprising event I mean one which is both very surprising to the individual and highly relevant to his judgments : that is, a very surprising change in some very important circumstance.

[3] Since *both* its focus outcomes will be reduced, he cannot tell anything as to whether any blueprint will be rendered more attractive or less attractive by the process of examination : either can happen.

than those assigned to $A_{[1]}$ by his provisional judgments ; and

(2) in case his new set of fully-considered judgments assigns to $A_{[1]}$ a much less attractive pair of focus outcomes than those assigned to it by his provisional judgments.

The former possibility will be made more insistent to his mind by the fact that the precautionary increases of focus gains and focus losses will, by their nature, have been such as to *level up* the attractiveness of different blueprints. These precautionary increases will have been generous in all cases, and more or less determined by a factor common to *all* the blueprints, namely the need to make sure that these increases shall be large enough. The individual will tend to push them all up to some common high level.

Our main conclusion from the argument of this Section is as follows : One effect of an event which causes surprise will be to heighten at first the attractiveness of liquidity, that is, of deferment of choice of a specific blueprint, and discourage the immediate construction of equipment. If a large number of investors are thus affected by the same event, the aggregate investment flow in some period closely[1] following this event will be lower than it would otherwise have been.

The time occupied by the process of examination may be considerable. The sorting-out and assembling of fresh impressions, the gradual evolution of new ideas, the tracing-out of all the bearings of the event on what was contemplated before, and the canvassing or waiting for signs of other people's reactions to the same event, will make an arduous process not completed in a day or two. We shall call this process the assimilation of the event into the structure of expectations. To this process may be added a *testing* of the new set of judgments by waiting to see if more events will come along such that *they would have been surprising had they occurred before the event which occasioned the process of examination, but are not so now that this event has been assimilated.*

If an event, after its meaning has been assessed, *increases* a focus-gain or a focus-loss, then by the definition of these latter it must have been surprising. A hitherto unthought of event, even though it turns out, after assimilation into the structure of expectations, to *decrease* a focus-gain or a focus-loss, will also at its occurrence have been surprising. And, as we have seen in Section V, it is possible for a hypothetical decrease of a focus-gain or loss, when this decrease exceeds a certain size, to carry a positive degree of potential surprise, and such a decrease if it occurred could therefore be the outcome of a *counter-expected* event. But many of the events which *decrease* a focus-gain or loss will be non-surprising : they will be some of those very events which the investor had in mind in assigning *nil* potential surprise to those profit-outcomes of the venture falling within the inner range ; such events will be assimilated easily and quickly into the individual's

---

[1] Closely, rather than immediately, since plans for the immediate future can only be altered at high cost.

structure of expectations, and he will be in as good a position to make a decision immediately after such an event as before it.   Thus we find that there is an important *asymmetry* between investment-stimulating and investment-depressing events.   Investment can be stimulated, after the assimilation of the event, by either an increase of focus-gains or a decrease of focus-losses.   But only in the latter case will the assimilation and therefore the effect be immediate.   In the former case the *impact effect* will be depressive.   Investment can be depressed by either an increase of focus-losses or a decrease of focus-gains, and the effect in *both* these cases will seem to be immediate, though in fact the downward movement following an event which is going to increase focus-losses will be due at first to the mere " stand-still " effect of the surprising event.   This asymmetry seems at least partly to explain why the decline of investment and employment after a boom is usually more abrupt and rapid than their recovery after a slump.

IX

Our final task will be to try to suggest a possible line of attack on the central problem of all, the question by what means and process does the individual select, for each different course of action that seems open to him, those hypotheses as to the outcome, or the path which the future course of events will follow, which are to carry less than indefinitely high potential surprise, and are therefore to provide his basis for comparing the attractiveness of this course of action with that of any other ?   When we think of the individual as being free to choose amongst a set of different courses of action, we mean strictly speaking that he can choose amongst the respective initial moves, or " gambits ", in these different plans.   He will not usually determine in advance a unique move for every stage of his plan, regardless of what shall have been the reactions of others to the preceding steps.

We shall regard the individual's power to choose his own immediate next action, or gambit, as a power to " choose " the immediate situation.   Thus we think of past history as a series of situations culminating in a " present " situation which hangs in suspense, as it were, until the individual has chosen his gambit.   When, for the purpose of weighing the attractiveness of a given course of action, he has provisionally done so, he has a complete series of known situations covering some period of time measured backwards from the present moment, and the *immediate* future, each of these situations being " known " in the sense that some of its attributes are uniquely determinate (others, of course, indeed the majority, will be forever unknown to any one individual), and his task is to determine some set of hypothetical situations, as few and mutually alike as possible, amongst which the next, future, situation will be found.

In seeking a basis for some conjecture as to how he proceeds, we can

perhaps get a hint from remembering what is the first and fundamental operation of all inductive science : classification. Thus the
first of our basic concepts is that of a *situation-type*. By this I mean
simply a specification of a state of affairs conceived to exist at a point
of time, the purpose of such specifications being to serve as a means of
classifying actual situations according to their degree of resemblance
to one or other of a set of situation-types. What we mean here by
resemblance will be touched on below (page 123). Instead of the term
situation-type we shall use the word *symbol*, since in the mental process
we are going to describe, the individual treats a situation-type as
equivalent to any of the actual situations which he classifies as belonging to it, and after once performing the classification, thenceforth
concerns himself with situation-types alone. Thus the latter *stand for*
actual situations, and we shall call them symbol-situations or merely
symbols.

The apparatus by means of which a person answers the question " If
I choose such and such an immediate action, and thus complete the
' existing ' situation, whose nature will then be fully determined,
what will be the next following situation ? " will consist according to
our hypothesis in a finite set of symbol-situations and a system of rules
prescribing a correspondence between sub-sets of these symbols. When
the members of any sub-set of these symbols are taken in a given order,
we shall have the left-hand side of what we may call an expectation-
equation. The system of rules will then prescribe one and only one[1]
sub-set of symbols, considered without regard to the order of its
members, as the right-hand side. The reason why the symbols on the
left-hand side must be taken in a given order is that the situations of
history occur in a given time-order, and their sequel would often be
different if their order were different. The reason why there is no
question of order on the right-hand side is that the situations there are
rival hypotheses, all referring to the same future point of time. In this
conception the flow of history is thought of as consisting in the passage
from one to another of a series of situations, the latter being conceived
in such a sense that there will be a finite number in any time interval of
given length. Thus history is thought of as resembling a cinema film,
wherein each of the " still " pictures, which when traversed in succession
yield the movement of events, corresponds to one particula point of
time. The process by which the individual will form his expectations
concerning the next future situation will be as follows : He will consider
a certain period of the past, extending back from the present moment,

---

[1] This does not and, of course, cannot imply that there will be a *different* sub-set on the right-
hand side for each different order of each different sub-set on the left-hand side, for even if we
count only the permutations which have no repetitions of symbols,

$$\sum_{r=1}^{n} {}_nP_r > \sum_{r=1}^{n} {}_nC_r,$$

and when we allow for repetitions of symbols (which will very frequently occur) on the left-
hand side, but not, of course, on the right-hand side, the disparity is even greater.

and formulate the history of this period so far as he knows it into a finite series of situations, including one representing the existing situation as determined by his own choice of an immediate action. He will then *classify* each of these actual situations as equivalent to one or other of his symbol-situations, and thus obtain a finite sub-set of symbol-situations in a given order. This by hypothesis will yield some other specific sub-set, regardless of internal order, of symbol-situations, and this latter sub-set constitutes his set of hypotheses concerning the situation which will come into being next. Within the sub-set there may be a sub-sub-set whose members carry *nil* potential surprise, while the remaining members of the sub-set carry it in increasing degree according as their resemblance to the most similar member of the sub-sub-set is less.

The above is the formal frame of our hypothesis. To develop this into something like a complete theory, we must try to answer the following questions :

1. By what criteria will an actual situation be assimilated to, i.e., classified as belonging to, some particular symbol-situation ?

2. How does the individual decide how long a past period to take as the basis of his expectations ?

3. How will an individual's system, consisting of his set of symbols and his rules for combining them (i.e., for assigning to each permutation one particular combination), come into being and develop ? How does he derive the rules which solve the expectation-equations ?

4. What will the individual do if, when he comes to add a situation which has just slid, as it were, into the past, on to his chain of past situations, its symbol proves *not to be a member* of the sub-set on the right-hand side of the equation of which that chain, before the addition of the new situation, formed the left-hand side ?

5. Does this conception imply that, from a knowledge of a few past situations, an answer can be obtained specifying the situation which will exist on any future date however remote ?

6. Is it possible for an individual to build up and retain in his mind, and have always available for application, a system of rules comprehensively capable of dealing with the vast number of possible permutations of symbols which can occur on the left-hand side of his expectation-equations ?

7. Are such systems as we have described the same for all people ? If not, are they sufficiently alike for generalisations applying to all or the majority of people to be built ?

No proper discussion of these points can be attempted here, but we shall touch on each of them briefly, in order to indicate a possible line of attack where it may be thought that our theory encounters a difficulty.

Let us represent a situation by a point in m-dimensional space. This is quite a convenient notion, as each of the orthogonal co-ordinates of this point can then be thought of as standing for one of the mutually independent features, attributes, or elements, whatever we prefer to call them, of the situation ; for example, the price of some commodity, the voting-strength of a political party, the size of a harvest. A change in any of these magnitudes will give us a different value for the co-ordinate representing it, and thus a different point, standing for what will, of course, be a changed situation. We can specify such a point by a vector, say $[r_1 r_2 \ldots r_m]$, wherein the elements $r_1 r_2, \ldots$ must always be retained in a fixed order so that we may know to which of the co-ordinates each of them corresponds. An actual situation can, of course, only be very imperfectly known to any one person. He is sure to be ignorant even of the existence of some of its most important features, for example, the ideas and intentions of influential persons, and amongst those of its co-ordinates which he is aware that he ought to take into account, the magnitudes of many will be unknown to him. Let the vector $[R_1 R_2 \ldots R_m]$ stand for one of his symbol-situations. This will prescribe the number and nature of the co-ordinates to be taken into account, and the corresponding co-ordinates of an actual situation can be represented by $[r_1 r_2 \ldots r_m]$. The individual may find that he knows nothing of the values of $r_1 r_2$ and r_3, but that the values of the remaining elements lie within certain distances of the corresponding elements $R_4 R_5 \ldots R_m$ of the symbol-situation. He then assimilate the actual situation to the symbol-situation.

When the individual is setting up the left-hand side of his equation, the series of successively earlier situations stretching back into the past, available for this purpose, is evidently indefinitely long. We have supposed him to take some finite, in practice quite small, number of these, classify them into situation-types, and, treating the result as a single entity, i.e., a set of given symbols in a given order, obtain from it by reference to a system of rules a set of rival hypotheses as to the next future situation, this entire set of hypotheses considered as a whole constituting the solution. Now suppose he has taken N past situations and obtained a particular set of hypotheses as the answer. And suppose he now takes one more, still earlier, situation : will this give him a different set of hypotheses ? If we think of actual attempts to interpret past history, we are bound to answer that it may. For example, if we are given that two successive harvests in a given region were each of a hundred million bushels, and are told nothing else, our conjecture as to the next harvest will be different from what it would have been had we been told that the next earlier harvest had been of two hundred million bushels. But how then does the individual decide when to stop taking more and more past situations, if each additional one may give him a different answer ? The principle we must adopt here, I think, is that, given the character of the most recent situations, the degree to which the interpretation of them need be modified or coloured by the nature of earlier situations will decrease according as the latter are more remote. As the familiar saying goes,

" It will be all the same a hundred years hence ".   However, so far as more remote past situations can contribute to our understanding of the recent past, the effect of taking them into account must surely be to narrow the range of our uncertainty.   It seems reasonable to suppose that the longer the chain of past situations we take, up to a point, the *more compact* will be the set of hypotheses obtained.   By " more compact " we mean either "less numerous " or " having its mutually most dissimilar members more similar " or both these things. The individual will lengthen the chain of past situations up to the point, which in practice will not be very remote, where the associated increase in compactness becomes negligible.

How will a person's system, consisting of his set of symbol-situations and his rules for combining them (i.e., for obtaining solutions from them), come into being ?   This system, as it exists at any moment, must evidently be the product of a process of growth which has gone on during his whole life up to the moment in question.   At an early stage it will comprise only a few symbols, and sooner or later he will encounter a real situation which is inordinately difficult to assimilate to any of his existing symbols.   He must then introduce into his system a new symbol, and prescribe for it rules of combination which will yield a determinate set of symbols for the right-hand side of any expectation-equation into whose left-hand side this new symbol is introduced ; and, of course, there must be a determinate " right-hand side " for every one of the possible different permutations of time-order in which the new symbol can occur.

What will the individual do if, having solved an expectation-equation for the situation at date [n], he finds when date [n] arrives that the actual situation of that date is not a member of the set of hypotheses obtained as the solution of the equation ?   He may decide that some of the actual situations on the left-hand side of the equation must be assimilated to different symbols.   But if they all appeared to be easily and unambiguously assimilated to the symbols first chosen, he may be impelled to modify his system of rules.   In such a way the rules of combination, as well as the set of symbols, could be gradually developed.

We may here notice that the individual will be guided and constrained somewhat in his choice of symbols to which to assimilate his actual past situations : the series of symbols he obtains on the left-hand side must be *internally self-consistent*.   Suppose, for example, that his set of symbols[1] is $[S_{[6]}\ S_{[7]}\ S_{[8]}\ S_{[9]}]$ where we again denote fixed, specific dates by numbers in square brackets, these dates being in this case *past* dates.   Then for the sake of logical consistency it is necessary that the set $[S_{[6]}\ S_{[7]}]$ when standing as the left-hand side of an equation should yield as the right-hand side a set of hypotheses which includes the symbol which appears as $S_{[8]}$ in the full series.   Similarly $[S_{[6]}\ S_{[7]}\ S_{[8]}]$ must give a right-hand side which includes $S_{[9]}$.

Does our hypothesis imply that, knowing a few past situations, a

[1] Since the left-hand side of an expectation-equation is a set of symbols in a given order, we can appropriately represent it by a vector.   To avoid confusion with the vectors we employed to specify the character of situations, we shall henceforth treat the latter as column-vectors.

person can compute, by successive steps, what will be the situation at *every* future date ?   No.   For the succession of answers, referring to more and more distant future dates, will be rapidly " divergent ", since *every* member of the set of hypotheses obtained as the right-hand side of the equation for future date [n] must be used in turn as the last symbol on the left-hand side of the equation for date [n + 1], and so on. Thus if the solution for date [n] contains M hypotheses, and each of these when used as the last symbol on the left-hand side for date [n + 1] gives a solution with M hypotheses, there will be M^2 hypotheses altogether for date [n + 1], M^3 for date [n + 2] and so on.   Thus it will not be worth while to go very far ahead.

We have suggested that the individual will have a completely comprehensive set of rules, able to give him the right-hand side of *any* expectation-equation which can be set up with the symbol-situations which exist in his system.   That is to say, any permutation of any subset of the symbols which at present exist in his system, when set down as the left-hand side of the equation, must be capable of solution by reference to his rules.   But this does not mean that he will have to create in his mind, and retain for reference, an immense number of separate, unsystematised results, in a process like learning to spell, that is, to attach separate, unsystematised meanings to arbitrary permutations of letters.   On the contrary, I conceive of the rules as analogous to such a system of rules as those for the multiplication of matrices.   In matrix algebra, multiplication is non-commutative, so that, for example, the product-matrix BA of the two matrices B and A is in general different from the product-matrix AB of the same two matrices, supposing that both products exist.   But the rule for multiplication, once established, enables us to obtain the product of any set of matrices arranged in some specific order, provided they are conformable for such product, simply by performing a series of ordinary multiplications and summations of ordinary scalar numbers.   Thus we conceive of the individual as having a compact *technique* for the combination of symbol-situations, which can be applied to any desired permutation of symbols.

The last of our questions asks whether such a system as we have adumbrated would differ in its concrete forms and details from person to person, or whether there is in the nature of things something which would lead them all to develop the same system ?   Since the personal experience of every individual is different from that of every other, and their minds are also different through hereditary causes, it seems perfectly clear that the systems will differ from each other in detail, and often in very important ways.   But the record of history " in the large ", that is, of those events which touch everybody in an obvious way, is roughly the same for everybody.   And since this record is an important part of the raw material for building up such a system as we have sketched, it seems possible that the systems developed by different individuals may show sufficient uniformities for generalisations to be possible.

X

We shall call a sequence of non-future situations which, in the framework suggested in the last section, we suppose to determine, regarding the next future situation, the set of hypotheses to which an individual will attach nil or low (as distinct from indefinitely high) potential surprise, a *gnomon-configuration* or *gnomon*. It will consist of a sequence of vectors each specifying the situation at one point of historical time, as that situation is now known to or conceived by the individual. The latest of these points of time will be the individual's viewpoint (Section 4 above), that is to say, the sequence includes the existing situation. Each vector will be a set of co-ordinates written in a column, say

$$\begin{bmatrix} R_1 \\ R_2 \\ \cdot \\ \cdot \\ R_m \end{bmatrix}$$

and each of these co-ordinates will stand for one element in the set of elements or variables which the individual regards as composing the main structure of every situation. A gnomon can thus be thought of as a matrix, say

$$\begin{bmatrix} R_{11} & R_{12} & \cdot & \cdot & R_{1n} \\ R_{21} & R_{22} & \cdot & \cdot & R_{2n} \\ \cdot & \cdot & \cdot & \cdot & \cdot \\ \cdot & \cdot & \cdot & \cdot & \cdot \\ R_{m1} & R_{m2} & \cdot & \cdot & R_{mn} \end{bmatrix}$$

of n columns or situations, and m rows or *time-series of the values of m different variables*. We shall not here attack the problem of the nature or detailed specification of the correspondence[1] on gnomons to sets of hypotheses. But it happens that we can suggest an answer to a simpler question which, for the purpose of applying our theory to the theory of investment, can take the place of the more fundamental one : Is there any *formal and general* characteristic of all gnomons, varying in degree between them, such that it can be pointed out and measured for any given gnomon the values of whose elements are given, *without our knowing what these elements stand for*,[2] and such that the " value " or " level " or " classification " (as high, low, etc.)

---

[1] As we pointed out in Section IX, there cannot be a one-to-one correspondence between gnomons and sets of hypotheses, since the former outnumber the latter, but we assume a correspondence on gnomons to sets of hypotheses. That is, each gnomon determines a unique set of hypotheses, but not *vice versa*.

[2] We seek a characteristic of gnomons *in general*, as a class. A characteristic would not be a *formal and general characteristic of gnomons as such*, if we needed to know the concrete meanings belonging to the elements of each gnomon before we could classify it.

of this characteristic will tell us whether the set of hypotheses, corresponding to this particular gnomon, is likely or unlikely to induce the individual to invest ?

The idea of constructing now a particular blueprint will seem highly attractive, if the investor believes that the demand for the services of this type of equipment will be very much stronger[1] in relation to the supply of the equipment, or of the resources for making it, in the next future situation than in the existing situation. For this belief will mean that the cost of constructing the blueprint now will be low, but that the present value attributed to it by the individual's view of the future will be high. In order that the two successive situations (existing and impending) may appear to stand in this relationship to each other, the investor must assume that some one or more of the variables composing the situations will show a wide change of value between the two situations[2]; that is, since the length of the period separating the two situations is regarded as fixed, he must assume that the variable in question will undergo a very rapid change over the immediately-ensuing period of the future. It must also be assumed that over this period, between the existing and the next future situation, no changes of other variables will occur such as to cancel the effect of the movement of that variable or group of variables which implies a strengthening of demand. Can we select any one type of gnomon as making it specially plausible that favourable[3] changes will indeed occur and that no unfavourable changes will occur ? I suggest that this will be specially plausible if the investor has seen a favourable movement of a single main variable occurring alone in what we may call *experimental conditions*, and that *these conditions are still operating*. By experimental conditions I mean a state of affairs where all the other main variables, except this single active one, remain constant. For if there has been such constancy of all but one variable over the immediate past, then (a) the constancy of all the other variables is evidently compatible with rapid change of the one in which the investor is interested ; and (b) certain factors or conditions have been operating such as to give rise to the movement of this variable, and these particular conditions, which brought about the rapid movement which the investor has just seen occurring in the immediate past, have remained in force and are still operating at the investor's viewpoint : for *all* the other main variables have remained constant, and hence so also have their derivatives of first

[1] I.e. that the demand curve will have shifted upwards, so that more will be bought at each given price.

[2] That is to say, that successive elements of some one or more rows of the gnomon-matrix will show large (positive or negative) differences.

[3] We assume that the investor will select for intensive consideration, out of a large number of widely different types of blueprint appropriate to widely differing products or methods, that type which is best adapted to take advantage of the movements of variables which he expects. But a movement or set of simultaneous movements which is favourable for one blueprint will be adverse for others. Thus the expressions 'favourable' and 'unfavourable' movements have meaning only in relation to each other, and to specific blueprints.

and all higher orders ; and thus if the movement of the single active variable depends only on the values, whether synchronous or lagged, of some or all of the other variables themselves or of their derivatives, or the relations between any of these magnitudes, it follows that since all such magnitudes, whether relevant or irrelevant to the determination of the path of the active variable, have remained constant, the *relevant* conditions must have remained constant, and the factors generating the favourable movement of the active variable, though we cannot specify nor identify them, are therefore still in force. Thus if we can assume that there will not be any *discontinuous* changes of the conditioning variables, a continuation of the movement of the active variable for some short period at least may be looked for. Moreover, since this particular change is the only one which has been occurring, there is no special reason to suppose that other changes, amongst which there might be ones adverse to the particular blueprint whose merits are being assessed, will begin in the immediate future.

There is one possible and important departure, which we must recognise, from our assumption that the movement of a variable is determined only by values, first or higher derivatives, or the relations between these, of the other variables : it may be that the subsequent path of the active variable is partly determined by some integral over time of its own past movement ; or, if some of the other main variables are themselves rates of flow, it may be that the path of the variable is influenced by some integral over time of these flows. Such considerations, however, will not destroy the appeal which the rapid movement of a single variable against a background of constancy will make to the investor's imagination : he will interpret it with much greater assurance than a state of affairs where a large proportion of the variables have all been changing at once.

If the view we have been putting forward is accepted, there are two powerful reasons why the type of gnomon here considered may be supposed to give a specially strong inducement to construct the appropriate blueprint. We have seen that it provides a presumption of *persistence into the future* of the recent movement of the one active variable, and some presumption that there will be no abrupt and immediate interference by unfavourable movements of other variables. The investor can thus attach nil potential surprise to a strengthening of demand for the services of the equipment between the existing and the next future situation. But besides this, the absence of movements of other variables over the immediate past increases the attractiveness of the blueprint in another way. Had there been such movements, the individual would have to attach nil potential surprise to their persisting into the future, and their total effect on the next future situation, comprising not merely their direct effect on the demand which will emerge at that time, but also their effect on the expectations which other individuals will then form about the further future, would have been incalculable as to its structure and its degree, and would have compelled the investor to attach nil potential surprise to the hypothesis of a great *deterioration* of the circumstances affecting the value of his equipment. For the multiplicity of simultaneous movements in the past would be the worst possible basis for discovering the influence of individual movements, and even if such knowledge were obtainable it would only apply to the circumstances which *have* existed, and not necessarily to those which will be created when the variables have continued their movements. An individual can grapple to some extent with the problem of what future situation will be created by the rapid movement of a single variable in an environment of constant values of other features : but if all variables appear to be simultaneously shifting at a variety of different speeds, he will feel compelled, from a mere recognition of his own inadequate knowledge of psychic and natural laws and the manifest *insufficiency of time* for him to trace out in his mind every possibility or investigate each individual problem, to make a wide comprehensive allowance for the outcome to be almost anything within a large region of the m-space in which his situations are defined. Thus the type of gnomon-configuration we have been considering will tend to give both a high focus gain and a small focus loss for that particular blueprint which is specially and peculiarly adapted to take advantage of the expected movement of the particular variable in question. The distinctive character of such a gnomon can be summarised by calling it a *high-contrast* gnomon : if we can find some way of rendering the variables comparable, e.g. by expressing each as a percentage deviation from its mean, this attribute can be quantified by taking the ratio of the highest rate of change to be found amongst the variables of the gnomon to the average rate of change of all the *other* variables, all the rates of change being taken without regard to sign. Let us suppose that the gnomon comprises only two situations : then the column describing one of these situations can be subtracted from the column describing the other, and the resulting vector of differences will be the set of rates of change in which we are interested. The ratio of the highest numerical value amongst these, to the average numerical value of the others, may be called the co-efficient of contrast.

Our proposition has been presented in this section in an extreme and hence an artificial form. It may seldom be the case that a rapid movement of a single one of the main variables will be generated by an environment of constancy of all the other variables. But many sequences of situations will approach in greater or less degree this extreme type, and our contention is that the more closely they do so, the more boldly will the investor attack the problem of **interpreting them.**

EXPECTATION AND CARDINALITY

I BELIEVE it is sometimes said that if we are to be able to claim that a given variable is cardinal, we must provide it with a unit interval and a zero point. If, by the nature of what we seek to measure, only one possible unit and only one possible zero point offer themselves, cardinality is complete. For some purposes, however, we shall be content, on a certain condition, with a lesser cardinality in which those two elements can be arbitrarily chosen; this condition is that the expression of a given magnitude in terms of one pair of these elements can always be re-expressed in terms of any other pair merely by a linear transformation. In the context with which I am specially concerned, the matter has presented itself to me from a somewhat different angle; for it seems to me that when the variable is *potential surprise* we are presented with not only a natural and inevitable zero point, the meaning of which will be the same for everybody, but also with another magnitude which satisfies this same condition of *absoluteness of meaning*, viz., the absolute maximum of potential surprise which I have habitually denoted $\bar{y}$. Now if $y = 0$ and $y = \bar{y}$ have fixed and universally constant meanings, and are distinct from each other, then if we can regard this distinctness as implying that they are separated by an interval, is not this a natural interval of fixed meaning which could meet the second of the two requirements of full cardinality? Plainly it cannot, for the entire range of the variable, to which we assign any meaning, is encompassed by and is identical with this interval. Thus it seems to me that, at any rate in my own context, the problem is to find some principle or method of *subdividing* the natural interval with which the context provides us. It is not appropriate or sufficient, as in some other contexts perhaps it may be, to assume that if the meanings of any two integers, taken to represent values of our variable, are fixed, then all other rational numbers will thus directly and automatically have their appropriate meanings assigned to them.

Our logical first step is to decide what conditions our principle of subdivision must satisfy, and to decide this we must consider what is our purpose in seeking to render cardinal, in some sense, the variable I have called " potential surprise." This purpose is analytical and descriptive. If an enterpriser chooses one rather than another of several technically specified investments that are open to him, we wish to be able to see this act as the consequence of several distinct elements, viz., some characteristics of his own temperament and some judgments that he makes about the range of different consequences which might follow from his committing his resources to this investment or that. Again, let us suppose him to have in mind three hypothetical outcomes, of respective face value x_1, x_2 and x_3, with degrees of potential surprise respectively y_1, y_2 and y_3 (see Fig.). Let us suppose that $x_1 < x_2 < x_3$, and that initially $\overset{1}{y}_1 = \overset{1}{y}_2 = \overset{1}{y}_3 = 0$, so that [1]

$$\phi(x_1, 0) < \phi(x_2, 0) < \phi(x_3, 0)$$

Then let us imagine his knowledge and inferences to change so that the outcome x_3 comes to be associated with such a degree $\overset{2}{y}_3$ of potential surprise that

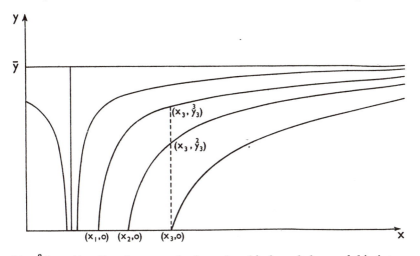

$\phi(x_3, \overset{2}{y}_3) = \phi(x_2, 0)$. Suppose, further, that his knowledge and his interpretation of it again change so that now x_3 is assigned $\overset{3}{y}_3$ such that $\phi(x_3, \overset{3}{y}_3) = \phi(x_1, 0)$. Finally, let us suppose that the change of information which assigns to outcome x_3 the degree of potential surprise $\overset{3}{y}_3$ occurs as it were in one movement, without the intervention of any stage where x_3 is associated with $\overset{2}{y}_3$. In the whole set of events that we have now imagined there are involved three distinct *differences* of degree of potential surprise, viz.,

$$\overset{3}{y}_3 - \overset{2}{y}_3 \qquad\qquad\qquad\qquad \text{(i)}$$
$$\overset{2}{y}_3 - \overset{1}{y}_3 = \overset{2}{y}_3 \qquad\qquad\qquad \text{(ii)}$$
$$\overset{3}{y}_3 - \overset{1}{y}_3 = \overset{3}{y}_3 \qquad\qquad\qquad \text{(iii)}$$

Then we wish to find some principle or method of subdivision of the range of definition of potential surprise, such that the sum of (i) and (ii) is equal to

[1] ϕ here stands, as in my *Expectation in Economics*, for the " attention–arresting power " of various " elements " (x, y).

(iii). It is in this sense that we must, I think, seek a *consistently additive* cardinality for potential surprise.

This introduction of the word " additive " in connection with potential surprise compels me to digress for a few moments, for there is another, and an essential, sense in which, as I have taken pains elsewhere to emphasise, potential surprise is non-additive.

If it is possible, *a priori* or empirically, to establish a table of the relative frequencies with which we obtain each distinct result out of an exhaustive set of possible results when some defined class of trial or performance is indefinitely repeated, and if some valuation is put on each distinct result, the so-called " mathematical expectation " is reckoned, in a way which is familiar to all of us, by multiplying the valuation of each contingency by its relative frequency, the latter being expressed as a proper fraction such that all the relative frequencies together sum to unity, and adding the products so obtained. The idea of the frequency-table has often been transferred from its proper use as a statement of " objective " knowledge about the outcome of an experiment consisting in the totality of some " large " number of trials, to an entirely different use for which it seems to me to be in several respects quite unsuitable, namely the description of a person's uncertain state of mind about the question what will come of a single unique or isolated act of his own. However, when our formal basis of discussion of uncertainty is the frequency-table, our process of thought involves *addition*, the summing and averaging of items each corresponding to a distinct contingency. It is addition for this sort of purpose which is entirely absent from my own construction based on potential surprise. My own construction recognises the different possible or conceivable results of a unique or isolated experiment (what I have elsewhere called a *non-divisible non-seriable* experiment) as mutually exclusive rivals the attempt to add which is a contradiction of their essential meaning.

Let us return to the problem of how to subdivide the range within which potential surprise is defined, the closed interval $0 \leq y \leq \bar{y}$. A proposal which introspection has strongly recommended to me is one which was made by Mr. W. E. Armstrong in 1939 in the context of utility theory.[1] Mr. Armstrong's idea as I understand it could be expressed as follows. In a given set of circumstances, I find that I prefer a cup of tea to a cup of coffee, and also that I prefer a cup of coffee to a cup of cocoa. But I also have a definite feeling which I can best express by saying that the difference between what the cup of tea does for me and what the cup of coffee does for me is less than the difference between the subjective benefit I get from the cup of coffee and that which I get from the cup of cocoa. The utility of the coffee can thus be said to be in some real sense *nearer* to that of the tea than that of the cocoa, there is an *interval* between the utility of the tea and that of the cocoa which is unequally divided by the utility of the coffee. Now if (Mr. Armstrong's argument proceeds) I can find some other object of consumption

---

[1] " The Determinateness of the Utility Function," by W. E. Armstrong, ECONOMIC JOURNAL, September 1939. I believe a similar suggestion had been made by Professor Frisch at an earlier date. Mr. Armstrong, however, arrived at his ideas quite independently.

concerning which I cannot decide whether its utility is nearer to that of the tea or that of the coffee, it can be claimed that this new utility exactly halves the interval. Each half of the interval can be similarly halved, and so on until, perhaps, a limit is set by my reaching the smallest difference between utilities which I can discriminate.

Does this method of subdivision furnish what I have called a consistently additive cardinality? We must notice that this question is not the same as the question whether the sub-intervals obtained by Mr. Armstrong's method are all equal in the same sense that the centimetre divisions on a scale of length are equal. The latter can be proved equal by being each compared with one and the same marked centimetre interval on a separate object which can be moved from one part of the length-scale to another. In our context and in that of utility no such procedure is possible. Yet by the nature of Mr. Armstrong's method it follows that, so long as my own subjective criteria, the correspondence in my own temperamental make-up between certain material states of affairs and certain feelings, remain stable, the additive test we have proposed is always met. For suppose I have in mind four objects of respective utilities $u_1 < u_2 < u_3 < u_4$ and that for the purpose of constructing a scale on Mr. Armstrong's principle I take the interval between u_1 and u_4 as my unit interval. Suppose also that u_2 and u_3 occupy the points obtained by the second halving operation in Mr. Armstrong's process of repeated halving, so that u_2 is " one-quarter " of the way from u_1 to u_4 and that u_3 is " three-quarters " of the distance from u_1 to u_4. Is it now necessarily true that the " distance " from u_1 to u_3 is the sum of the distances from u_1 to u_2 and from u_2 to u_3? Yes, for both u_2 and u_3 were determined or fixed with reference to the mid-point (in Mr. Armstrong's sense) of the unit interval separating u_1 and u_4. Let us call this mid-point u_M. Then if we start, as it were, from u_M and traverse a certain distance in one sense we reach u_2, while if we traverse a certain distance from u_M in the opposite sense we reach u_3. Having reached u_3, we can plainly reverse the sense of the movement and go right back through u_M to u_2 and on to u_1. It follows, I think, that we have in Mr. Armstrong's principle a means of obtaining a consistently additive cardinality in the sense which I have tried to give these words above.

We have *a* cardinality. But, according to Professor Carter,[1] whose criticism was the main cause of my attempting this exploration of the subject, it is not sufficient for my purpose to show that potential surprise can be cardinalised, I must show that there is one and only one cardinal scale. For let us assume that the function, according to which ϕ depends on gain or loss, x, and on potential surprise, y, is simply the product $x.\overset{1}{y}$. Then if, for example, two amounts of gain, $x_1 = 16$ and $x_2 = 27$, are respectively associated with degrees of potential surprise represented, on one scale, by

[1] " A Revised Theory of Expectations," by C. F. Carter, ECONOMIC JOURNAL, Vol. LXIII, No. 252, December 1953, reprinted in *Uncertainty and Business Decisions*, ed. Carter, Meredith and Shackle (Liverpool University Press, 1954).

4 and 9, the corresponding values of ϕ will be $\phi_1 = 16 \times \frac{1}{4} = 4$, and $\phi_2 = 27 \times \frac{1}{9} = 3$. But if we regard the particular scale by which we have assigned numerical values to particular degrees of potential surprise as simply *one* scale out of many, and if, for example, we assume that any monotonic increasing or decreasing function of that first scale will serve equally well, we might instead have $\phi_1 = 16 \times \frac{1}{2} = 8$ and $\phi_2 = 27 \times \frac{1}{3} = 9$. Thus by choosing a different scale for y we should have reversed the size-ranking of ϕ_1 and ϕ_2.

The fact that several different methods have been proposed for demonstrating the measurability of utility, or the " determinateness (that is to say, the uniqueness) of the utility function," may well set up in our minds a presumption against such uniqueness, not merely in regard to utility, the only context in which there has been any general discussion of the matter, but in any similar context, such as that of potential surprise. For is there any reason *a priori* why different methods should lead to the same result? In a luminous article [1] Mr. D. Ellsberg has indeed pointed out that if two concepts are defined by two different operational procedures they are in strictness two different concepts, and the onus of proving them to be effectively identical, in any context or argument, lies on the person who wishes to treat them so. Mr. Ellsberg's article is admirably lucid, exact and thorough, but its subject matter is inherently so difficult that perhaps I may be excused for having still in mind, after several readings, a number of points on which I do not feel quite clear or satisfied. His main concern is with two possible operations in particular, by which some concept of cardinal utility might be defined, namely that of von Neumann and Morgenstern consisting in the observation of a person's choices in so-called " risk situations," and that which the neo-classical economists such as Jevons had in mind, consisting in the subjective " weighing " by the person himself of the amounts of satisfaction associated with different events. I must confess myself here still puzzled by what is meant by a " risk-situation." What precisely is it that the person has to do? He is offered the choice between, for example, the certainty of receiving a stated sum of money B, on the one hand, and a lottery ticket which will give him " with a probability " p a sum $A > B$ or " with a probability " $(1 - p)$ a sum $C < B$. Does this mean that if he chooses the lottery ticket the lottery will be drawn *just once* and he will in fact receive either A or C? If this is indeed the meaning, whatever can be meant by saying that he will receive A " with a probability " p? The interpretation he puts on this statement must be entirely subjective, something evolved in his own mind and different, in general, from the interpretation which would be put on it by another person. There seems to me to be no ground on which we could say that if, for example, $p = \frac{1}{2}$ and $\frac{1}{2}A + \frac{1}{2}C = B$, he " ought " or " it would be rational " to be indifferent between the sure outcome B and the lottery ticket $(A, p; C)$. We simply do not and cannot know, without further information, what a lottery ticket in this sense of a *unique* drawing means to him,

[1] " Classic and Current Notions of ' Measurable Utility,' " by D. Ellsberg, ECONOMIC JOURNAL, Vol. LXIV, No. 255, September 1954.

what its essential quality or significance in his mind is. The idea " *A* with a probability *p* " involves *two* subjective elements and not one, the so-called probability cannot play the role of something objective that will enable us to pin down a single remaining element of " satisfaction," this probability is no more, *at most*, than the objective base or correlate of a dimension or aspect or element of *feeling*, that very strand of feeling to which I have sought to give precise definition under the name of potential surprise. Thus to me Mr. Ellsberg's insistence that we cannot treat the " utility " arrived at by von Neumann and Morgenstern's procedure as being identical with that resulting from Jevonsian introspection, is rather like an insistence that we cannot discover the altitude of a mountain peak by manipulating its latitude and longitude.

Suppose, however, that the meaning of the lottery ticket is quite different, and that instead of being drawn just once the lottery is going to be drawn, say, 10,000 times, so that the probability *p* means a statistical frequency which will be approximately realised in fact. In this case if the lottery ticket offers, for example, £1,000 with a probability of $\frac{1}{4}$ and £200 with a probability of $\frac{3}{4}$, the actuarial valuation of the lottery ticket is £250 + £150 = £400, and this is what, to a quite good approximation, the person can look forward with virtual certainty to receiving. But on what ground, in this case, can we speak of a risk situation?

How fallacy can flow from this ambiguity of the expression " a risk-situation " is most strikingly illustrated by Professor Wold in his note on " Ordinal Preferences or Cardinal Utility? " in *Econometrica*, Vol. 20, No. 4. This Note Mr. Ellsberg dismisses without any reasoning or discussion whatever, with an *ipse dixit* which seems something of a blemish on his otherwise fine article. The assertion " The argument . . . by H. Wold . . . is definitely invalid " ought surely not to have been made without a demonstration that would have rendered the word " definitely " superfluous.

My contention is, then, that if von Neumann and Morgenstern's operation, by which they seek to define utility, refers to a *unique* lottery drawing, the resulting observed behaviour will spring from the *combined* effect of two subjective judgments, one concerned with degrees of belief in outcomes and the other concerned with degrees of satisfaction arising from given face-values of outcomes, and that it will be impossible, by observation alone of the kind Mr. Ellsberg and others have in mind, to disentangle the effects of these two elements. If, on the other hand, von Neumann and Morgenstern have in mind an indefinitely long series of drawings of the same lottery, then risk and uncertainty are eliminated and the proposed method breaks down in the way that I think is implied in Professor Wold's note.[1]

However, even if we claim that, whatever is distilled by von Neumann and Morgenstern's operation, this distillate is not pure utility or satisfaction and that their procedure cannot be included in the list of methods of car-

---

[1] Uncertainty enters only in regard to the *temporal sequence* in which the various outcomes will occur, a matter which, as Professor Wold has pointed out in his Note in *Econometrica*, is quite inadmissible when we are considering a static model.

dinalising utility, still this elimination of one suggested method does not imply that there are no others.   Mr. Armstrong himself has in fact suggested an alternative to his first method.   He proposes to use as the cardinal unit of utility the *smallest discriminable difference* between utilities.   This method would indeed eliminate altogether the difficulty, if it be one, that even when we have established a unit for measuring the intensity of some mental phenomenon such as satisfaction or potential surprise, we may need, and be unable, to propose a method of sub-dividing it.   Plainly, we can attach no meaning to the idea of sub-dividing the least discriminable difference.   If Mr. Armstrong's second method can be validly applied to certain psychic variables, it follows that these variables are in fact discontinuous, and only a discontinuous cardinality can be established for them.   It is not evident that such variables would entail any greater strain on our consciences, when we apply to them the methods of the differential calculus, than such things as population or money value do already.

But the real question I have to face is whether Mr. Armstrong's two methods are bound to give us concepts of cardinal utility, or in my own context, of cardinal potential surprise, which it will be legitimate for us to treat as identical.   I feel bound to ask whether, in supposing it to be possible that there are many different cardinal utilities, we are not losing sight of psychic reality, the character and essential processes of the human mind, and allowing ourselves to be led astray by considerations of technical mathematical or logical procedure.   It is true that, for example, the " distance " between two points in any space can be measured, if we will, along any number of different paths, and we are quite at liberty, in the abstract, to postulate any space.   But the physical space of nature, whether it be Euclidean or of some non-Euclidean variety, is surely of a *unique* character, and gravity or whatever we care to call the principle which manifests itself in the apparent behaviour of massive objects operates in just one and only one way, and it operates in just one and only one kind of space, whatever that kind may be.   Can we suppose that the structure of human thought, feeling and consciousness is any more capricious and " multi-principled " in its essential nature than the physical universe?

I have one suggestion to make, in regard to the particular question whether Mr. Armstrong's two methods will lead us to one and the same or to two different cardinal utilities.   I wish to suggest what may seem to you a rather far-fetched analogy, and I wish to ask whether in this matter we could not usefully pay some attention to the difference between the methods open to us for measuring, say, length or mass and those open to us for measuring *time*.   In measuring length in practice we are absolved from any need to resort to methods essentially involving *integration*, but when we measure time by means of clocks, candles or sand glasses we are, it seems to me, using a principle closely bound up with integration, and even if we measure time by observing the different positions of the sun, or of its shadow on the sun-dial, we are in effect assuming that the sun moved from one position to the other by traversing (as it were) the distance between those positions " a bit at a time," at a speed corresponding, of course, to that of the earth's rotation. Now can we not imagine a person who is contemplating the degree of utility, or of potential surprise, associated with some event or state of affairs allowing himself to traverse in his own mind the distance separating that degree from some other definite degree, such, let us say, as zero potential surprise, by a series of steps each of the smallest size he can discriminate? If so, we can imagine him to make the following experiment: Having selected two particular levels of utility or of potential surprise, he first selects by a direct and immediate judgment the mid-point, in Mr. Armstrong's sense, between them. He then proceeds to move, as it were, from one of the initial levels towards the mid-point, reckoning the distance by some process rather like that by which we subjectively reckon *duration* in time, or even, if you like, by counting the number of the *minima sensibilia* he needs to carry him to the mid-point. Lastly, he moves from the mid-point to the other of the two initially selected levels and again reckons the distance by this process of quasi-integration. Will the two distances thus reckoned, between the two initial levels and the mid-point selected by direct judgment, turn out equal? I do not assert that they will, I scarcely venture to assert that the experiment that I have described has a clear meaning, but if it has I see no reason why the two distances should not be equal.

However, my real answer to Professor Carter's objections is not along the lines of technical analysis. The solution appears to me to lie in a radically different argument concerned with the essence of the matter rather than with formal analysis of it, and this argument can perhaps be best introduced by means of a brief anecdote. In a certain village the grocer and the baker lived just opposite one another. One day the baker entered the grocer's shop in a state of high indignation, and charged his neighbour with repeatedly selling him bags of sugar that were several ounces short in weight. " I am really very sorry," replied the grocer, " but the fact is that I always weigh out my sugar by putting one of your loaves in the other pan of the scales." In assigning numerical values to certain intensities of feeling we are at most making explicit a cardinality which may already reside in these intensities. The cardinality itself, if it exists, is a psychological reality. If cardinality inheres in the intensities of one kind of feeling, in one emotion, it must surely inhere in all. But if we admit this, can we then suppose that any kind or aspect whatever of reality can be reflected by the practice, which Professor Carter's argument would by implication make legitimate, of adopting one unchanging method of conferring explicit cardinality upon one variable, representing one emotion, while holding ourselves free to use in combination with it any one of several methods of making explicit the cardinality of another variable representing some other feeling? The two feelings must surely in the nature of things be linked with each other like the measures used by the grocer and the baker in my story. Or perhaps we can say, they are linked in the same way as the measures of length we use in reckoning the volume of a cuboid. If we decide to measure the length of the cuboid in centimetres, we shall not feel free to measure its breadth and height in centimetres or in inches as the fancy takes us, and then express the volume as the product of the resulting three numbers without any explanation.

Surely we must believe, if we are to make sense of life at all, that nature guarantees us against making a *practical* mistake of the kind that would be possible if the human mind itself were free to use, as it were, one method of " measuring " one kind of feeling and some other method of " measuring " another kind of feeling, in such a way that its judgment, which is the greater of two values of some variable depending on both these feelings, could be made *inconsistently* at different times.   In saying " inconsistently " I mean, of course, *differently* without any justifying change in the person's knowledge, inferences or tastes.   And this brings me back to my statement that my purpose, in seeking to show that potential surprise can be treated as a cardinal variable, is analytical.   The task we are charged with is not that of *designing* the human mind but of *describing* and understanding how, overtly, it proceeds.

G. L. S. SHACKLE

Liverpool University.

An Analysis of Speculative Choice

By G. L. S. Shackle

A MAN who feels sure that he knows the time-rates at which the prices of all kinds of assets are going to change during some short interval measured forward from his viewpoint[1] will decide, if all assets can at his viewpoint be exchanged at given prices, to hold the whole value of his existing set of assets through this interval in the form of that *one* asset whose money price is going to increase most. But if instead of looking on a unique time-rate of price change for each kind of asset as *certain*, he entertains several hypotheses as to this time-rate, we can no longer speak of him simply as expecting one price to increase faster than any other: the degree of belief he accords to each hypothesis has now to be also considered. On what principle will he then make his choice of assets, and what actually-observed market phenomena can be accounted for by supposing that all or many individuals make use of this principle? This problem seemed to invite the application of a group of associated new concepts which I had originally devised and used in previous articles to study some problems of investment in durable equipment. These concepts are fully described, under the names of potential surprise, and focus gain and focus loss, in my " Expectational Dynamics of the Individual " (ECONOMICA, May, 1943), to which for reasons of space I must ask the reader to refer. The concept of focus outcomes makes possible a new variant of the indifference curve technique. Our main result from the use of this technique is an explanation of the sensitiveness of speculative markets to events small in themselves, minute straws in the wind which seem to have disproportionate effects. Finally our justification in substituting the concept of potential surprise for that of numerical probability, in such problems as the present, is sought in an actual market phenomenon of the highest interest both topical and permanent, namely, the nature of ' floating value ' of land mentioned in the Uthwatt Report.[2]

We suppose our enterpriser to possess at date $[i-1]$ a given collection of assets, and to be faced with a set of *given* prices at which at that date he can exchange any quantities of these assets for others. We suppose him to look forward to a date $[i]$ which is so near to date $[i-1]$ that price-changes over the interval as a whole can be regarded as linear functions of time, so that he need not concern himself with changes occurring in sub-intervals within this interval. The interval thus defined, beginning at a named date $[i-1]$ and ending at a named date $[i]$, we shall refer to throughout as interval $[i]$. The date $[i-1]$ can be thought of as his viewpoint or as a date still in the future. Prices and other variable quantities will be assigned to particular dates by writing $[i-1]$ and $[i]$ as subscripts to the symbols concerned. Let $B, C, \cdots, M$ be the entire list of different kinds of assets or goods with which the enterpriser concerns himself, and let $a_B, a_C \cdots, a_M$ be the ratios in which, according to some hypothesis in his mind, the money prices of these goods will respectively change in interval $[i]$. That is to say, if $x_{B, [i-1]}$ is the price of good B at date $[i-1]$, and $x_{B, [i]}$ is the price it will have at date $[i]$, then $a_B = \dfrac{x_{B, [i]}}{x_{B, [i-1]}}$. Then if each of the ratios $a_B, a_C, \cdots, a_M$ has in his mind a unique value which he looks on as *certain*, he will decide to exchange on date $[i-1]$ all the assets he then possesses for goods of that *one* kind, say B, whose ratio a_B is highest: where there is no subjective uncertainty, his preference will be for a *single* good. (If the ratios of expected price change are equal for two or more goods, he will be indifferent between these goods or any combinations of them:)

In reality however the ratios $a_B, a_C, \cdots, a_M$ in which the prices of the different

[1] By the individual's viewpoint I mean the point of time at which the thoughts and decisions, which we are studying, are occurring in his mind.

[2] Expert Committee on Compensation and Betterment, Final Report (Cmd. 6386), paragraphs 23, 24.

10

goods will change in any interval [*i*] are not known for certain to anyone. For each such ratio the enterpriser will have in mind not a unique value but a function associating with each of a number of hypotheses concerning this ratio a particular degree *p* of potential surprise. Suppose that for two goods *B* and *C* the respective potential surprise functions are $p_B = p_B (a_B)$ and $p_C = p_C (a_C)$, and let us also assume for the purpose of our later argument, that these goods are not subject to any natural physical change. The condition $p_B = p_C > O$, for the increasing branch of each curve, will determine a one–one correspondence between values of a_B and values of a_C, each specific pair of values being associated with a specific degree of potential surprise ; and similarly for the decreasing branches. We shall call such a pair of values a pair of linked values. For any specific set of quantities of the two goods, any particular pair of linked values a_B and a_C will correspond to some specific amount of gain to be had from holding this set of quantities through interval [*i*]. There will be one particular pair of linked values for which the corresponding gain will be the focus gain from holding the given set of quantities through interval [*i*]; and there will be another linked pair to which there will correspond the focus loss.[1] Now the forms of the potential surprise functions may be such that in every pair of linked ratios the same member, say a_B, is greater than the other. In this case the focus gain will be greatest, and the focus loss smallest, when the set of quantities held consists exclusively of good *B*, with none of good *C*. But more often one of the ratios, say a_B, will be greater than the other when both are greater than unity, but less than the other when both are less than unity.[2] In this case, by holding less of good *B* and more of good *C*, the enterpriser can have a smaller focus loss at the cost of having also a smaller focus gain. Measuring focus losses along the horizontal and focus gains along the vertical axis of Figure 3, we can display the range of choice open to the enterpriser as a curve *QQ* such that the two focus outcomes increase together. If one of the two goods in question is money, this curve will start from the origin, otherwise it will in general start some distance from the origin. For by gain and loss we mean gain and loss of money value, and by holding all his capital in the form of money, the enterpriser can make sure of having neither gain nor loss, and the situation in which he has this assurance is represented by the origin. The curve, which we shall call the gambler opportunity curve, will approximate closely to a straight line. Indeed, if instead of the focus outcomes we plotted against each other the upper and lower extremes of the inner range (that is, those amounts of gain and loss which, for the various mutually equivalent combinations[3] of goods, are associated with potential surprise barely exceeding zero) we should get a straight line. For suppose a unit of *C* exchanges, at the prices prevailing at the threshold of interval [*i*], for *U* units of *B*, that before re-arranging his holdings the enterpriser has *B* units of *B* and *C* units of *C*, and that he considers the effect of giving up *r* units of *C* in exchange for some units of *B*. And let us take as our money unit the value, at the beginning of interval [*i*], of a unit of *B*. Then for given (algebraic) values of a_H and a_C the total worth of the enterpriser's stocks of goods at the end of interval [*i*] will be

$$Z_{[i]} = a_B (B + rU) + a_C U(C - r)$$
$$= rU(a_B - a_C) + a_B B + a_C UC$$

while the worth at the beginning of interval [*i*] is

$$Z_{[i-1]} = B + UC$$

Thus his gain or loss is

$$Z_{[i]} - Z_{[i-1]} = rU(a_B - a_C) + B(a_B - 1) + CU(a_C - 1)$$

which is linear in *r*. If in this expression we insert the pair of linked values of a_B and a_C which are greater than one and carry potential surprise barely exceeding

---

[1] Thus if *g* is a variable hypothesis as to the amount of gain to be had from holding a given set of quantities through interval [*i*], and $p = p_B = p_C$ is the degree of potential surprise associated with each value of *g*, and ϕ is the power of any associated pair of values *g* and *p* to concentrate the enterpriser's interest and attention upon themselves, the focus gain is defined as that value of *g* for which $\phi = \phi [g, p(g)]$ is a maximum ; and the focus loss is similarly defined, *mutatis mutandis*.

[2] The potential surprise function for a_C will then lie wholly 'inside' that for a_B in the manner illustrated for three functions in Figure 6.

[3] I.e. combinations amongst which the enterpriser, faced by a given set of prices of these goods at the beginning of interval [*i*], and possessing goods of a given total value at these prices, is free to choose, when deciding what set of stocks of goods he shall hold through interval [*i*].

zero, we have for each value of r the upper extreme of the inner range. Thus the latter is a linear function of r, and so in a similar way is the lower extreme. Since all the quantities other than r which enter into the expressions for the upper and lower extremes are constants, these extremes are linear functions of each other. The upper and lower extremes are shown as functions of r in Figure 1, and as functions of each other in Figure 2. However, when we turn to consider focus outcomes we have to take account of possible variation in the relative weight which the enterpriser attaches to a given increment of hypothetical gain or loss and to the associated increase in potential surprise, when the increment is added to a different level of hypothetical gain or loss. Such variation would alter the distance between the upper extreme of the inner range and the focus gain, and between the lower extreme of

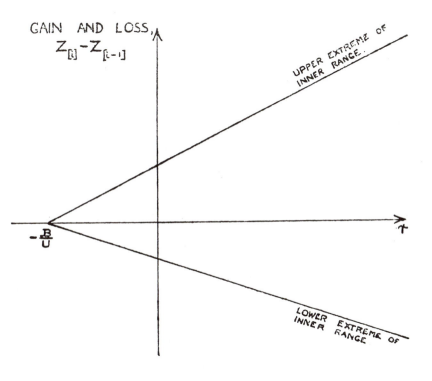

GAIN AND LOSS, $Z_{[i]} - Z_{[i-1]}$

UPPER EXTREME OF INNER RANGE

LOWER INNER EXTREME OF RANGE

$-\dfrac{B}{U}$

r

FIGURE 1

In Figure 1, those two specific pairs of linked values of a_{B} and a_{C}, which each carry potential surprise barely exceeding zero, and those two only, are considered. One of these pairs gives the upper and one the lower extreme of the inner range of $(Z_{[i]} - Z_{[i-1]})$ for each value of r. This diagram illustrates a case where one of the two goods, namely good C, is money. Then a_{C} is always unity, and if in the expression

$$Z_{[i]} - Z_{[i-1]} = rU(a_{B} - a_{C}) + B(a_{B} - 1) + CU(a_{C} - 1)$$

we put $r = -\dfrac{B}{U}$ we have

$$Z_{[i]} - Z_{[i-1]} = B(1 - a_{B}) - B(1 - a_{B}) = 0$$

that is to say, if the enterpriser turns all his initial stock of B into C, namely money, and holds all his capital in the form of money, his gain or loss of money value will be zero.

the inner range and the focus loss.[1] Thus where two goods only are involved the 'gambler opportunity curve', as we may call the curve expressing the enterpriser's range of choice between different combinations of focus gain and focus loss, will be approximately linear but perhaps not perfectly so; and it will approximately coincide with the curve in Figure 2 which shows the upper extreme of the inner range as a function of the lower extreme. In each of these curves the relevant part is a segment of finite length bounded at one end by a point corresponding to the holding of the whole of the enterpriser's capital in the form of one good only, say *B*, with none of *C*, and at the other by a point similarly corresponding to the holding

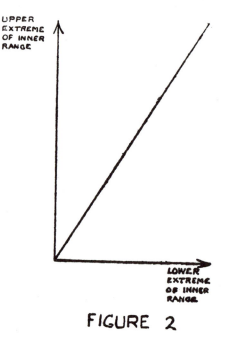

UPPER EXTREME OF INNER RANGE

LOWER EXTREME OF INNER RANGE

FIGURE 2

of *C* only with none of *B*; any extension of the curve beyond these points has no meaning. In the curve of Figure 2 these points are obtained by putting $r = C$ and $r = -\dfrac{B}{U}$ and the curve is a straight line segment joining these points.

Every point with both co-ordinates positive on the plane of Figure 3 stands for a distinct pair of focus outcomes: the combination of some specific focus gain

---

[1] It is hard to say *a priori* whether these distances will increase or diminish as the enterpriser turns his attention to combinations of goods giving higher levels of the upper extreme of the inner range, or lower levels of the lower extreme. As a simplification which does not involve anything palpably absurd we shall assume below that the highest gain carrying nil potential surprise, and the focus gain, will change in a constant ratio to each other. Against this it might be urged that when he contemplates a low hypothetical gain the attractiveness to the enterpriser of any *given* increase in it will be stronger than when he turns to a high level of gain. In this case, if we write *g* for gain, *p* for potential surprise, and $\phi\,(g, p)$ for the power to focus the enterpriser's attention, $\dfrac{\partial\phi}{\partial g}\Big/\dfrac{\partial\phi}{\partial p}$ will be numerically greater when *g* is low than when *g* is high, and if the values of $\dfrac{\partial p}{\partial g}$ at given distances from the upper extreme of the inner range are the same for all values of the latter, the focus gain will be *further* from the upper extreme of the inner range when the latter is low.

and some specific focus loss. Starting with any one such point it will be possible to find others which, to a specified person with a specified total value of stocks of goods, will be neither more nor less attractive than this point. An entire set of points mutually equal in their attractiveness to a given person at a given point of time, lying within some relevant range of focus losses (say from zero up to the total value of the particular individual's possessions) we may call a ' gambler indifference curve '. For any one person there will be a family of these curves such that any point on the plane will lie on one or other of them. Every member of this family of curves, or indifference map, will be altered in shape by any alteration in the total value of the enterpriser's possessions, for the significance to him of a given hypothetical gain or loss per unit of time depends on its ratio to his total capital (as well as to his habitual level of consumption and some other standards).. Thus a gambler indifference map describes the tastes, in regard to hopes and uncertainty, of a given individual in given circumstances.

The gambler indifference curve which passes through the origin will indicate all those combinations of focus gain and focus loss which to the particular person concerned, in his circumstances of a particular instant, are no more or less attractive

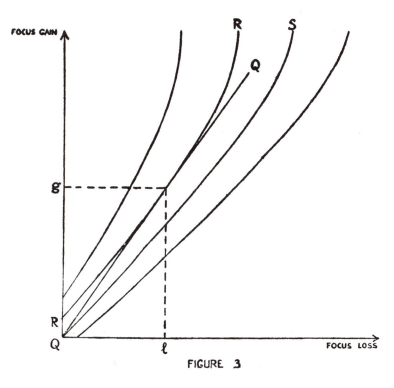

FIGURE 3

Figure 3 is drawn on the assumption that one of the two goods is money. The gambler opportunity curve QQ therefore starts from the origin. Amongst the gambler indifference curves which it encounters (cuts, meets, or is tangent to) the one representing the most desired situations is the curve RR, with which it has a point of tangency (g, l) representing a focus gain g and a focus loss l. The enterpriser will choose those determinate quantities of the two goods, B and C, which correspond to the point (g, l) on the opportunity curve. The curve QS is the origin indifference curve.

to him than a high degree of confidence[1] that he will experience neither gain nor loss. It seems reasonable to suppose that the gambler indifference curves will all resemble each other in the main features of their shape, and it follows that if we can infer from a general knowledge of human nature and circumstances the general shape of that particular indifference curve which passes through the origin, which we will call the ' origin indifference curve ', we shall have a clue to the general shape of the indifference map as a whole. Now this origin indifference curve is likely to slope upwards to the right with increasing steepness: for a focus loss equal to the whole of one's capital would in the minds of most people need a focus gain many times as large as itself to compensate it (i.e. to render the combination equivalent to an assurance of constancy of one's capital in terms of money), while a focus loss which is a hardly noticeable proportion of one's capital can perhaps be offset by a focus gain equal to itself; and as we consider successively larger focus losses in the range

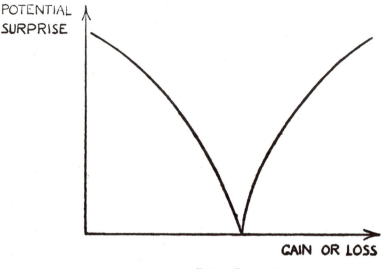

POTENTIAL SURPRISE

GAIN OR LOSS

FIGURE 4

between these extremes, the focus gain just sufficient to compensate each size of loss is likely to bear a larger and larger ratio to the latter. Thus in some neighbourhood of the origin we may expect the origin indifference curve to have fairly typically a constant slope of unity (half right angle) and thence to rise with increasing steepness, perhaps in some cases eventually becoming asymptotic to a finite focus loss. The typical 'gambler indifference map' will therefore resemble the one indicated by means of a few sample curves in Figure 3. In an indifference map where the

---

[1] The origin in Figure 3 represents the combination of a focus gain and a focus loss both equal to zero. Now a focus outcome is by definition the amount of gain (or loss) associated with such a degree of potential surprise that if this amount of gain is slightly increased the associated increase of potential surprise will more than outweigh the extra attractiveness of the gain, so that on balance the enterpriser will be *less* interested in the new combination of hypothetical gain and associated doubt as to its possibility of realisation. In order that the focus gain may be a *zero* gain, it is necessary that the potential surprise associated with any positive gain however small should be considerable ; that is to say, the amount of gain must vanish to a higher order than the associated potential surprise. But zero is not only the focus gain, it is also the focus loss, and a parallel argument applies. It follows that the potential surprise function must resemble in shape Figure 4 or Figure 5. Thus we are justified in referring to the origin in Figure 3 as representing "a high degree of confidence" that there will be neither gain nor loss : for this outcome is the *only* one carrying nil potential surprise, all others carrying some positive degree of it.

axes have the meanings here assigned to them, the combination of focus outcomes represented by any point on an indifference curve is preferred, by the individual whose map it is, to every combination represented by a point on any curve lying below and to the right of the former curve.

We have now to superpose the gambler opportunity curve on the gambler indifference map. We shall assume in what follows that the focus gain and loss always change in proportion respectively to the upper and lower extremes of the inner range.[1] Thus not only will the opportunity curve be a straight line, but when we consider the proportions in which *the inner range of a_B, or of a_C*, is divided by the value $a_B = 1$, or $a_C = 1$, these proportions will also apply if we consider the distances from $a_B = 1$ to those values of a_B which correspond to the focus outcomes. Thus if we assume, for example, that the inner range of a_B is *bisected* by the value unity, this will imply that, whatever the value of r, the values of a_B which correspond to the focus outcomes lie equal distances above and below $a_B = 1$. Let us indeed

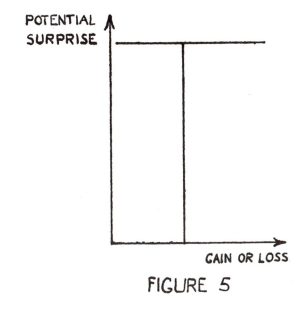

POTENTIAL SURPRISE

GAIN OR LOSS

FIGURE 5

begin by making this latter assumption in regard to both a_B and a_C. The opportunity curve will then be a straight line bisecting the angle between the axes; and we have seen that there will be an indifference curve which in some neighbourhood of the origin also bisects this angle. If the opportunity curve extends near enough to the origin, it will coincide over some part of its length with this indifference curve, and elsewhere will lie below and to the right of it. Thus the latter will be the highest (i.e. most desirable) indifference curve which the opportunity curve encounters. If the opportunity curve and the origin indifference curve should chance to have only one point in common (which would necessarily be the extreme end of the opportunity curve nearest the origin), the enterpriser will choose that combination of quantities of B and C which corresponds to this point on the opportunity curve. In this particular case, then, his preference will be to hold his whole capital in the form of the less exciting, the more narrowly predictable in value (according to his own judgment) of the two goods. And this will still be approximately true if the two curves have a range of points, instead of a single point, in common, since this range is not likely to be large in relation to the length of the opportunity curve as a whole.

---

[1] I.e. in proportion to the distances of these from the point representing zero gain and loss.

Now suppose that, instead of lying equally above and below the value unity, the inner range of a_B extends further above than below unity, while the inner range of a_C, lying wholly within the inner range of a_B, is still bisected by the value unity. In this case that end of the opportunity curve which is nearest the origin will represent two equal focus outcomes, while the other end will represent a focus gain larger than the corresponding focus loss. An opportunity curve tilted in this fashion will be common enough, since equality of the focus outcomes at one end of it will always occur if one of the two goods is money, and the other end of the curve is as likely to be nearer to one axis as to the other. The origin indifference curve will now no longer be the highest indifference curve touched by the opportunity curve: the latter, if it is long enough, will evidently be tangent at some point to one of the indifference curves lying above and to the left of the origin indifference curve, and this point of tangency will no longer be the extreme end of the opportunity curve nearest the origin, but will be some way along it, and will represent a combination of goods no longer consisting exclusively of C but comprising also some B. If the increase in the slope of the indifference curves is very gentle, so that they approximate somewhat to straight lines, a relatively small pivoting shift of the opportunity curve, in such a way as to increase its slope, will carry the point of tangency a long way up the opportunity curve to a point which implies a combination of goods consisting mainly of B. It is possible indeed, as a by no means exceptional case, that this combination will consist *exclusively* of B; for what we have called the opportunity curve is in fact a finite segment only (since the gain or loss from holding a finite quantity of any goods through a specific interval cannot be infinite) and hence although if produced far enough it would eventually have a point of tangency such as we have described, it may in fact stop short of this point, and have its extreme furthest from the origin resting on an indifference curve which it meets at an angle greater than zero.

We have in the foregoing an explanation of how some event which attracts little direct notice in its own right can initiate a boom of activity in the market, first inducing, for each of many enterprisers, a small, bodily upward shift of the inner range of, say, a_B, thus causing a slight tilting of the opportunity curve and thus a *great* change in the relative quantities of two goods (one of which may be money) which individuals wish to hold *at the initial prices*, thus inducing large offers to buy one good and causing a rise of its price, a rise which will seem to justify, or probably more than justify, the small bodily upward shift of the inner range of a_B which expressed each individual's interpretation[1] of the originating event itself, and lead, in this latter case, to a further revision of expectations and a new cycle of the same sequence of events. The validity of this explanation, it will be remembered, depends on certain assumed characteristics of the gambler indifference map which we suppose to be typical of the indifference maps of a substantial proportion of the enterprisers: these characteristics are, first, an origin indifference curve which in some neighbourhood of the origin approximately bisects the angle between the axes, and second, only a gentle curvature in the indifference curves, so that a small pivoting shift of the opportunity curve causes the point of tangency to sweep more or less from one end to the other of the opportunity curve. The shape of the indifference curves is, of course, a mathematical or graphic description of the temperament of the enterpriser concerned. The particular shape which we assume in the above argument represents what we may express in rough and ready language as a low rate of increase of the reluctance to gamble as the amount at stake, considered as a proportion of the individual's total capital, increases. Common sense approves the conclusion that, if such temperaments abound, small events will be the more readily able to generate booms of market activity.

Let us turn now to the case where more than two goods are involved. We have seen that if, say, $a_B > a_C$ in *every* pair of linked values, both above and below unity, the good C can be neglected. Thus when we consider more than two goods, we need only concern ourselves with cases where, say, $a_B > a_C > a_D > \ldots > a_M$ in every *linked set* in which all these ratios are greater than unity, and where $a_B < a_C < a_D < \ldots < a_M$ in every linked set in which all these ratios are less than unity. The potential surprise functions in such a case are illustrated in Figure 6. Now if, taking each of the goods $B, C, \ldots, M$ in turn, we suppose the enterpriser to

---

[1] I do not mean to suggest that the upper and lower extremes of any one individual's inner range for a_B will usually move by equal amounts; still less is it suggested that the amounts of the shifts will be the same for all individuals,

hold the whole value of his capital in the form of the equivalent quantity of this good alone, we shall have on the plane of Figure 3 a number of points, each of which we may label with the name of the good concerned. Each of these points will represent a higher focus gain than any point which shows a smaller focus loss. For the value, at the beginning of interval [*i*], of the stock of goods then held by the enterpriser is the same no matter what its form. Its value at the end of the interval [*i*] will have risen (or fallen) in a ratio a_B if it is wholly in the form of good B, in a ratio a_C if it is a pure stock of good C, and so on. If, then, the potential surprise function of a lies wholly 'inside' that of a_B, and the function for a_D inside that of a_C, and so on, it is plain that a lower focus gain implies a smaller focus loss. Thus the points representing the paired focus outcomes attached to a pure stock of B, a pure stock of C, etc., will form a chain of straight line segments all sloping upwards to the right. But it is possible that even some of these points can be neglected : for suppose that one of them, representing, say, good C, lies below and to the right of a straight line segment joining two others of the points, say B and D, and within a triangle bounded by this line segment and by a straight line parallel to the loss axis and another parallel to the gain axis, as shown in Figure 7. Then it will be possible to find a point on the line joining B and D which stands for the same gain but a smaller loss than C, and another which stands for the same loss but a larger gain than C, and between these two latter points there will be a sub-segment every point of which will represent *both a larger focus gain and a smaller focus loss than C.* Plainly the enterpriser will

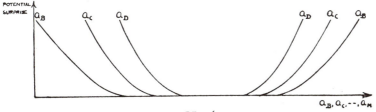

FIGURE 6

prefer a combination of B and D corresponding to some point of this sub-segment, to the holding of a pure stock of C, or any combination of B or D with C. When all points such as C have been eliminated, the remainder will determine a chain of straight line segments lying *convex to the gain axis.* This chain will constitute the curve of most favourable opportunities, and the enterpriser will choose that combination of goods which corresponds to the point of tangency, or other contact, of this chain with the highest indifference curve which it meets. What combination of goods will such a point represent ? Evidently it will be the combination, in determinate proportions, of that *pair* of goods which correspond to the *adjacent* ' *corners* ' of the opportunity chain. We are at once led to ask " Will it never seem to the enterpriser advantageous to hold a set of more than two goods ? " This question opens up a theoretical issue of basic importance, We have indeed to consider whether, as we have been tacitly assuming above, the potential surprise functions for a_B, a_C, etc., are really *independent of each other when a large number of goods are considered together.*

So long as the potential surprise functions for the ratios of price change remain valid in unchanging form, no matter how many goods are involved, there will always be, for any combination of more than two goods, some combination of not more than two goods which is superior (or, at least, not inferior) to it. In order to see this, let us first see how we can plot on the plane of Figure 7 a point representing the focus gain and loss from holding some specific combination of three goods, say B, C and D. We first plot the three points corresponding to pure holdings of these goods. Then, as we have seen, the opportunity curve for combinations of any two of them, say B and D, will be (on our assumptions concerning the relation of focus outcomes to extremes of the inner range) the straight line segment joining the two points B and D corresponding to pure holdings of these goods. Now any point on

this straight line segment can be looked on as representing the focus outcomes from
holding a specific quantity of a composite good made up of *B* and *D* in fixed proportions. Let us call this new composite good *E*. We can then join this fixed point,
labelled *E*, to the one remaining point *C* of the three original points and thus obtain
a new straight line segment each of whose points will represent the focus outcomes
from holding some specific combination of *E* and *C*, that is to say, some combination
of specific quantities of *B*, *D* and *C*. By a similar procedure we can determine a
point representing the pair of focus outcomes corresponding to *any* combination of
three goods, and analogously, for any combination of any number of goods. We
shall thus get a ' swarm ' of points, which will evidently cover entirely a simply-

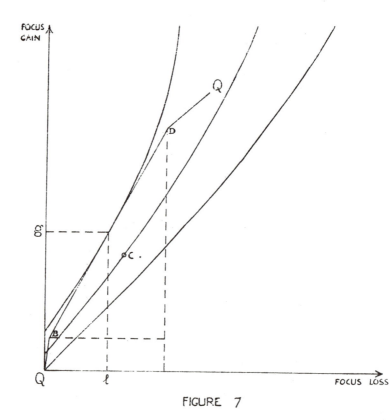

FIGURE 7

connected region of the plane. leaving no ' holes ', or interstices, between the points
within its outer boundary. But this outer boundary, above and to the left of the
swarm, will be simply the gambler opportunity chain of Figure 7, and we know that
any point lying below and to the right of this chain will be inferior to some point
of the chain itself, that is, some point on one of the straight line segments composing
the chain. Thus (except in the case where the points for three goods all lie on the
same straight ' link ' of the chain) any combination of more than two goods will
be inferior to some combination of not more than two goods.

If, then, combinations of more than two goods are ever chosen, one or other
of two things must in such cases be true: either. some qualities of the combination
besides its focus gain and loss are being taken into account; or else the assumption

that the focus gain and loss of such a combination can be obtained from the potential surprise functions for the ratios of price change of the individual goods in the direct way we have described does not always hold. Let us consider this latter possibility first. It is not easy to think of any simple (mental) mechanism by which a combination of many goods could be assigned a *higher* focus gain than a pure stock, equivalent in initial value, of the most promising of the constituent goods of the combination. But there has recently come to light an exceedingly interesting phenomenon of an actual market, namely the market for land adjacent to towns, and this phenomenon, and our own immediate problem, seem to throw some light on each other. Evidence taken by the Uthwatt Committee[1] shows that, where the belt of land encircling a town is parcelled up amongst a large number of separate ownerships, the market value of each piece is such that, when the separate values are aggregated, the total is several times as great as would be warranted by any reasonable estimate of *aggregate* future building development round the town as a whole. It is as though each actual and potential owner of a plot of land near the town were convinced that, out of a far more than adequate total supply of similarly situated land, the particular plot in question was almost *certain* to be selected as part of the site for such new houses as will be required during, say, the next twenty years. We can, I think, go a long way towards explaining this curious phenomenon by supposing that, instead of assigning to his own plot the value it would have if development of it within a moderate time were *certain*, multiplied by the *probability* of this particular plot being chosen out of, say, fifty equally good plots each sufficient by itself for all likely development within a period short enough to influence current values, each owner in effect considers what I have called the focus outcomes from holding such a plot. He believes that there will certainly be some extension of the built-up area of the town: he sees no reason, other than pure accident, why his plot should *not* be the one chosen; no positive disability tending to exclude it; consequently he attaches nil or very low *potential surprise* to the hypothesis that his plot will be required; and though he must also attach nil potential surprise to the hypothesis that it will *not* be required, yet the price he assigns to the plot must be well above that which would emerge from a calculation of numerical probabilities, in order that the focus gain may not be out of all proportion to the focus loss: for if the market valuation were as low as that based on probability, the plot would offer any potential buyer a very high focus gain, even perhaps of the same order of magnitude as the difference between the value of the plot if development were *certain* and its value if non-development were certain.

Now let us suppose that the relevant belt of land surrounding a town is divided into ten equal plots each divided into ten equal sub-plots, and that the amount of land likely to be required for building development within a period short enough to influence current values appreciably is equal to one plot. Let us further assume it to be publicly known that the land required will not be taken from a number of different plots but will consist of one or other of the individual plots as a whole. And let us suppose that our enterpriser, intending to buy some of the land in the hope that the pieces he acquires, or some of them, will be selected for development, finds his capital sufficient, at the current prices, for the equivalent of one plot. He has the choice, then, of buying one whole plot or, for example, one sub-plot in each of ten plots. If he chooses this second course, his focus gain may, for some temperaments, be only *one-tenth* of what it would be if he bought the whole of one plot. This assertion will raise immediate objection from those accustomed to think only in terms of numerical probability: for they will say that, though admittedly the largest gain which the enterpriser can hope for is in the second case only one-tenth that of the first case, yet in the second case he is *certain* to make this gain, while in the first case his chances are only one in ten. This brings out, albeit in a rather exaggerated form, the essence of my contention regarding the difference between numerical probability and potential surprise. In order to enjoy with a high intensity, or even to the full, the anticipation of some gratifying outcome, a man requires only that there should be *no solid, identifiable reason to disbelieve in the possibility* of this outcome: he does *not* require solid grounds for feeling sure that it will be the true outcome. If we look upon the ten sub-plots, each from a different plot, as ten distinct commodities, it is plain that this is a case where it is by no means legitimate to derive the focus outcomes of a combination of the commodities from the potential surprise

---

[1] Expert Committee on Compensation and Betterment, Final Report (Cmd. 6386), paragraphs 23, 24.

functions of price change of the individual commodities.   In this particular concrete example it is the focus *gain* which is smaller for the combination of several goods than for a quantity, equal in initial value, of a single good.   But there is no evident basic reason why some analogous mechanism should not operate in the case of the focus *loss*: if it did of course the combination would be preferred to any single commodity.

There is not space here to consider the other class of reasons why a combination of many goods might be preferred, namely that qualities of other kinds besides its profitability as a store of value are taken into account: amongst such other qualities *liquidity* or marketability will no doubt be prominent.

AUTHOR'S NOTE :

Some months after writing this article, and just as the proofs of it have come to hand, I have seen the admirable article by Evsey D. Domar and Richard A. Musgrave on " Proportional Income Taxation and Risk-Taking " in the *Quarterly Journal of Economics* for May 1944.   These authors make use, as I do, of an indifference map in which the curves have a positive slope, in contrast to the negative slope of the indifference curves used in value theory.   The positive sloping curves are of course appropriate wherever one of the two variables is a *disutility* and the other a utility :   and I understand that an indifference map of this type has been habitually used by Professor Hayek in his lectures to explain the individual's distribution of his time between work and leisure.

A THEORY OF INVESTMENT-DECISIONS

By G. L. S. SHACKLE

ECONOMIC theory has conceded an ever more important place to men's *preferences*, but hardly any place to their ignorance or knowledge,[1] their feelings of hope, doubt, and fear,[2] and their power of imagination. Economists are no longer satisfied with a 'timeless' theory. But the importance of time in economic theory is mainly due to the necessity it imposes on us to take account of our *ignorance* about the relevant consequences of different alternatives of action. We have to decide what course to follow when we do not know what respective outcomes the different possible courses stand for. To find any motive for taking one decision rather than another we have to put something in place of this foreknowledge which does not exist. The nature of what we substitute for it is the subject of this article.[3] The suggestions developed hereafter apply to the *general* problem of expectation in any field of activity. I have chosen an economic illustration as being more readily within my reach.

Out of all the different paths which the individual can imagine

---

[1] The importance of realistic assumptions as to what the individual can or cannot know has been discussed with a different reference in Professor F. A. Hayek's article 'Economics and Knowledge', *Economica*, New Series, No. 13.

[2] Some writers, such as Professor F. H. Knight and Professor Gunnar Myrdal, have given uncertainty a high importance. But it has been left to Mr. J. M. Keynes to make the 'utter doubt, precariousness, hope, and fear' which are the condition of human activity the focus of his whole theory. (See especially his article 'The General Theory of Employment', *Quarterly Journal of Economics*, February 1937.)

[3] I have here tried to draw together into a systematic whole and to push a stage farther the suggestions put forward in my articles 'Expectations and Employment', *Economic Journal*, September 1939, 'The Nature of the Inducement to Invest', and 'A Reply to Professor Hart', *Review of Economic Studies*, October 1940, and 'A Means of Promoting Investment', *Economic Journal*, June–September 1941.

In his article 'Uncertainty and Inducements to Invest' (*Review of Economic Studies*, October 1940), Professor A. G. Hart has pointed out that an entrepreneur may prefer a production-plan which offers a rather lower income than would otherwise be obtained in case of the 'most likely' contingency, in exchange for a rather higher income in case of some rather less likely contingencies. He develops the theory of the planning policy which must be adopted to meet the fact that we are likely to gain more and more knowledge about the market conditions of a given date as that date approaches. I fully recognize the interest and importance of these ideas, but, except that I think it is seldom possible to distinguish an unique 'most likely' contingency, they in no way conflict with my own ideas.

Professor Hart's new book, *Anticipations, Uncertainty, and Dynamic Planning* (Chicago University Press), reached me at the moment of finishing this article, too late to be discussed here.

the future course of events to take there is a large number any one
of which would cause him some degree of *surprise* if it were to turn
out to be the actual path without there having been in the meantime any change in the knowledge on which he is now basing his
expectations. The degree of this *potential surprise* will differ between
different hypotheses about the future: some will involve assumptions so dissimilar to anything in the individual's past experience,
and so difficult a search for special factors which could be imagined
to dissolve some obvious barriers in the way of such a path being
followed, that the potential surprise attached to these hypotheses
will be extreme; other hypotheses will seem potentially less surprising, and others less still, in descending steps which will lead
ultimately to the other group of hypotheses, those, namely, for each
of which the potential surprise is *nil*. Now it is clear that this 'inner'
group must comprise at least one hypothesis: but our knowledge
of future natural events, and still more, of the present intentions of
other people and what will be their reactions in the further future
to each other's more immediately future acts, is so extremely slight
and insecure that, in reality, the inner group will always consist of
a large number of hypotheses whose mutually most dissimilar
members will differ from each other very widely. In what follows
we shall speak of one complete set of hypotheses existing in an
individual's mind about the future, in which each hypothesis is
associated with one and only one degree of potential surprise, which
may be positive or *nil*, as a *set of variants*.

Above we have spoken as though the individual would have only
one set of variants in his mind at any moment. This tacitly assumes
that his own course of action is already decided on. If he has still to
choose between a number of different courses which are open to
him, then it follows that, since the nature of his own actions in the
immediate future will help to determine what happens afterwards,
he must have one complete set of variant hypotheses, such as we
have described above, as to the course of events in general, for *each*
hypothesis as to his own immediate action. This brings us to the
definition of our problem: How will he choose between different
courses of action when the outcome of each cannot be known, but
is only represented in his mind by a whole set of differing hypotheses?

When we feel that we know for certain what will be the outcome
of a given course of action, that outcome, if it is a desirable one, can

be *enjoyed by anticipation* as soon as we have decided to take that course. This promised experience, due to begin the moment we are committed to the given course of action, is the real incentive for taking the decision. When the outcome is represented in our mind by a whole range of differing hypotheses, this enjoyment derived from an act of imagination can still be obtained, even though, in place of the feeling of certainty that the imagined outcome will later become actual, there is only the *absence of certainty* that it will *not* become actual. Between a feeling of certainty that a given hypo-thetical outcome will become actual and a feeling of certainty that it will not, there is a continuous range of variation which we have described as a variable degree of potential surprise attached to the idea that the outcome will become actual. Now the intensity of enjoyment of a given hypothetical outcome by imagining it in advance is a function of more than one variable, but it is surely a *decreasing* function of the degree of potential surprise attached to this outcome. It is also evidently an *increasing* function of the desirability of the outcome. In the same way the distress the individual will feel at the thought of a positively hurtful outcome will be a decreasing function of the potential surprise and an increas-ing function of the hurtfulness. Out of the whole assembly of hypotheses as to the outcome of any one course of action, those hypotheses the thought of which causes him the most enjoyment or the most distress will mainly focus his attention and influence him in assessing the attractiveness of this course of action in comparison with others. Thus in general there are two possible reasons for the individual to pay more attention to one of a pair of hypotheses than the other: first, there may be a difference in the respective degrees of potential surprise he associates with them, and second, one out-come may be more advantageous or more hurtful than the other. But among all the outcomes for which his potential surprise is *nil*, there will be only one reason for him to concentrate his attention on some rather than others, namely, that some are more to be desired or the reverse. I suggest, therefore, that when he contemplates this inner range of outcomes each of which carries no potential surprise, the individual concentrates his attention on the *best* and the *worst* hypotheses in this range. Evidently he need not confine himself to considering only the inner group; outside it there may be outcomes even more desirable or hurtful than any of those inside it. But it will usually be true that outside the inner range, the greater the desirability or hurtfulness of a given outcome the higher the degree of potential surprise it will carry; and since, for some outcomes, the potential surprise is indefinitely great, amounting to absolute disbelief in the possibility of these outcomes, there will be a point beyond which no outcome offers a sufficient extra advantage (or

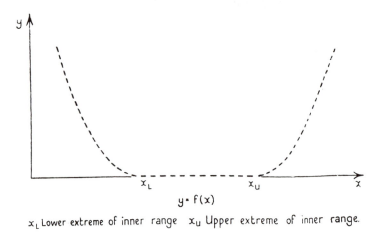

$y = f(x)$

x_L Lower extreme of inner range x_U Upper extreme of inner range.

Fɪɢ. 1.

extra detriment) over the next most desirable (or hurtful) to compensate for the extra potential surprise which it carries. At such a point the total differential of the degree of enjoyment by anticipation, or distress by anticipation, will be zero, and the degree of enjoyment or distress a maximum. At these two points will be found that particular pair of hypotheses which will mainly capture the individual's attention and will represent for him the attractiveness of the particular course of action in question.

   The set of variants we have been speaking of can consist of all the possible values of a continuously variable quantity x. Let y stand for the degree of potential surprise associated with x. Then we have seen that there will usually be a range of values of x for all of which $y = o$, this range being what we described above as the 'inner' group of variants. We shall call it the 'inner range'. For all values of x above the upper extreme of the inner range, y will be an increasing function of x, and for all values of x below the lower extreme of the inner range, y will be a decreasing function of x. Thus the shape of the function $y=f(x)$ will usually be of the general type illustrated in Fig. 1. It is reasonable to suppose that the segment of y corresponding to the inner range will merge smoothly into the decreasing and increasing segments of y, so that $\dfrac{dy}{dx}$ will be everywhere continuous.

We shall call the function of $y=f(x)$ the potential surprise function.

The degree of enjoyment or distress caused by the thought of any hypothetical outcome will be a function, first, of the degree of success or advantage represented by this hypothesis, and second, of the degree of potential surprise associated with it. For this degree of feeling let us write ϕ. Then ϕ will depend on x in two ways, first directly, and second through its dependence on y which itself depends on x. Thus we can write $\phi=\phi(x, y)$ or $\phi=\phi\{x, f(x)\}$. Now let us suppose that at some value *within* the inner range x is neither advantageous nor hurtful, and for simplicity let us assume that this neutral value of x happens to be $x=o$. Over the interval of x between zero and the upper extreme of the inner range $\dfrac{dy}{dx}=o$ and therefore $\dfrac{\partial\phi}{\partial y}\dfrac{dy}{dx}=o$, while $\dfrac{\partial\phi}{\partial x}$ is positive. Over this interval, therefore, ϕ will increase as x increases. Beyond the upper extreme of the inner range, $\dfrac{dy}{dx}$ is positive, and therefore, since $\dfrac{\partial\phi}{\partial y}$ is everywhere negative, $\dfrac{\partial\phi}{\partial y}\dfrac{dy}{dx}$ is here negative, while $\dfrac{\partial\phi}{\partial x}$ is of course still positive. Now when y approaches a value amounting to absolute certainty that the outcome will not be realized, ϕ will be reduced to zero whatever the value of x. But clearly in most concrete cases there are finite values of x for which y will be indefinitely great. There will therefore be some value of x at which $\dfrac{\partial\phi}{\partial x}=-\dfrac{\partial\phi}{\partial y}\dfrac{dy}{dx}$, and at this point ϕ will be a maximum. Turning to the negative values of x let us put $z=-x$, so that increasing values of z stand for increasing degrees of hurtfulness or disadvantage in the outcome. Then an argument symmetrical with the one above shows that there will be a point where $\dfrac{\partial\phi}{\partial z}=-\dfrac{\partial\phi}{\partial y}\dfrac{dy}{dz}$ and here ϕ will again have a maximum value. These two values of x, we suggest, where ϕ is a maximum, will attract to

4520.6

themselves the greater part of the individual's attention, and we shall call them the *focus-values* of x. His basis for comparing the attractiveness of the course of action in question with that of another course will consist in these two values.

The function $\phi = \phi\{x, f(x)\}$ will resemble in shape the one shown

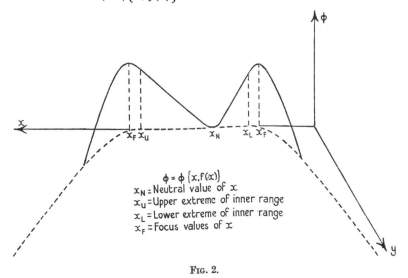

$$\phi = \phi\ \{x, f(x)\}$$
x_N = Neutral value of x
x_U = Upper extreme of inner range
x_L = Lower extreme of inner range
x_F = Focus values of x

Fig. 2.

in Fig. 2. Here a three-dimensional diagram is shown in perspective, the x, y plane being considered horizontal and the ϕ axis vertical. $\phi = \phi\{x, f(x)\}$ is a twisted curve lying vertically above the curve $y = f(x)$.

By the earnings of a piece of equipment in any year we mean the difference between the receipts in that year from selling its produ st and the outlay in that year for the materials and the services needed to operate it. If the assumed earnings of each future year of its useful life are discounted to the present and the results for all these years added together, we get a 'present value' for the plant. The difference between the present value of a proposed new plant and what this would cost to construct is what we mean by the gain or loss from constructing such a plant. This gain or loss is a specially clear-cut example of an outcome to which the conception of focus-values described above is appropriate. Even the construction-cost, though it refers to proposed operations in the immediate future, cannot be exactly known in advance. The present value, which clearly depends on the circumstances of a long series of years stretching into the future, is far more conjectural still. Thus the outcome will present itself as a wide range of hypotheses varying from a gain of several times the amount laid out on construction to the loss of the whole of it, and a considerable inner range of these hypotheses will carry *nil* potential surprise. The choice which faces the holder of a large sum of cash, between putting into execution one or other of a large number of projects for constructing equipment of widely differing characters, or retaining the cash or lending it at fixed interest, will be resolved according to our theory by comparing the pairs of focus-values assigned to the different courses of action.

For shortness we will hereafter use the term 'blueprint' to mean a project, existing only as an idea or on paper, for constructing a block of equipment of a specific character. One of the focus-values which the individual assigns to the outcome of each blueprint will usually represent a gain and the other a loss, and we shall call these the 'focus gain' and the 'focus loss' of this blueprint. It would be more elegant to think of a loss as a negative gain and representing the outcome, whether gain or loss, by a variable x, to describe the passage from a specific loss to a numerically larger loss as a decrease of x. But for simplicity of statement we shall say that the loss increases when we mean that it increases *numerically*, passing to an algebraically smaller value of x. We shall sometimes speak of the focus-values of x as the 'focus-outcomes' of a given course of action. Suppose that for a blueprint A the focus gain is g_A times the construction cost and the focus loss a proportion h_A of the construction cost, while for a blueprint B the ratios are g_B and h_B. For each ratio $\dfrac{h_B}{h_A}$ there will be some critical ratio $\dfrac{g_B}{g_A}$ which would make blueprint B neither more nor less attractive than blueprint A. If $\dfrac{g_B}{g_A}$ exceeds this critical level, the investor will decide, so far as the choice between A and B is concerned, in favour of B. All other pairs of uses for his cash can be compared in the same way and his course thus decided on.

In the next two sections we have to consider a special factor which may influence the potential investor in favour of retaining his cash or lending it at fixed interest for the time being. We are all of us sharply aware at times of the depth of our ignorance about the future. But this alone would not offer us any incentive to postpone a decision. It is only if we feel that our means of looking into the future will at some near date *improve*, that the most widely different hypotheses in the inner group of those representing the outcome of each possible course of action will become more nearly like each other, and that the potential surprise attaching to all other hypotheses outside this inner group will increase, that we shall feel the temptation to wait and see, that is, to retain *liquidity*. For there is no point in putting off a decision if the conditions for making it, the coherence, number, and decisiveness of the signs on which we can base our expectations, and the authority of the intuitions we draw from them, are never going to be better than now.

III

A blueprint has amongst its attributes not only the nature of its product and its own technical design and its location, but also the specific period of future time in which it is intended to be operated. An investor who has in mind at a particular date a given type of plant will assign to it different pairs of focus-outcomes according as he considers constructing it now or at various distances in future time. For not only will he expect the circumstances of two different specific periods to differ, but the more distant the period considered, the less light his present knowledge will seem to throw on it, and the wider will be the range of values of each important variable[1] in that period which he must regard as non-surprising. Thus if we designate different physical types of plant by letters A, B, etc., we must also attach to each letter a subscript indicating the particular fixed[2] date at which we are supposing that the plant will be completed and begin its operating life. We will write A_o, B_o, etc., when the hypothetical construction date is in the very close future, and A_n, B_n, etc., when it is some moderate distance into the future. In the following it will be understood, then, that a pair of focus-outcomes belong to a specified type of plant which is imagined to begin operating at a specified date.

[1] Such as prices, total value of backlogs of orders, size of inventories in various hands, rates of taxation, relative numerical strength of parties in Congress or Parliament, relative strength of national air forces or fleets, etc., etc.

[2] i.e. identified date such as 1st January 1942. Since we shall be considering what goes on in the individual's mind in a fixed identified short interval, designated by o, the subscript n will imply a specific distance into future time measured from this fixed short interval.

Now it is in the nature of focus-outcomes that the investor will attach high potential surprise to the idea that the focus-gain or the focus-loss of a blueprint of rather distant construction date, might increase as the present moment advances towards that date. But he will attach *nil* potential surprise to the idea that either of them may decrease. For the only judgment which a potential surprise function expresses is that the eventual *ex post* outcome from constructing the plant will not turn out to have been a gain greater than one specified amount nor a loss greater than another specified amount. This judgment will not be discredited by any signs which may arise in the meantime, before the end of the plant's useful life, pointing to an *ex post* value anywhere within the original inner range. But if through new indications the individual has to extend the inner range, and include within it some values which formerly carried some positive degree of potential surprise, he is admitting that his first judgment was wrong.

Besides an extension of the inner range itself, there are two other ways in which the focus-outcomes can be moved outwards away from the neutral outcome. First, the investor may lessen the degree of potential surprise he assigns to some hypotheses without reducing it to *nil*. That is, he may shift the increasing and decreasing segments of the potential surprise function[1] by pivoting them as it were about the extremes of the inner range, in the sense of making them less rapidly increasing or decreasing. But the necessity to make this change in his attitude to certain contingencies will itself be surprising to him, for it differs only in degree from an actual extension of the inner range. Secondly, the investor may change the form of the function ϕ so that a *given* form of potential surprise function gives different positions for the focus outcomes. This represents a change in taste or temperament. Such a change in his own personality is peculiarly difficult for a person to imagine in advance, and its rapid occurrence must surely be rare in the extreme. If such a change does occur rapidly, it will usually be surprising to the individual.

The possibility that the focus-gain or the focus-loss of a blueprint of distant[2] construction-date may get smaller as that date approaches will usually arise in the individual's mind in a special form: he may

---

[1] The function $y=f(x)$ shown by itself in Fig. 1.

[2] i.e. non-immediate.

have in mind one or more particular question, such as what will be
the result of some election, the provisions of some new statute, a
Cabinet decision on foreign policy, or the character of a Budget,
which if answered in one way will greatly decrease the focus-gain
of the blueprint B_n and if answered in some particular different way
will greatly decrease its focus-loss. The answer to such a question
may be due, as in the case of a Budget or election, at some particular
date, and the idea that the event might be postponed may carry
very high potential surprise. When the investor is making a comparison, such as we shall describe below, between the advantages
of committing himself at once to the construction of a particular
blueprint and the advantages of waiting for extra knowledge, a
factor in this comparison will be the length of time he would have
to wait and whether this time is known or indefinite. His feelings
as to whether or not a particular question will be answered on a
particular date could be expressed as potential surprise varying as
we consider successive fixed future dates. If the potential surprise
fell to *nil* for some short range of dates, rising steeply for dates both
nearer the present and more remote than that range, the investor
might treat that as equivalent to knowing when the question will
be answered.

   In what follows we shall at first *assume* that the total outlay of
cash which an investor can hope to make in a given period in exploiting investment-opportunities is not unlimited: 'total outlay'
meaning here simply the result of adding up the amounts he pays
out in the given period in buying or constructing equipment for his
own use, regardless of whether he sells any of the equipment again
within the period. This implies that in exploiting investment-
opportunities, he must make a *choice*: he cannot construct every
blueprint which seems fairly attractive, but must try to select the
most profitable. The grounds which justify this assumption are quite
simple and will be given after we have completed the main thread
of our argument.

IV

   Let us suppose that the investor has in mind a blueprint for
immediate construction A_o which is more attractive to him than the
lending of his cash at fixed interest, and a blueprint for deferred
construction B_n which couples an extremely high focus-gain with a

focus-loss so catastrophic as to render the blueprint unattractive. We have seen that he will attach *nil* potential surprise to the idea that either the focus-gain or the focus-loss of B_n may greatly decrease before its hypothetical construction-date is reached. He may even feel that he will be very surprised unless one or other of these things does happen. Now if, from being disastrous, the focus-loss becomes only moderate while the focus-gain remains very high, this will transform the blueprint B_n into an extremely attractive proposition. The existence in his mind of a blueprint for deferred construction which is, in the above sense, *potentially* a brilliant investment-opportunity is an *inducement to the investor to wait and see* instead of beginning at once the construction of a plant of more moderate promise and hazard. Two rival attractions will in this case be competing in his mind: if he embarks on A_o he will have the hope of a specific gain tempered by the fear of a specific loss, the focus-gain and loss of A_o: if he retains his cash or lends it at fixed interest for a suitable term he will have *the hope of being able later on to have the hope* of a much greater gain, tempered by the fear of a still only moderate loss: hope meaning in these sentences the state where nothing of knowledge or intuition in the individual's mind makes the desired result potentially surprising, or more than a certain degree surprising. To have committed himself to A_o, when the focus-gain is at least equal to a certain function of the focus-loss, is to his taste and temperament a desirable situation. In the other alternative a much superior situation is in question, one in which the focus-gain far exceeds the critical function of the focus-loss: but this situation is not one into which he can actually put himself, or feel certain that later on he will be able to put himself: for all he can now tell he may find when the time comes that the best in-vestment-opportunity then offered him is not a better but a poorer one than A_o was. The choice is between a gamble actually available of a certain attractiveness (more attractive than the mere lending of the cash at fixed interest, with no further purpose in sight) and a much more attractive gamble which could present itself at some more or less specific future date without surprising him, and which could, without surprising him, altogether fail to present itself. We have to consider what are the variables on which the strength of the inducement to wait and see will depend. For if the investor does decide to wait and see, this will cause the community's aggregate investment flow to be lower in the immediately following period than it would otherwise have been by the average speed of outlay on constructing A_o.

The inducement to wait and see whether the focus loss of B_n will diminish will be stronger if the investor not only attaches *nil* potential surprise to the idea that either the focus-gain or the focus-loss, or both, will decrease, but actually assigns some positive degree of potential surprise to the idea that the focus outcomes will remain unchanged. And it will be stronger, the higher the degree of this surprise. Thus we can say, first of all, that the investor is specially likely to refrain from embarking on A_o if there are in his mind one or more special questions of the type we have discussed above, the answers to which will greatly affect the focus-gain or loss of B_n. For the existence of such questions will make him feel almost certain that the focus-gain and focus-loss will not *both* stay put at their present levels: one or other is bound to be altered as soon as these questions have been answered. Next it is clear that the *length of time* he must wait in order to know the answers to the special questions is an influence on the inducement to wait. For, by assumption, there is something he would prefer to do with his cash rather than lend it at fixed interest. To wait therefore involves an item on the debit side, a cost, and the longer the prospective time which it will be necessary to wait, the stronger the temptation to choose the other alternative, the immediate construction of A_o. Finally it is clear that, besides the actual attractiveness of A_o and the potential attractiveness of B_n, the investor must consider what alternative will be available to him at date n if the focus-loss of B_n should have failed to decrease. Does he, for example, assign the same focus-gain and loss to A_n as to A_o, so that if B_n remains unattractive he will still have an investment-opportunity no less attractive than he has now? There is, of course, an infinite variety of possibilities: besides B_n he may have in mind other blueprints for deferred construction, some of which may have their focus-*loss* reduced by that very set of answers to the special questions which would be *unfavourable* to B_n, reducing its focus-gain instead of its focus-loss. Thus the next best alternative, if B_n fails to become attractive, may itself be quite attractive. We can, of course, make no attempt to explore the possible complexities of the choice which might face the investor. What we have done is to pick out the essential element which must be present in any such choice where he hesitates to invest *immediately* because he expects the basis of his expectations soon to become, as it were, more coherent or authoritative.

If the argument of the preceding paragraphs is accepted, it is clear that the approach of some event, such as a Presidential election or an international conference, some conceivable outcomes of which are widely different from each other and would have extremely different effects on the valuation of a specific investment blueprint, is likely to throttle for a time the aggregate national investment-flow. There will be a *general* tendency to wait and see. At a date when such an event is still remote, most of the entrepreneurs who are then making such comparisons as that between A_o and B_n, which we described above, will feel that the waiting time would be too long, and each of these will decide to construct at once the plant representing his A_o. But at a date nearer to the event, most of them will feel it worth while to wait and see.

It follows that such an event when it actually occurs may release a large number of investment-decisions, *even though it has not lessened the focus-loss nor raised the focus-gain of any blueprint in the mind of any investor.* The investor will now feel himself to be at the beginning of one of the best-illuminated periods that one can reasonably look for. To wait longer now would be to allow this period to slip into the past without having exploited it, while its place is gradually taken by months which were beyond the range of the special indicator of clustering of consistent signs, i.e. the answers to the special questions, and whose character is likely to remain more hidden, even when they have come into the immediate foreground, than that of the period which now lies ahead. Moderately attractive blueprints such as A_n will no longer have attention diverted from them by the thought of more brilliant opportunities which might be rendered practicable by a sudden clarifying of the future, and many such blueprints as A_n may begin to be constructed.

The temptation to wait and see does not arise only when there is some particular event, due at a fixed future date, which we think will throw light on some aspect of the future. The means available to us for forming expectations are at best mere glimpses and suggestions, utterly unequal to determining even the main character of future periods. The sense of this inability to know the future and to know what each possible course of action on our own part would lead to may not normally oppress us, but it becomes acute when important decisions must be taken, and perpetually tempts us to wait just a little longer in the hope of getting some sort of inspiration from events. The investor's motive for waiting is the same in this case as when he has a more definite reason for believing that his expectations will shortly become clearer: it is the feeling that out of several investment-ideas at the back of his mind and perhaps only partly developed into complete blueprints, all having extremely high focus-gains but comparable focus-losses, one or other may suddenly shed a great part of its focus-loss and thus immediately transcend in attractiveness all of the investment-opportunities which at present seem to him practicable. The fear of missing such an opportunity constrains him to defer his choice until one of those moments when his intuitions about the future will seem at their most clear-cut and authoritative. The condition for such a moment to be recognized is the occurrence all together in quick succession in a short time interval of a number of those special events which do seem to restrict somewhat the number of different paths along which the course of events can develop in the near future. If such events were evenly spaced out in time we should seldom be better off at one time than another, for as soon as a new indication arrived the relevance of a former one would be near to ceasing. But in fact such clusterings in time of special clues to the future do occur, while their periods of relevance are of unequal lengths. The occurrence of such a clustering, even when quite unexpected, may generate an exceptional number of decisions to invest, thus giving that small extra impulse which may start a boom.

We must turn now to consider the question we deferred from the end of Section III. Why should a decision to invest now in blueprint *A* preclude the enterpriser from investing a little later on in blueprint *B*, if by then he has come to prefer the latter, even supposing his cash resources, owned and borrowed together, are only sufficient to pay for one or other of the blueprints at a time? Could he not sell plant *A* when it is complete, or obtain a loan secured on it? This is the heart of the problem of *liquidity*, which consists essentially in the fact that a man can hold with perfect sincerity (and often, as it turns out afterwards, with justice), expectations which imply a far higher value for a plant than he can persuade others to believe in. The focus-gain which he himself assigns to *A* may be larger, and the focus-loss smaller, than the corresponding ones in the mind of any potential buyer of plant A. If in such a case he yet insists on selling A, he will make, according to his own expectations and corresponding valuation of A, a loss, and this may well offset the superior attractiveness which blueprint B may by then have acquired. Thus, if having constructed A he finds when date n is reached that B has become a very attractive proposition, it may seem better none the less to hold on to A: *but he will regret not having retained his cash*. If at date o he foresees that this position may arise at date n, he will decide to retain his cash.

A liquid asset is fundamentally one about which *one can feel sure that at any future moment the same value will be assigned to it by all or a great many people, as will then be assigned to it by oneself*. For where this condition is satisfied, it will be possible to cash in fully on an investment which time seems to be justifying, without waiting till the arrival of the end of the plant's useful life actually fulfils the hopes. Now a newly completed plant, built probably by a man who has made a special study of the particular line of production and the potential market, will not usually be very liquid. The investor cannot be sure of selling it quickly for anything like the upper focus value of its present value or even, perhaps, for its construction-cost. If he decides that the hope of gain represented by A is not so attractive as the hope of a hope of much greater gain represented by the idea that B's focus-loss may shortly be decreased by new indications, then he must, if his cash resources will only cover one plant at a time, decide to retain his cash: the community's aggregate investment-flow, during the immediately future interval up to the date when the new indications are due, will be lower by the average unit-time outlay on A than they would have been.

V

Our conclusions can be summarized as follows:

1. Those qualities of an investment blueprint, which are relevant to a decision whether to construct it or not, can with logical justification be expressed by means of only two hypothetical values for the profit-outcome of the venture. These values, though they cannot be *identified* without the help of the potential surprise function, do not have to be multiplied by any coefficients representing 'likelihood' in order to express, between them, the blueprint's claim to attention.

Orthodox theory would express the attractiveness of a blueprint as the sum of a large number of terms, each term being a possible outcome multiplied by its 'probability'. We reject this conception on two grounds: first, the setting-up of a particular type of equipment in a particular place in a particular historical period is an *unique* experiment, the conditions of which can in few cases be even broadly repeated, and for whose outcome probability in the numerical sense has no meaning. It is not possible, and it does not make sense, to assign a numerical probability to each hypothetical outcome of such an experiment, whether on logical or on actuarial grounds. Second, the investor needs a clear-cut and simple basis of comparison, arrived at by an intuitional rather than an arithmetical mental process. We cannot suppose him to go through an elaborate calculation of probabilities, even if the data for doing so existed.

2. The desire for liquidity is the desire to wait for more penetrating means of looking into the future before committing ourselves. Though these means are always poor, there is a wide variation in their strength from time to time, on account of the time-clustering of events which answer particular questions. The approach of a date when a strengthening of these means is generally expected will tend to reduce the aggregate flow of investment, and the actual occurrence of a generally-recognized strengthening, whether previously expected or not, will tend to increase this flow. These changes in the penetrating-power of our means for looking into the future are thus a second source of changes in the flow of investment, additional to *and distinct from* the source consisting in movements of focus-outcomes themselves. These latter will be considered under the next head.

3. An actual occurrence which causes surprise proves that the individual's structure of expectations[1] either contained a misjudgment or was incomplete. Either the event was included amongst his hypotheses but excluded from the inner group, where clearly it ought to have been, or else it formed no part of any hypothesis. If his exclusion of this event from the inner group was wrong, so may be that of other hypotheses still to be tested, and he must consider again his other judgments of this kind. If the event was something entirely unthought of he must consider a mass of new ideas which it will generate about the paths which the course of events may follow. Thus an important surprising event will require him more

---

[1] i.e. the whole assemblage of sets of variants in his mind.

or less to create afresh his structure of expectations. The sorting-out and assembling of fresh ideas, the tracing-out of all the bearings of the event on what was in his mind before, and the canvassing or waiting for signs of other people's reactions to the same event, will take time. We shall call this process the assimilation of the event into the structure of expectations. He will feel it imperative to wait until this process is completed before he commits himself to a particular blueprint, even though the event itself has sown the idea of some new and brilliant ones in his mind, for evidently at the moment of starting this process he is in one of the worst possible positions for judging the merits of rival blueprints. Thus one effect of an event which causes surprise will be to heighten at first the attractiveness of liquidity, that is, of *deferment of choice* of a specific blueprint, and discourage the immediate construction of equipment. If a large number of investors are thus affected by the same event, the aggregate investment-flow in some period closely[1] following this event will be lower than it would otherwise have been.

If an event, after its meaning has been assessed, *increases* a focus-gain or a focus-loss, then by the definition of these latter it must have been surprising. A hitherto unthought of event, even though it turns out, after assimilation into the structure of expectations, to *decrease* a focus-gain or a focus-loss, may also at its occurrence have been surprising. But the majority of events which *decrease* a focus-gain or loss will be non-surprising; they will be assimilated easily and quickly into the individual's existing structure of expectations, and he will be in as good a position to make a decision immediately after such an event as before it. Thus we find that there is an important *asymmetry* between investment-stimulating and invest-ment-depressing events. Investment can be stimulated, after the assimilation of the event, by either an increase of focus-gains or a decrease of focus-losses. But only in the latter case will the assimila-tion and therefore the effect be immediate. In the former case the *impact effect* will be depressive. Investment can be depressed by either an increase of focus-losses or a decrease of focus-gains, and the effect in *both* these cases will seem to be immediate, though in fact the downward movement following an event which is going to increase focus-losses will be due at first to the mere 'stand-still'

---

[1] Closely, rather than immediately, since plans for the immediate future can only be altered at high cost.

effect of the surprising event. This asymmetry seems at least partly to explain why the downturn of investment and employment after a boom is usually more abrupt and rapid than their upturn after a slump.

4. We have thus found three distinct initiating sources of change of the aggregate investment-flow. First, an event which, after its assimilation by a number of investors, causes them to move up or down the focus-gains or losses of blueprints which they have in mind, or to create new blueprints. Second, the recognition by many investors of a future date which will bring the answers to specially significant questions and thus restrict the number and narrow the divergence of the different paths which the course of events can reasonably be imagined to follow. Third, the invalidation of existing structures of expectations by a surprising event, which will make individuals feel sure that their means of looking forward are, for the time being, in an exceptionally poor condition and are going to improve.

5. The concept of focus-gain and focus-loss offers us a new and extremely simple definition of an individual's risk preference, and enables us to measure it. Writing g for the ratio of focus-gain to construction cost of a particular blueprint, and h for the ratio of focus-loss to construction cost of this blueprint, we ask what value of g/h would be just sufficient to induce the individual to construct the blueprint, rather than retain his money in cash, supposing there were no other way of using this money, except these two, visible to him. This critical value of g/h is then the definition and measure of his risk preference or, as I should prefer to call it for the sake of avoiding any suggestion that we are concerned with *measurable risk*, his 'gambler-preference'. Inter-personal comparisons of gambler-preference can evidently be made only between persons possessing roughly equal total resources, and on the supposition that the respective blueprints that they have in mind are of roughly equal construction cost, so that they are being asked on what terms each would risk equal proportions of equal total resources.

Part III

EXPECTATIONS, INVESTMENT, MONEY AND THE BUSINESS CYCLE

Dynamics of the Crisis : A Suggestion

THE suggestion made in this paper as to a possible mechanism of the crisis invokes two classes of considerations :

(i) Each entrepreneur's ignorance [1] of many of the magnitudes relevant to his decisions, and especially of their time-shapes in the future. In particular, his ignorance of the intentions of other entrepreneurs.
(ii) The technical conditions of constructing large systems of durable equipment.

No mention is made in what follows of any monetary causation in which an unexpected rise in the long-term rate of interest might bring on the crisis before any such mechanism as is here described could come into play. This article develops a particular suggestion in isolation from other and possibly more important aspects of the crisis.

In order to give an exact definition of investment, we suppose all members of the economy to take decisions simultaneously at the beginning of a short interval during which these decisions cannot be revised. Investment refers to the consequences of these decisions, which having worked themselves out during the interval are seen in the light of each entrepreneur's knowledge of his own affairs as it exists at the *end* of the interval. Investment is measured per unit of time as follows : each entrepreneur's prime costs of the marginal unit of output comprise—(1) payments to workers, lenders, etc., and (2) the present or discounted expected future cost of any power, materials, or apparatus which he buys now or intends to buy, which he would not buy if he did not produce the marginal unit of present output. Sale-proceeds of output of the interval, minus the integral of marginal prime costs, is the entrepreneur's income. His payments to workers, etc., excluding other entrepreneurs, are their income. Summed for the whole economy, these two categories of income give the economy's income. Total payments of consumers for consumables during the interval is consumption. Income minus consumption is investment. Let an entrepreneur value each item of his equipment of n identical items at A at the beginning of an interval, and let one item be destroyed in production during the interval. If, during the interval, the entrepreneur's conception of the future changes, he will revise his valuation both of the destroyed and the remaining items. Suppose that at the end of the interval his revised valuation is hA per item. Then the prime equipment-cost is hA, while his gain or loss on capital account is $h(n-1)A$. Such revisions may result from any change of an entrepreneur's *expectation*, including expectations of the bundle of interest-rates, but cannot result from the time-approach of events whose expected characteristics are unchanged.

[1] I wish to acknowledge a debt to Professor Hayek, who in his latest work has been the first to stress the vital significance of the differences between the sets of facts and beliefs in the minds of different individuals, and of the mechanism of the diffusion of knowledge.

To Mr. Keynes I owe the basis of the concepts of investment and income, which, however, I have formulated a little differently from the " General Theory of Employment, Interest and Money " ; and to Mr. Kahn and to Mr. Keynes jointly, the extremely important concept of the Multiplier.

Four components make up the magnitude we have labelled investment :

(1) The aggregate value of items of durable equipment newly brought to the operable condition during the interval.

(2) Any change (excluding those due to changes of expectation) in the value of stocks of materials for making durable equipment, or of partly finished durable equipment.

(3) Changes in stocks of partly finished *consumers'* goods.

(4) Value (determined by the discounted intended cost of replacement with similar or improved items) of durable equipment actually destroyed by the operations of the interval.

Of these, (1) is the most important, and any large change in it in either direction implies a change of investment in the same direction. We shall assume that if (1) begins to increase, the stocks or goods in process under (2) will a short time afterwards begin to increase, or at least cease to decline. Since (4) will not show wide absolute variations in comparison with (1), any considerable offset against an increase of (1) can come only under (3). We shall therefore distribute all kinds of enterprise into two main classes :

I. Those whose product does not contribute directly or indirectly to the making of durable equipment.

II. Those which manufacture or assemble durable equipment.

The operations performed by plants of class I stand in simple sequences, such as : wheat-farm, flour-mill, bakery. We shall therefore call such industries " straight-sequence " industries. It is otherwise with class II. *Every* type of plant, whatever its function in the general activity, must from time to time have its apparatus replaced or its functions taken over by items newly produced with the help of *existing* equipment. It follows that some types of plant must be helping directly or indirectly to replace themselves with similar or improved equipment, as well as providing the equipment of the straight-sequence industries. These plants are those of class II, and we shall call them the growth-elements of the general productive complex.

The fact that one of the two main provinces of industry is concerned largely or exclusively with the construction of durable equipment is almost bound to intensify any initial change in the rate of investment. For any strengthening of the demand for durable equipment will make it seem profitable to improve the scale or design of plants producing it, and this development of the growth-elements will itself add to the demand for their own output. A drop in the rate of money-input into construction of straight-sequence plants will in the same way discourage construction of new projects of class II. This is one element in the mechanism of an upward or downward cumulative movement.

At the beginning of recovery there are considerable unemployed potential flows of almost all kinds of resources. If now the output of the durable-equip-ment-making industries is increased by their taking on more men, the com-munity's attempt to spend some of the addition to aggregate income will result, according to the multiplier principle of Mr. Kahn and Mr. Keynes, first in some depletion of stocks at various stages of the straight-sequence industries, and some rise of prices, and then in an increase of the output of these industries effected by taking on additional men. As soon as this second addition to aggregate income begins to be spent, the process will be repeated, and so on until eventually aggregate income attains a combination of size and distribution with which its excess over aggregate consumption equals the concurrent investment in durable equipment without any offsetting disinvestment of consumption-goods.

All this will happen because some individual entrepreneurs, in the light of their knowledge in the initial situation, *then* thought it profitable to construct new plants. Did each take account of the multiplier effect of his own and the others' action, or will the increased demand for consumables appear to these entrepreneurs as an unexpected event warranting still further investment ? Seeing how little each can currently know of the aggregate scale of all the others' operations, or of the shape of the community's propensity to consume, we are justified in finding here a second element in the mechanism of the boom, which like the former can act in reverse and produce a downward cumulation.

Thus an initial tendency to raise the level of the flow of investment causes increased consumption through the multiplier effect, and further increased investment in the growth-elements. The higher level of consumption-spending encourages a further raising of the investment-flow, and so on. We have a process of self-increasing activity called the boom. The main purpose of this article is to suggest one way in which this process could break down.

This explanation assumes that the boom carries some resource or group of resources essential for constructing durable equipment some distance up a steeply-rising segment of its short-period supply curve without causing anything similar to happen in the straight-sequence industries, and that this situation causes the number and scale of projects being planned, which determines an important component of the time-rate of investment some months later, to fall sharply, thus initiating, when that date is reached, a downward cumulation through the multiplier mechanism and the effect on the durable-equipment-making industries.

" Resource " means the power, whether possessed by human beings, nature, or equipment, to perform some technically defined operation or group of similar operations. Time-rates of flow of the resource are measured in natural units of performance, e.g. in ton-miles transported. By a resource essential to, e.g., the growth-elements we mean one without which some proportion, say 20 per cent, of their output measured in value (at a particular phase of the cycle, say, after two years of increasing activity) could not be produced. A given technically defined operation, such as excavation, can be performed by different agencies, e.g. by men with hand-tools or by machines. The short-period supply-curve of a resource thus defined will rise steeply as agencies which are less well adapted to this than to another operation have to be taken into this employment. Thus if the resource in question is desert transport of oil, this resource (transport) will be cheap up to the capacity of the pipe-line, dearer if this has to be supplemented by railway tank-cars, and dearer still if lorries have to be called into service as well.

DYNAMICS OF THE CRISIS : A SUGGESTION   III

This explanation makes the following assumptions :

1. Entrepreneurs base their conceptions of the future time-shape of each economic magnitude largely on the present level and first and second derivatives of the main relevant magnitudes. That they do this in a fairly naïve way, especially when we include as entrepreneurs not merely the actual promoters of new enterprises but the public to whom they sell new equities representing these enterprises.

2. Entrepreneurs are largely ignorant of each other's intentions and of the time-rates of potential flows of resources which at any moment are not actually employed.

3. There are some resources essential for constructing durable plant, but not essential, once the durable equipment of the straight-sequence industries exists, for producing consumables.

4. Some of these are absorbed in the construction of each project (sub-system of durable equipment) at a low time-rate in the early phases of construction but at a high time-rate later.

5. Alternative assumptions :

   A. Once the contract for a new plant has been placed, this plant will be completed within the stipulated time or nearly so.

   B. For a reason which we shall develop below a plant which has attained a certain stage of advancement towards completion will be completed without delay in spite of a large unexpected rise of prices of some essential resources happening after construction of the project is begun.

The construction of an equipment-system requires many different types of services and materials, each of which will have its own time-shape of input. The programme of construction by which these time-shapes are implied will be largely determined by technical necessities. Thus when the building of a new underground railway, for instance, has been decided on, much time and large sums of money must be spent on survey, designing, acquisition of land and preliminary clearance and excavation before steel, cement, electrical equipment, and skilled labour can begin to be absorbed at high time-rates. This necessity creates a lag between the decision to construct a project and the the peak absorption of certain resources.

Many of these resources will be of kinds not required for the operation of straight-sequence plants in the production of consumables. The knowledge and ability of designers and technicians and the skill of many workers is specialised. Many types of materials and component apparatus which are built into durable plants are not embodied in consumables. Let us label resources which are both specific and essential to the construction of durable equipment G-essential resources, and those which are both specific and essential to the production of consumables L-essential resources.

The boom is a process in which each increase of activity in either of the two divisions of the general productive complex, namely, the straight sequences and the growth-elements, leads to increased activity in the other. Thus so long as no G-essential resource reaches a steeply rising segment of its short-period supply curve, each increase in the time-rate of durable equipment construction will, through the mechanism described above, make a further increase in this rate seem profitable, and at each position t of the moving present moment the time-rate at which G-essential resources are actually being absorbed is less than their rate of absorption implied for some future moment by the combined effect of plans made and constructions already in progress at t. If the self-stimulating growth of activity continues a level must eventually be reached where some essential resource begins to move up a steeply-rising segment of its short-period supply-curve. This resource may be G-essential, L-essential, or both G- and L-essential. Our purpose here is to trace the consequences, supposing that it is G-essential, and that all L-essential resources have still some room to move along their short-period supply-curves before a steeply rising segment is reached.

We have seen that there is likely to be a lag between the date t_q when the price of the G-essential resource begins to rise steeply, and the future date at which, if intentions existing at t_q are carried out, its rate of absorption will be at a maximum. Thus, unless existing intentions are modified, the price of the resource will rise considerably, and the cost of completing partly constructed plants from whatever stage each has reached at date t_q, will be higher than was expected when these systems were planned. Will not this cause the construction of those plants which are least advanced towards completion or which are promoted by the less sanguine entrepreneurs, to be postponed or abandoned one after the other as pressure on the supply of the G-essential resource tends to increase, so that this pressure is in fact kept down ? This is unlikely to happen for two reasons. The first is that the firms who are actually building the plants may have contracted with the promoters to complete them at a certain cost within a certain time. There is, however, an economic reason which will have the same effect whether this institutional reason operates or not.

At the moment when the price of some G-essential resource begins to rise steeply, some projects have only just been started, and in each case only a small proportion of the quantity of this resource, measured in natural units, which will have been absorbed by the whole project when completed, has yet been applied. If these projects are to be completed, large physical quantities of the resource will have to be bought at the unexpected higher price. But other projects have already at the date t_q, when the error of foresight is perceived, reached a fairly advanced phase. The question for each entrepreneur at such a moment is whether the cost which would have to be incurred from this moment onwards in order to complete the project from its existing stage, according to the original or a changed construction-programme, can be kept less than total discounted returns according to the new expectations of this moment (costs and returns being respectively accumulated and discounted to the new completion-date). According to the answer he will decide to proceed with or abandon the project. What has been already spent counts only in this way, that it has reduced the quantities of resources in terms of natural units, which are needed to carry the project from the already attained stage to the point where it can begin to earn. For by definition an equipment-system is a technical organism which can operate so as to produce something

DYNAMICS OF THE CRISIS: A SUGGESTION

saleable only when this organism is complete, so that the partly built system, if it has no prospect of being completed, is valueless. In some cases the conformity of actual projects to this definition is necessary and obvious, e.g. oil pipe-line, dock, etc. But even an ordinary factory must be designed to link some definite points in the web of production, that is, to absorb certain outputs of other plants and to pass on a given product for further purposes. The nature of this intended product cannot be arbitrarily altered when the plant is partly constructed so that some technical processes are left for some one else to perform elsewhere. This, even if technically possible, would upset the calculations on which the project is based. Moreover, sequences of transformations are actually grouped in one plant according to technical convenience. Since, then, a partly constructed plant usually has a value only because of the possibility of completing it, the money which already at any moment has been spent cannot be counted as a cost in deciding whether it is worth while to complete the plant.

The entrepreneur must consider his problem entirely afresh, and make new forecasts of all the elements under the newly perceived conditions : cost of remainder of construction at a range of different possible completion-dates, undiscounted returns during a working life beginning at each of these possible completion-dates ; a different complete set of these estimates for each of a reasonable number of different scales of the plant ; and, at each scale, a different set for various more or less mechanised and initially expensive technical designs. The extent of such changes of scale and design which are worth while will depend largely on the adaptability of the beginnings of the plant which have already been made.

Now we shall see that a sharp price-rise of some G-essential resource or group of resources will not necessarily check itself before the price has gone very high, by causing enough entrepreneurs to postpone completion of their projects.

Until we make further assumptions, we cannot decide *a priori* whether the unexpected price-rise of the G-essential resource will cause the entrepreneur to revise upwards or downwards his estimate of the prospective yield of the plant if completed at the originally intended date. If this resource is required for operation as well as for construction of the plant, he may revise upwards his expectation of running-costs. If the resource in question is a produced means of production of a kind to whose making his own output will contribute, he may revise upward his expectation of sale-proceeds. In any case the expected working life of his plant is a period of many years, while the consequences of the present situation can be judged only for the immediate future. We shall therefore assume that the entrepreneur retains unchanged his original estimate of the undiscounted prospective yield of his plant for the originally intended completion-date, and treats this undiscounted prospective yield as constant for any completion-date.

There are then two problems :

1. As the present moment advances through time, an entrepreneur who is constructing a plant has at each stage of this construction an expectation of the prices at which he will be able to buy the resources he still needs to

complete the plant from the stage it has reached at the moment in question. If for simplicity we treat the prices of all needed resources at all dates during the remainder of construction as a single price, we can speak of the time-shape of changes of the entrepreneur's expectation of this price *as his present moment advances through time.* Our first problem asks what is the limiting case of this time-shape, in which resource-price is considered as a function of the quantity still required, which will just make it *seem* to him worth while, *at each successive change of expectation,* to persist in the construction of the plant. Since, as we have seen, the money already sunk in the plant cannot be treated as a cost in deciding whether or not to complete it, we may say briefly that the resource-prices, in spite of which it will be worth while for the entrepreneur to persist in construction, will be higher and higher the farther construction has already proceeded when he makes an upward revision of his expectation of these prices. An exact analytical formulation of this answer will be given below.

2. If the entrepreneur expects the price of the particular combination of quantities of resources required for completion to fall back again in the near future, it may seem to him profitable to postpone completion even if the cost of immediate completion would be less than the present value of the prospective yield. Our second problem asks under what conditions this will be the case. As construction proceeds, the money destined by the entrepreneur for buying resources for the project, but not yet invested in it, grows steadily less. Whatever the quantity of this diminishing fund on any date, this sum can earn interest for the entrepreneur. But as instalments of it are used to buy resources for the project, these instalments surrender their current fruitfulness in exchange for the prospective returns from the project when completed. If at any date t_q during construction the entrepreneur considers postponing completion, he will have to balance a loss and an offsetting gain. The loss will consist in the difference between the present value of expected returns from the project if this is completed at an earlier date, and their present value if completion is postponed to a more remote date. Against this will be offset the difference between the present value of whatever series of future direct outlays will be required to complete the project by the earlier date, and the corresponding present value for completion at the more remote date. Evidently the further construction has proceeded the nearer will be the originally intended completion-date, and the larger will be the *absolute* reduction of the value, discounted back to t_q of returns of a given time-shape, when the completion-date at which they will start is postponed by any given interval. But the absolute difference between the present values of the respective series of future direct outlays, which could be used to complete the project at an earlier or later date, is smaller, assuming resource prices unchanged, the farther construction has proceeded. It follows that the average rate of expected fall of resource prices over the period between now and some future date, which will suffice to make postponement of completion until this future date seem profitable, will be higher the farther construction has already proceeded when the decision is taken. This answer also will be formulated analytically below.

DYNAMICS OF THE CRISIS : A SUGGESTION   115

We can deal with the first problem as follows : We measure quantities of resources in natural units of physical performance. Suppose that the plant can be constructed in one way only, namely, by applying flows of certain resources each at a constant time-rate so long as construction is proceeding. This is equivalent to saying that a composite flow of unchanging quantitative composition must be applied at a uniform rate throughout the process of construction. We assume that the only alternative is complete suspension of the work. Thus the rate of application of the composite resource has two possible values, a fixed positive rate and zero. Let ω be the period needed to construct the plant from start to finish (i.e. from the entrepreneur's first outlay on it to the date when it is ready for operation), provided there is no interruption. Let s be the time during which, when any given date has been reached, the uniform rate of input of the composite resource must continue without interruption in order to complete the plant. Thus at the beginning of construction $s = \omega$, at the end $s = 0$. Now suppose that at each stage of construction the entrepreneur expects that the quantity of the composite resource still to be applied will be obtainable at a single price, which, however, may be different from the various expectations of it which he has held at earlier moments. Thus, if at some date when construction has been in progress for some time, he intends to buy the remaining quantity in three instalments at different dates, he will expect to get all of these at the same price, though not necessarily at the price he initially expected. On the hypothesis, the conditions for whose realisation we are now testing, that construction once begun will be completed without interruption, this expected price (which varies as the "present moment" at which the expectation is held moves forward through time) may be written as a function of s

$$p = f(s)$$

Now the quantity of the composite resource which at any moment still remains to be applied varies directly with s, and by the choice of suitable units may itself be represented by s. Let the rate of interest (r) be supposed the same for loans of all terms starting at any date. Then the expected cost of executing the remainder of construction without interruption from the stage reached on any date, discounted to this date, is approximately

$$K = sf(s)(1+r)^{-s/2} = sf(s)e^{-\rho s/2}$$

where $\rho = \log(1+r)$. As regards the accumulation of interest, the period $s/2$ is short, and the factor $e^{-\rho s/2}$ therefore approximates to unity and may for the purpose of our present argument be omitted. We therefore write

$$K = sf(s)$$

We have decided to treat the prospective yield of the plant, namely, the series of differences between expected sale proceeds and expected running costs in the succession of intervals making up the working life of the plant, as constant. With the rate of interest also constant, the value g of the prospective yield discounted back *to a fixed completion date* is also a constant. Treating the factor $e^{-\rho s}$ as approximating to unity, we may say that g is the present value of the plant. Now we have seen that when, after an unexpected rise in the price of resources for construction, the entrepreneur has to decide whether or not to complete the project, it is only the outlay which remains to be incurred, namely K, which he compares with the present value of the plant. He will therefore not be throwing good money after bad if he decides to complete the plant, provided he is confident that

$$sf(s) \leqq g \qquad\qquad \text{where } g = \text{constant.}$$

At the moment of beginning construction, the expected construction-cost is $\omega f(\omega)$. Suppose that this equals g. Then the critical level of $f(s)$, which must not be exceeded if construction is to continue, is in the ratio $\dfrac{\omega}{s}$ to the price $f(\omega)$ expected when construction was begun. For this critical expected price $f(s)$ at any stage of construction will be such that $sf(s) = \omega f(\omega)$, or $\dfrac{f(s)}{f(\omega)} = \dfrac{\omega}{s}$.

Thus, if price-expectations begin to be falsified from the start, the time-shape which the series of critical levels of the expected price forms as s diminishes, is a rectangular hyperbola referred to its asymptotes, the latter being the time-axis and an ordinate measuring price erected at the completion-date.

It is clear that if some G-essential resource is at the threshold of a steeply rising segment of its supply-curve, and will climb this segment unless a growing rate of absorption is slackened by the postponement of completion of a number of plants already under construction, the first unexpected movement of the price will have to cause very large upward shifts of some of those conceptions of the future time-shape of this price, which exist in the minds of individual entrepreneurs, in order to cause a sufficient number of plants to be abandoned, so that the price may not, in fact, rise very far. This example is interesting, apart from our main purpose, for two truths which it throws into sharp relief :

1. It emphasises the essential *multiple* nature of expectations, each individual having his own, which may be different from any one else's.

2. It shows that an entrepreneur has to forecast *two* things : (*a*) the economic " set-up " or whole complex of elements which may from some particular aspect be regarded as passive, e.g. in the example above, the impending insufficiency of flow of a G-essential resource for a rapidly growing rate of absorption ; (*b*) the actions of individuals, different actions being bound to call forth different results from this complex. In our example a price-rise of resources will occur unless a certain number of entrepreneurs abandon construction of their plants. But if many entrepreneurs realise this, and *too many of them assume that an insufficient number will actually abandon their plants, the price rise will not happen* !

We shall show in what follows that the avoidance of a price-rise of construction resources can in some circumstances depend on the actual abandonment of plants already under construction, and that the slackening of the rate at which new constructions are begun may be insufficient by itself.

Our second problem to which we now turn requires the formulation of fresh assumptions.

Suppose that in order to complete the plant from the stage of construction it has reached on some date $p = 0$, a fixed combination of quantities of resources, measured in natural units of physical performance, will have to be applied. Suppose that the actual application of these resources, that is, the execution of the remainder of the construction programme, can be done in a negligibly short time at a date P variable at the choice of the entrepreneur. Then the expected cost *as at P* of completing the plant will vary directly with the expected price of the fixed combination of resources, and can be treated as a function of the intended period of postponment, P. All these quantities are hypotheses in the mind of the entrepreneur, thinking on date $p = 0$. Completion-cost as at P is labelled k.

$$k = \Phi(P)$$

The cost *as at $p = 0$* of completing construction depends further on the rate of interest r at which money could be lent for the period P, and on the length of this period. It is also probable that the rate of interest itself depends on P, i.e. the term of a potential loan, but this we can neglect without injuring the argument. The cost of completion discounted to $p = 0$ is

$$K = \Phi(P)(1+r)^{-P} = \Phi(P)e^{-\rho P} \qquad \text{where } \rho = \log(1+r)$$

The expected working life of the plant is a period of many years. If the entrepreneur considers that the price of his product or his running costs will show a definite trend over such a period, then postponement of completion will alter his expectation of the series of differences between sale-proceeds and running-costs in the succession of intervals making up the working life. There is, however, no presumption in the situation which this chapter discusses that the trends will be either up or down. We therefore assume both that the undiscounted prospective yield remains unchanged if the completion-date, when this yield begins to accrue, is postponed, and that the rate of interest connecting any pair of dates is the same. Then let us call the prospective yield discounted back *to the completion-date g. g* will be constant. Then the value as at $p = 0$ of the prospective yield is

$$G = g(1+r)^{-P} = ge^{-\rho P}$$

We can now state the conditions under which the entrepreneur will postpone completion.

(i) He will certainly do so if $K > G$ for *immediate* completion, i.e. if $\Phi(0) > g$.

(ii) He will do so even if $\Phi(0) < g$, if he is confident that $G-K$ will be made greater by postponement.

We have further to ask under what conditions he will be confident that $G-K$ can be increased by postponement. It is possible that $G-K$ will be greater by a certain postponement than by immediate completion, even if $\Phi(P)$, so far as the entrepreneur can judge, is at the present moment increasing ; for it may fall very steeply in the future. But to act on such a belief will be a gamble, and if $\Phi(0) < g$ and $\Phi'(0) \geqq 0$ immediate completion will probably be decided on. The condition of postponement if $K < G$ for immediate completion, i.e. if $\Phi(0) < g$, is therefore probably that K is *now* decreasing faster than G with increase of postponement (from zero postponement), that is, $\dfrac{dK}{dP} < \dfrac{dG}{dP}$

where we know that $\frac{dG}{dP}$ is negative. Writing out these derivatives at $P=0$ we get for this condition

$$\Phi'(0)-\rho\Phi(0)<-\rho g$$

or

$$-\Phi'(0)>\rho[g-\Phi(0)]$$

This means that the time-rate at which completion-cost is falling with increase of postponement (from zero postponement) must be *numerically greater than the absolute flow of interest on the difference between immediate completion-cost and present value of prospective yield with immediate completion.*

As a numerical illustration, let us put $g=\pounds 100,000$ and see at what average rate the price of resources needed for completion must be expected to fall after an unexpected rise, in order to make postponement of completion seem profitable.

Case I. Suppose that the cost of completion from the stage already attained at some date $p=0$ according to the revised expectations of resource-prices which the entrepreneur has in mind at this date is $\Phi(0)=\pounds 80,000$. Then if $\rho=5\%$ construction will be completed immediately unless it is confidently believed that resource-prices will, by some date in the future, turn out to have fallen as compared with their level at $p=0$ by an average of at least

$$\frac{100,000-80,000}{20\times 80,000}=1.25\% \text{ per annum.}$$

Case 2. $\Phi(0)=\pounds 30,000$. Resource-prices must be expected to fall by at least

$$\frac{100,000-30,000}{20\times 30,000}=11.7\% \text{ per annum.}$$

Case 3. $\Phi(0)=\pounds 10,000$. Resource-prices must be expected to fall by at least

$$\frac{100,000-10,000}{20\times 10,000}=45\% \text{ per annum.}$$

It may be well to repeat more explicitly the relation between the two problems we have discussed above. When we spoke of $G-K$ being made greater by the decision to postpone completion by a certain interval, we were describing the thoughts of the entrepreneur, occupying a time so short compared with that required for the execution of his decisions that we may consider them to be instantaneous. For whereas his thinking occupies a few hours his decisions relate to periods of months or years. For algebraic simplicity we assumed in our second problem that the actual execution of the remainder of the construction-programme would occupy a time negligibly short as regards the accumulation of interest. But we cannot assume this time negligible from the point of view of price-changes which can happen while the project is being completed. While our second problem was concerned with a survey of various possible actions and their outcomes by the entrepreneur *at a moment of time*, our first problem traces a process in time, namely, the changes of the entrepreneurs' expectations which happen *as time advances*. The combined result will be applied to our main investigation.

We must next gain some notion of the probable time-shapes of the *aggregate* rates of absorption of resources in constructing durable equipment during the boom. For this purpose we assume that all plants are constructed by means of a composite resource, whose quantitative composition remains the same throughout the construction of each plant and is the same for all plants. However, instead of assuming that this resource must be applied to each plant at a uniform rate from start to finish, we suppose that it must be applied at a *uniformly increasing* rate, starting from zero. This supposition represents in a manageable form the condition of a time-lag between the starting of construction and the peak absorption of some essential resources, the reason for assuming which was explained above. It is further assumed both that the rate of increase *z* of the time-rate at which the resource is absorbed in the construction of each plant, and the period *ω* occupied by this construction, are the same for all plants. Thus the time-shape of absorption of the resource in an individual plant is represented by a straight line inclined at an angle arc tan *z* to the time-axis. This line, it should be noticed, is *not* a cumulative curve. Its ordinates, and not its slope, represent the rate of absorption at each stage of construction. We have thus the following set of magnitudes:

Distance of the moving present moment from some arbitrary fixed date in the past = *t*

Number of plants started in unit-time = *f(t)*

Period occupied by construction of each plant = *ω*

Time which has elapsed since the moment of starting the plant, when any stage of construction is reached = *v*

Time-rate of absorption of the composite resource in each plant = *zv*

Aggregate rate of increase of absorption in all plants under construction at time *T* = *Z*

Then the rate of absorption into an individual plant at the moment of completion is *zω*, and the aggregate flow of absorption is reduced, *ceteris paribus*, by this quantity as soon as the plant is completed. This quantity multiplied by the number of plants being completed in unit time therefore gives us the negative term of our formula. Thus:

$$Z = z \int_{T-\omega}^{T} f(t)dt - z\omega f(T-\omega)$$

$$= z \left[\int_{T-\omega}^{T} f(t)dt - \omega f(T-\omega) \right] \quad \dots\dots\dots\dots(a)$$

As an illustration of how this formula works we may take the special case where *f(t)* has been constant over a period of the past longer than *ω*. Then:

$$\int_{T-\omega}^{T} f(t)dt = \omega f(T) = \omega f(T-\omega) \text{ and } Z = 0$$

Study of formula (a) yields some interesting results.

1. The *sign* of the aggregate momentary rate of increase of absorption Z depends on that of the second factor, since z by assumption is positive. The sign of the second factor, namely, the expression in square brackets, depends on the form of $f(t)$ in the interval $T-\omega \leq t \leq T$. If in this interval $f(t)$ has at any time risen above $f(T-\omega)$ but has never fallen below it, the second factor, and therefore Z, is positive ; and vice versa.

2. For a given value of the second factor the absolute size of Z, whether positive or negative, varies directly with z. Thus if the second factor is negative, the aggregate rate of *decrease* of absorption is greater, the greater the rate of increase in the individual plant. The meaning of this paradox is that since ω and z are constants, it would take a given number of plants under construction to balance a given number being completed per unit-time, in order to keep $Z=0$. The rate of increase or decrease of absorption represented by any given *numerical* shortage or excess of the number of plants being completed in unit-time, over that required exactly to offset the effect of a given number under construction, depends on the *scale* of the operations represented by the construction of an individual plant. For given ω, this scale is measured by z, so that the larger is z the larger is the decrease of absorption represented by the cessation of work on any one plant at its completion.

If the second factor has a given positive value, Z varies directly with z.

Thus, even if $\int_{T-\omega}^{T} f(t)dt$ only exceeds $\omega f(T-\omega)$ by a little, Z may be large (i.e. the rate of aggregate absorption may be rising steeply) if z is large, i.e. if the rate of absorption in individual plants increases steeply as construction proceeds. Z may be considerable for some fraction u of a period equal to ω, even if during this u period $f(t)$ is already less than $f(T-\omega)$.

At this point it may be well to answer an objection which will probably occur to the reader. Granting that the rate of absorption of the resource in the construction of an individual plant probably ascends to a maximum, have we the right to assume that it continues to increase throughout the construction, so that the maximum occurs at the completion-date ? The answer is that we are merely treating the point of maximum absorption as the completion-date, and assuming an instantaneous instead of a gradual fall to zero.

We have, therefore, only to substitute a period ζ during which the rate of absorption into an individual plant is increasing, instead of the period ω, and our statement above will hold in the more general case where the individual rate of absorption may not increase throughout the construction period, but may decline gradually after the peak.

In what follows we consider T as the moving present moment, and the interval between $T-\omega$ and T as a moving time-segment located successively between different pairs of dates as T advances through time.

Now during the boom $f(T)$ will always be greater than $f(T-\omega)$ until, and perhaps some while after, the moment x_1, when some G-essential resource begins to climb a steeply-rising segment of its short-period supply curve. Thus, when the moving present moment T reaches x_1, Z will be positive, and no fall of $f(T)$ occurring at x_1, however great and even if instantaneous, can render Z negative until some interval has elapsed. Unless, therefore, some plants already under construction are abandoned, pressure on the supply of the G-essential resource will during this interval continue to increase, forcing up its price and the cost of construction of durable equipment very rapidly. *We have seen above why this rise is unlikely to be checked by suspension of work on plants whose construction has already been begun.* If such a rise happens, the decision whether to build any given unstarted project or not will depend on what is happening to the most sanguine entrepreneur's estimation of its prospective yield. If a considerable proportion of the projects which entrepreneurs are considering do not seem likely to cover the higher costs, the number of new projects begun in unit-time will fall. Leaving the discussion of prospective yield to the next paragraph let us assume that at x_1, $f(T)$ begins to fall. So long as Z remains positive the price of the G-essential resource will go on rising, and $f(T)$ will fall with increasing steepness. As $f(T)$ falls, $f(T-\omega)$ follows the rising path traced by $f(T)$ one ω-period ago. At the date x_2 at which $f(T)$ and $f(T-\omega)$ become equal, $f(T-\omega)$ is still rising, for the date x_1, where $f(T)$ passed its maximum, lies between $x_2-\omega$ and x_2. At x_2 the second factor of Z, and therefore Z itself, will still be positive, for $\int_{T-\omega}^{T} f(t)dt$ will be greater than $\omega f(T-\omega)$.

$f(T)$ will therefore continue to fall. If $f(T)$ continues to fall until the date $x_1+\omega$, at which $f(T-\omega)$ reaches a maximum, Z will be negative at $x_1+\omega$, since $\int_{T-\omega}^{T} f(t)dt$ will now be less than $\omega f(T-\omega)$. It follows that Z will fall to zero at some date x_3 lying between x_2 and $x_1+\omega$, this latter being the date where $f(T-\omega)$ reaches its maximum. At x_3, therefore, we have :

$$f(T)<f(T-\omega)$$
$$f'(T-\omega)>0$$

Now $$\frac{dZ}{dT}=z[f(T)-f(T-\omega)-\omega f'(T-\omega)]$$

As T approaches x_3, therefore, $\frac{dZ}{dT}$ is negative. If Z is to avoid becoming negative when T passes x_3, $\frac{dZ}{dT}$ must here jump suddenly from a negative to a zero or positive value. Since the second and third terms of $\frac{dZ}{dT}$ are fixed by history, this jump can only be effected if $f(T)$, the number of new projects started in unit time, itself undergoes a large instantaneous increase at the moment when the pressure on the G-essential resource ceases to increase. If we admit that this is unlikely, *Z must become negative at x_3.* Z stands in our simplified scheme for the rate of increase of flow of absorption of a uniform composite resource which is the exclusive means of constructing all durable plants. Translated into terms applicable to the real world, a negative value of Z will correspond, *for given output of the straight-sequence industries,* to a falling rate of investment. The rapidity of this fall will be somewhat checked at first by the piling-up of stocks of ready consumables, but as the straight-sequence industries cut down their output investment will fall steeply. We have seen reason to suppose that such a fall will lead to a downward cumulative movement. We have, therefore, to examine what is likely to happen to the prospective yield (*a*) of " straight-sequence " projects (*b*) of growth-element projects.

We have assumed that no L-essential resource is brought to the threshold of a steep price-rise by that increment of the time-rate of durable construction which causes a G-essential resource to climb a steeply-rising segment of its supply-curve. There will, therefore, be no corresponding sharp rise in the prices of consumables, though there will be the multiplier effect on the scale on which they are produced. Thus the movement of the demand-conditions for consumables, which we have suggested will cause during the boom a series of upward revisions of the prospective yield of contemplated new straight-sequence plants, will have no greater influence than before, while the cost of constructing new straight-sequence plants has undergone a sudden rapid rise. It is extremely likely, therefore, that there will be a large fall in the rate of increase of the number of new plants begun in unit-time, probably amounting to an actual decrease of this number. In any case, however, this fall will as we have seen imply a very large proportionate drop in the rate of absorption of the output of the growth-elements. The construction of new growth-element plants is, therefore, likely to cease entirely. With this further effect, it becomes easy to understand how $f(T)$ can fall. We have seen that if the rate of absorption of resources in individual plants under construction increases as they progress, the pressure on these resources will not be relaxed until a position is reached where a fall in the rate of investment is almost inevitable. This will bring in its train a downwards multiplier effect, further discouragement to investment, and the whole downwards cumulative process.

London.   G. L. S. SHACKLE.

Some Notes on Monetary Theories of the Trade Cycle

By G. L. S. SHACKLE

No reader of Dr. Hayek's *Prices and Production* and of Mr. Keynes' *Treatise on Money* can doubt that each of these authors has developed new aspects of monetary theory which have not been explored by the other. There are also manifestly certain grounds of actual divergence of opinion between them, the interest of which is heightened by the fact that they acknowledge a common starting-point in the work of Wicksell. Since these authors represent schools which are the spearhead of the attack on monetary problems to-day, and have paid each other the tribute of systematic and penetrating mutual criticism, a comparison of their work is inevitable. In the following notes, it is proposed first to consider individually the chief points which have been raised in this criticism, and after this, in view of the charge of obscurity which more than one reviewer has brought against Dr. Hayek's theory, to attempt an outline of his central conception.

There are two chief questions to which these investigators have sought the answers :

(1) What factors can cause a change in the effective demand for intermediate products?

(2) What are the successive effects of such a change, on the direction and character of production as a whole?

In regard to the first question, the chief point at issue is as to whether an increase in the rate of money-saving does, or does not, *necessarily* stimulate a shift of productive effort from consumers' goods to intermediate products. In contending that it does not, Mr. Keynes assumes that losses suffered by producers of consumption goods as a result of increased money-saving by the public will not necessarily cause them to reduce the scale of their operations. In order, then, that they may be able to maintain their output of consumers' goods at the former level, they must reimburse their business-deposits which have been depleted as a result of their failure to sell their output for as much as it cost. Apart from an extension of bank-credit, with which we are not now concerned, there is only one source from which they can reimburse their deposits, namely the extra savings *which have caused, and are equal in amount to, their losses*. They must, therefore, obtain the use of the *whole* of these extra savings, either by borrowing direct from the savers, or by selling enough of their own non-liquid assets to bring in an equal amount. In either case the whole of the extra savings will be absorbed in replenishing the business-deposits of the entrepreneurs.

27

The objection to the initial assumption on which this result depends is thus expressed by Dr. Hayek (*Economica*, No. 35, p. 31).

" It seems to me that a complete neglect of the part played by rate of interest is involved in the assumption that, after investment in the production of consumption goods has become relatively less profitable, some other openings for investment which are now more profitable, will not be found."

The point seems clear : an increase of saving will provide an increased supply of money lying in the savers' bank accounts ready to be used either

> (a) To make good the losses which this very increase of saving has caused producers of consumption goods to suffer ;
> or (b) for increased output by producers of intermediate products.

The decision as to who gets the use of the money will depend on who is willing to pay the highest interest, that is, who has reason to suppose he can use the money most profitably. Is it likely, in the circumstances, that putting the money back into consumers' goods will seem to hold out such good prospects of profit that it will pay the producers of these goods to outbid the producers of intermediate products for the use of it ?

It is true that the lower rate of interest, resulting from the larger volume of savings seeking employment, will lower the cost of production of consumers' goods. But there will be no such lowering of the rate of interest if producers of consumption-goods seek to borrow the *whole* of these extra savings, since any lowering of the rate will make it profitable for producers of intermediate products to borrow a part of them. Unless, therefore, producers of consumption-goods are prepared, in spite of their losses, to maintain the same output at the same cost, at least a part of the new savings will represent additional demand for intermediate products.

The point may perhaps be summed up by considering the following passage from Mr. Keynes' " Reply " (*Economica*, No. 34, p. 393) :

" In my view, saving and investment (as I define them) can get out of gear without any change on the part of the banking system from ' neutrality ' as defined by Dr. Hayek, merely as a result of the public changing their rate of saving, or the entrepreneurs changing their rate of investment, there being no automatic mechanism in the economic system (as Dr. Hayek's view would imply there must be) to keep the two rates equal, provided the effective quantity of money is unchanged." Dr. Hayek's comment on this passage may be readily guessed : such a mechanism does exist, in the rate of interest, which differentiates between those stages of production which offer the better, and those which offer the poorer, prospects of profit, and causes the available resources to be invested where they will bring in the greatest return.

In the absence, then, of changes in the amount of the effective industrial circulation, and in the co-efficient of money transactions (*Prices and Production*, p. 105), there would be a natural tendency for a new equilibrium to be attained after changes on the side of the real structure and technique of production, or on the side of money, had upset the old one. The next

SOME NOTES ON MONETARY THEORIES OF THE TRADE CYCLE 29

point at issue concerns the causes, and the effects, of changes in the effective circulation. It is as to whether the effective industrial circulation (=the quantity of money used in industry multiplied by its velocity of circulation) can, or cannot, be increased under normal circumstances and to a material extent, without causing a change in the ratio of saving to investment. Mr. Keynes holds that it can, Dr. Hayek that it cannot.

Mr. Keynes says : " The point, put very briefly, is, firstly, that money may be advanced to entrepreneurs (directly by the banks, or through the new issue market or by the sale by them of their existing assets) either to meet losses or to provide for new investment, and that statistics of the quantity of money do not enable us to distinguish between the two cases ; and, secondly (to indicate a general principle by means of an illustration), that, if desiring to be more liquid I sell Consols to my bank in exchange for a bank deposit, and my bank does not choose to offset this transaction but allows its deposits to be correspondingly increased, the quantity of money is changed without anything having happened either to saving or to investment."

In the first sentence, Mr. Keynes seems to mean that if the banks increase the amount of outstanding credit in order to make up for losses suffered by producers of consumption-goods, then this extra credit, *although it increases the effective industrial circulation,* will *not* provide anybody with means or inducement to lengthen the process of production. Yet the losses suffered by producers of consumption-goods can only mean that consumers have spent less on consumption-goods than they were paid for making them. Their extra savings have not been absorbed in making good the losses they have caused, since these losses have been made good by extra bank-credit. Therefore these savings are seeking employment, and will tend to improve the terms on which entrepreneurs can borrow for the purchase of intermediate products, and initiate a lengthening of the process of production.

As to whether the effective industrial circulation can be increased by open-market operations without any stimulus being given to investment, this is purely a question of what is done with the extra money. If it is put into savings deposits, this is *not* an increase of the industrial circulation. If it is merely allowed to lie idle in swollen business-deposits, this is merely a slowing down of the velocity of circulation, offsetting the increase of volume, and does not constitute an increase of the effective circulation for the purpose of this discussion. If it is spent on consumers' goods, then this is indeed a means whereby an increase in the output of consumers' goods could conceivably be matched by an increase of the effective circulation, so as to maintain the price-level without disturbing the equality of saving and investment. But to what extent do capitalists actually dissipate their capital in this way?

Mr. Keynes' theory of the mechanism of open-market operations is discussed by Dr. Hayek in *Economica*, No. 35, where he criticises Mr. Keynes' assertion that " given the volume of savings-deposits created by

the banking-system, the price-level of investment goods is solely determined by the disposition of the public towards ' hoarding money.' "

Dr. Hayek says, " If we concede both assumptions : the direct dependence of the demand for securities on their present price, and the power
of the banking-system to determine the volume of savings-deposits, then,
indeed, this conclusion certainly follows.   But both assumptions are highly
questionable " ; the second " depends, obviously, on the assumption that
the amount of money required by the industrial circulation is determined
independently of the terms on which the banking-system is willing to
lend."   Dr. Hayek's point is that the banking-system, when it creates
deposits by buying securities in the open market, is increasing the amount
of money potentially available for the purchase of other securities or of
new intermediate products : this constitutes a lowering of the rate of interest,
and will normally cause some of the extra money, available as a result of the
open-market purchases, to flow into the active deposits and be used for
buying new intermediate products.

I do not think Mr. Keynes would deny this, but I believe the lines of
his answer may be discerned :

It will not pay anybody to buy *new* intermediate products at so high
a price that the yield on them is lower than the yield on old securities at
their current price.   Yet if the public believe that old securities are likely
to fall in value, there will be a general movement to sell, with the result
of a fall in the price of old securities which will necessarily bring down the
value of new intermediate products in its train. Thus a " bear " movement of
public opinion will tend to reduce the amount of money seeking investment in
new intermediate products ; that is, it will cause the rate of interest to rise.
The effects of such a " bear " movement may be counteracted by the banking-system, if it is willing to buy all those securities which the holders
wish to exchange for deposits.   Provided it confines its open-market operations to just the amount necessary to counteract the " bearishness " of the
public, *it will not have increased the active circulation*; it will not have
lowered the rate of interest, but merely prevented it from rising.

Mr. Keynes does not, I think, mean that the banking-system can determine the disposition of the money it provides by open-market purchases of
securities, but merely that it can *counteract the " bearishness " of the public*
in a varying degree : either inadequately, fully, or too much ; so that as a
net result the rate of interest rises, remains constant, or falls.

Dr. Hayek's other contention is that " any fall in the price of securities
is just as likely to create a fear of a further fall as the expectation of a
rise."   Mr. Keynes does not mean that *every* fall in the price of securities
is likely to create the expectation of a rise ; but that, if the price of securities
falls far enough, it will reach a point where the holders of securities, on the
average, feel that the sacrifice of selling at this low price is too much to
pay for safety from a further fall, in view of the probability that prices will
ultimately recover ; or where, if they still desire to sell, purchasers can
be found who consider that the risk is worth assuming at this low price.

Now it is clear that open-market operations on the lines indicated by

SOME NOTES ON MONETARY THEORIES OF THE TRADE CYCLE 31

Mr. Keynes would constitute an essential part of the means at the disposal of the banking-system for preventing the volume of the industrial circulation from varying. A " bear " swing of public opinion constitutes a raising of the rate of interest, since it means that entrepreneurs must offer a higher rate to tempt savings from savings-deposits into investment. In the event of such a " bear " swing of opinion, the banks would have to maintain the price of securities by buying them in the open market, and so keep down the yield to a level at which the demand for new intermediate products continued in equality with the public's flow of new saving. Otherwise, in this event, there would be no inducement to entrepreneurs to compensate any reduction in the output of consumption-goods, which might take place as a consequence of an increase in the rate of saving, by an increased output of intermediate products of higher stages. Similarly, open-market sales would be needed to prevent a " bull " trend from stimulating investment for which no provision was being made by voluntary deferment of consumption.

The chief points at issue regarding the answer to the first question have now been mentioned. In approaching the second question, we find so significant a difference of treatment on a fundamental matter, that Dr. Hayek has taken it as the starting-point of his criticism (*Economica*, No. 33, p. 273). It concerns the origin and nature of profits, which he and Mr. Keynes are at one in regarding as the prime-mover in economic change. Dr. Hayek's contention is this : that Mr. Keynes considers " total profits " accruing to the entre-preneurs as being necessarily derived either from a disparity between the costs, and the sale-proceeds of consumers' goods, or from a similar disparity between costs and sale-proceeds of *new* intermediate products : whereas such total profits can also arise because of changes in the value of *existing* inter-mediate products. In Dr. Hayek's view, " total profits " can arise because *existing* intermediate products have increased in value on account of a rise in their marginal productivity, such rise coming about because more of these existing intermediate products are needed for the production or operation of *new* intermediate products.

What is the real significance of this? It is that an increase in the flow of money coming forward for the purchase of new intermediate products does not mean that the whole of the resulting profit will be reaped by the producers of *new* intermediate products : the prices they pay for their cost goods will also be raised, and a part of the profits will go to the sellers of these cost goods, some of which are needed for the *operation* of existing instrumental capital. The operators of this instrumental capital will no longer be able, at prices which they can afford, to command an adequate supply of the intermediate products which they need for the operation of their plant, and the marginal productivity and hence the value of this plant will fall. Thus, in Dr. Hayek's words (*Economica*, No. 33, p. 276) " . . . a divergence between current expenditure and current receipts will always tend to cause changes in the value of existing capital which are by no means constituted by that difference, and that because of this, the effects of a difference between current receipts and current expenditure (i.e. profits in Mr. Keynes' sense) may lead to a change in the value of existing capital which may more than balance the money profits.'' Capital whose value had thus declined would not, of course, be fully renewed as it wore out, and thus when a breakdown of the effort to lengthen the process of production necessitated a return to less capitalistic methods, it would not be adequately available, and its absence would delay the re-employment of labour.

In the passage quoted above, Dr. Hayek is touching on what is the key idea of his whole theory—namely, that a stimulus to increased investment may result in the *disproportional creation of various kinds of intermediate products,* that is, in the attempt to create one part of a new, longer process of production, the operation of which will be impossible without such economies of non-specific goods as can only be expected when the *whole* of the new, longer process has been put into operation. Thus, for instance, so much plant for making machines might be laid down, that the operation of all this plant would be impossible with the available supply of, e.g. labour and electric power until the need for these in the consumers' goods stages has been economised by a completed longer process of production; the completion of the process demanding a temporary sacrifice of consumption which the receivers of income will not tolerate. The receivers of income express their disapproval by spending a larger proportion of their incomes, now augmented by the flow of fresh money which has stimulated the increased investment, on consumers' goods. The resulting profits accruing to producers of consumption goods enable these to outbid the operators of machinery-producing plant for the non-specific goods which they need, and they are compelled to cease operations and throw out of work a quantity of labour, etc., which the producers of consumption goods will only gradually be able to absorb.

The chief points raised by the authors in criticism of each other have now been touched upon. Briefly summed up, the position is this : Mr. Keynes believes that the volume of currency media used in payments to the factors of production can be allowed to vary, under suitable conditions, without upsetting the equality of savings and investment. He therefore contemplates the simultaneous maintenance by the banking-system both of a stable or uniformly-varying price level of consumers' goods, and of a harmony between saving and investment. Dr. Hayek holds that in a dynamic economy, the consumption price-level can be maintained only by constantly injecting fresh currency media into the industrial circulation; that the point in the money-circuit at which this fresh currency is injected is of primary significance; that, in fact, such injection can only take place to a material extent through investment; in consequence, any variation in the amount of the industrial circulation which does not correspond to changes in the co-efficient of money transactions must inevitably affect the rate of investment; and finally, that an acceleration of the rate of investment, which is not the result of increased voluntary saving, will result in the disproportionate creation of complementary intermediate products; that this disproportionality will only disappear when *the whole process of production, and not merely a part of it,* has been adapted to a more capitalised technique; and that usually, the completion of the new lengthened process will prove impossible, those parts of it which have been established will find no sufficient market for their products, and a shortage of their cost goods, and will become inoperable and derelict. Since, in his view, the only condition under which a lengthening of the process of production can be initiated, with the assurance of its being completed, is that it shall conform to the rate at which the public voluntarily saves its money-income, he believes that entrepreneurs must borrow no more nor less than what has been saved. Since what has not been saved has been spent, the volume of the industrial circulation must be kept *constant,* by a rate of interest which equalises the public's desire to save and the entrepreneurs' readiness to borrow. Thus, it is the very elasticity of the circulating medium under the modern system of banking, the most inherent and characteristic feature of that system, which makes disturbances of production self-intensifying instead of self-rectifying. To eliminate this, to make money " neutral " towards production and ensure that it shall leave the forces of equilibrium free to operate, the elasticity must be replaced by constancy.

It will be seen that the conclusion depends on whether, in fact, any change in the volume of the industrial circulation does necessarily disturb the equality of saving and investment, and it has been shown that, except under conditions of panic where the rate of interest ceases to operate in the normal manner contemplated by equilibrium theory, conditions which are the result rather than a spontaneous cause of disturbance, the volume cannot be changed without affecting investment.

It is, however, in describing the mechanism of such disturbances, the successive changes in the real structure of production which are initiated by an expansion of the circulating medium, that Dr. Hayek has shown a new horizon.

In his conception, the significant aspects of capitalistic production are :

(1) The length of the periods which elapse between the input of the various units of original resources (labour and land) at successive stages of the process, and the ultimate sale of the consumers' good in which they are embodied ; the longer the weighted average of these periods is, the greater will be the aggregate costs embodied in the intermediate products existing at a given moment, in relation to those embodied in the output of final products in unit time, and hence the greater also will be the proportionate quantity of intermediate products, measured in costs, being moved from stage to stage in unit time. This is beautifully demonstrated by the right-angled triangle diagram of capital, in which the base represents costs embodied in the output of final products, and the vertical distances from base to points on the hypotenuse represent the periods for which successive units of original resources are invested, changes in the relation between area and base therefore illustrating changes in the quantity of intermediate products which must exist simultaneously to maintain a given output of final products, with processes of varying length.

(2) The ratio of those inter-stage movements of intermediate products which are effected by exchanges against money, to the total of such movements. This ratio, which Dr. Hayek has called the co-efficient of money transactions, is lowered, if the ratio of costs embodied in intermediate products existing at any moment to costs embodied in final output of unit time, is increased without any increase in the number of separate ownerships of the intermediate products of different stages.

Such an increase in the number of stages, without a corresponding increase in the number of times exchanges must take place against money, is equivalent for the purpose of monetary theory to vertical integration of industrial concerns.

(3) The three distinct streams in which money is being used in production and distribution :

> (a) By entrepreneurs in paying for the factors of production, that is, in paying for original resources (labour and land), interest to lenders, and a composite return of interest and profits to themselves as risk-bearing capitalists.
>
> (b) By the providers of factors of production in buying consumers' goods.
>
> (c) In payments by entrepreneurs to other entrepreneurs for intermediate products.

It is clear that so long as the process of production is being lengthened, the increase in the relative quantity of intermediate products to output of final products, measured in costs, must, in the absence of any change in the co-efficient of money transactions, be accompanied *pari passu* by a growth of the ratio of stream (c) to stream (b), and that a lengthened process of production will remain in equilibrium only so long as the ratio of (c) to (b) remains higher, since otherwise a larger quantity of goods will have to be exchanged against a given quantity of money in the higher stages of production, than in the final stage and those immediately above it.

(4) The set of ratios fixed by the existing technique, between the quantities of various kinds of intermediate products and original resources, which are used together at any given stage.

(5) The distinction between the more specific kinds of intermediate products which can be used only at one or a few different stages, and those the supply of which can be diverted to any stage where, owing to a change in monetary or technical conditions, their marginal productivity is for the time being higher.

Lengthening the process of production really consists in rearranging and multiplying the connections between streams of intermediate products and introducing new sections of the " grid," so that a given unit of original resources goes a longer way round, and is embodied in a larger number of different products and stages before it emerges as a consumable good. The purpose of this lengthening is to realise the economies of a higher degree of specialisation : typically, special plant and equipment will be created for turning out a single product which before was an " internal " product

SOME NOTES ON MONETARY THEORIES OF THE TRADE CYCLE 35

of a more generalised plant, where its production was carried on with less capital but more labour per unit of output. Unless the marginal productivity of capital is raised by new discovery or invention, such increased specialisation will be profitable only when the rate of interest has declined relatively to the cost of labour. A fall in the rate of interest will therefore set up a demand for an increased output of industrial equipment, power, etc., the production of which can now itself be more highly capitalised, for the double reason of the increased demand and the lower rate of interest. If the rate of interest rises again, the operation of even the lowest of the new stages will be less profitable, and some of the new plant used at this stage, which may be labelled plant B, will not be replaced as it wears out. Therefore the plant, representing a higher stage, which manufactures equipment for plant B, will find the demand for its output decline or disappear, while its own costs will also have been raised by the rise in the rate of interest. Thus the effect of a given change in the rate of interest on the profitability of a stage becomes *cumulatively greater,* the greater the number of stages which separate this from the final stage (i.e. the longer the process and the higher the relative position of the stage).

Any increase in the quantity of money available for the purchase of producers' goods (that is, both original resources and intermediate products) relative to the quantity being spent on consumers' goods, implies a fall in the rate of interest, as compared with that prevailing in an initial equilibrium, since only thus will the extra money find borrowers.

Suppose that, through the banking-system making available a greater volume of credit, such relative increase in the quantity of money coming forward for the purchase of producers' goods takes place. The entrepreneurs seeking to adopt a new technique will now find their opportunity. They can borrow at what appears to be a cheap rate the money needed to divert non-specific intermediate products and original resources to the creation of a new extended structure of production. Thus the additional supply of money will be used to increase the demand for these producers' goods and raise their prices, and the producers of non-specific intermediate products will be encouraged themselves to adopt more highly capitalised methods and so carry on the work of extension. All those, therefore, who contribute real resources of any kind to the new structure will, *during its creation,* receive extra gains which they must distribute between saving and spending.

Though it is reasonable to assume that part of this additional money-income, particularly in the case of the profits of entrepreneurs, will be saved and invested, there is no reason to assume that consumers whose money incomes have increased will voluntarily consume less real goods than before. But if the receivers of extra gains do not invest the *whole* of them the cessation of injection of extra credit will result, not merely in a *cessation of the growth* of the money streams available for buying original resources and intermediate products, relative to the flow being spent on consumption, but in an *actual reaction towards the former ratio,* since such of their extra gains as they are spending are no longer being replaced by fresh injection

of credit. As a consequence, the profitability of the higher stages will necessarily bcome less than that of the lower stages, where more money is now
circulating against a given quantity of goods, and a draining away of
resources from the higher stages will result.

The length of process at which equilibrium can eventually be attained
will only be greater than the initial length of process, for a given co-efficient
of money transactions, if the proportion of the extra gains which has been
invested to that which has been added to the flow of consumption-spending,
is greater than the initial proportion of the production-flow of money (streams
(*a*) and (*c*)), to the consumption flow.

But will they, in fact, invest the bulk of their extra gains? A lengthening of the process of production involves a temporary reduction in the output
of consumers' goods, for the resources which were formerly employed at
the lower stages have been diverted to higher stages, and a longer period
will now elapse before the goods in which they are embodied reach the
consumers' market. If the stimulus to investment had come from an increased rate of money-saving, this temporary reduction would correspond
to the voluntary deferment of consumption which had made the increased
money-saving possible, and no one except the savers would have had to
forgo any of their usual consumption. But when the stimulus comes from
inflation, the reduction of output of consumption goods represents a com-
pulsory sacrifice on the part of consumers, some of whom are just now
enjoying increased money incomes. It will be surprising if they do not
attempt to restore their standard of living by increased spending on consumption. The extra bank-credit which began by causing a rapid rise of
prices and large profits in the higher stages, will thus be drawn off from
those stages to compete for the deficient supply of consumers' goods and
cause large profits in the lower stages. These large profits, which themselves represent a swing back towards the former proportions in which
money was being used to move goods in the lowest stages, as compared
with other stages, will impel the producers of consumption-goods to increase
their output as rapidly as possible, and for this purpose they will consider
it worth while to borrow at a rate of interest higher than that representing
the marginal productivity of capital in the newly-created higher stages
(that is to say, the rate which was high enough to stop borrowing by those
engaged in lengthening the process) money with which to outbid the operators
of higher stages for the means of production.

Non-specific intermediate products which have been used at high stages,
and have thus themselves represented still higher stages, will now be re-
diverted and used at low stages. Those high stages which represent the
operation of specific capital, incapable of being used elsewhere, will thus
find themselves as it were short-circuited, the economies of using the
specific capital being less, now, than the extra cost in interest which its use
entails. The demand for new or renewed specific goods in these high stages
will consequently cease, and those still higher stages which manufacture
their equipment will cease to be operated. In other words, the cumulative
effect of a rise in the rate of interest will be felt in the higher stages of the

SOME NOTES ON MONETARY THEORIES OF THE TRADE CYCLE 37

new lengthened process, and those of them which, by their nature, are incapable of becoming part of a shortened process will be immediately rendered inoperable.

The labour thus thrown out of work cannot, however, be absorbed immediately into a shortened process, for a sufficient quantity of complementary intermediate products adapted to the shortened process can only gradually be built up, and without them there is nothing to which the unemployed labour can apply its effort.

Dr. Hayek has thus shown that, starting from a position of equilibrium in which all the available resources are fully employed, a situation can arise through the self-intensifying character of disturbances in an elastic-money economy, where some of these resources are for the time being unemployable.

It is perhaps not out of place here to consider a criticism of Mr. Hawtrey's (*Economica*, No. 35, February 1932, pp. 121-2) who says : " This explanation requires a more adequate analysis of capital accumulation than Dr. Hayek has offered us. In reality only a part, and probably quite a small part, of the annual capital outlay of a community is applied to ' prolonging the process of production.' Most of it is devoted either (*a*) to providing increased output within the existing structure of production, or (*b*) to carrying out improvements due not to intensified capitalisation, but to technical progress and invention."

On the assumption, explicit in Dr. Hayek's argument, that all labour is initially fully employed, an increase of output " within the existing structure of production " can only be effected by technical improvements which do not involve any replacement of labour by machines. But any large increase of output, involving the treatment of larger physical quantities of intermediate products, must almost inevitably entail increased mechanisation, and the accompanying increase of power supply and plant for renewal, all of which, of course, constitutes a lengthening of the process of production.

The essence of Mr. Hawtrey's criticism under (*b*) is that if a supply of extra credit became available, it would largely be used to introduce new technical methods and new final products such as do *not* involve a lengthening of the process of production. But new methods which are of higher technical efficiency, or result in a better final product, than those in current use, but *do not imply a lower marginal productivity of capital,* need not await a fall in the rate of interest before they can be adopted : if they do not involve increased capitalisation, they can be introduced in replacement of worn-out plant, by means of the depreciation fund which this plant normally provides ; while even methods implying a lengthened process can be introduced without waiting for a fall in the rate of interest, if they represent so great an improvement as to raise the marginal productivity of capital at the existing degree of capitalisation ; since these will tend to raise the natural rate of interest, and increase the rate of voluntary saving until the extra capital required has been provided. What is relevant to Mr. Hawtrey's criticism, however, is that new methods of production which are compelled to await a fall in the rate of interest, will normally be those which imply a lengthening of the process of production.

There is one further aspect of the causation of the crisis, distinct from the question of whether the stimulus to investment has come from voluntary saving or from inflation. Dr. Hayek has, perhaps, not made the distinction quite clear. The *pace* of extension of the structure of production is a factor which can by itself cause disproportionate development; that is, creation of specific intermediate products which will become redundant, even if there is no reversal of the increase in the ratio of production-flow to consumption-flow of money. For if the pace is accelerated unduly, the demand for new plant and machines may increase so fast, and thus cause such large short-period profits, as to induce makers of this equipment to embark on methods of production, capitalised to an extent which is justified *only while very rapid extension is going on,* so that the specific instruments they create for the production of other specific instruments will be made redundant merely by the stopping of extension, quite apart from any reaction in the ratio of production-flow to consumption-flow of money. Changes in the pace at which capital equipment is being extended, large enough to cause such disproportionate development and redundancy, could theoretically be brought about through changes in the rate of voluntary saving. Hence they only enter into a monetary theory of the trade cycle in so far as they are, in fact, more likely to arise from inflation than from changes in voluntary saving.

THE MULTIPLIER IN CLOSED AND OPEN SYSTEMS

By G. L. S. SHACKLE (*St. Andrew's*)

THE Multiplier theorem of Mr. Keynes has two stages of elaboration. In the first it is an immediate inference from an assumption about the tastes of individuals in the choice between consuming and accumulating income. In the second, a further assumption is added about the change in the quantity of consumption goods produced in unit time, which will be induced by a change, realized or expected, in sales in unit time to consumers. This second assumption could take any one of many specific forms. Hitherto in expressing the Multiplier principle authors have assumed *equality*. From the two assumptions together, the more immediate consequences of an attempt by entrepreneurs to change the aggregate speed of equipment-growth are deduced.

To predict what a consumer will do in face of a change in the set of market prices confronting him, we assume that certain *tastes* are an inherent part of his make-up. We are equally entitled to assume a certain quality of mind in the individual which, in the case of any change in his own income,[1] or his estimate of it, would dictate that *in given circumstances* some particular proportion of the increment should be spent on additional consumption, and the rest either allowed to constitute a continuing growth of his cash-holding or be continually exchanged for securities. In either case the non-spending of this latter part permits the *accumulation* of output, i.e. the growth of equipment, instead of requiring the consumption, i.e. current destruction, of output. Human nature is not so widely various but that, if the incomes of any considerable sample of the population are increased, the resultant of these individual tastes in the matter of spending or not-spending will be much the same as if the increases were enjoyed by any other sample of equal size. Thus we are entitled to think of *the economy as a whole* as having a certain inherent quality

[1] The variables considered in this article are of dimension ux^{-1}, where u is either money value or physical quantity, and x is time. That is to say, each of these variables represents a *speed* (or *time-rate*) and is measured as so many units of money value *per unit of time*, or so many units of physical quantity *per unit of time*. The terms 'income', 'output', 'consumption', 'accumulation', 'growth of equipment', denote variables of this kind. I have used the words 'income', 'output', and 'consumption' without any explanatory phrase, in the belief that they will convey the above meaning without ambiguity. But I have written 'speed of accumulation' in order to avoid any confusion between a flow having a time-dimension, on the one hand, and a stock, on the other.

which we call its propensity to consume, and which implies that its aggregate spending per unit time on consumption can be regarded as a function of certain variables amongst which its aggregate income, or net output, is the most important.[1] We can take the partial derivative of aggregate consumption-spending per unit time with respect to aggregate income, and call this the economy's marginal propensity to consume. It is a reasonable assumption that this derivative will be greater than zero but less than unity: an individual who gets, e.g., an increase of salary will both spend more and save more in each unit of time than he did before.[2]

This inherent behaviour-pattern of income-receivers is not capable by *itself* of explaining why an increase in the output of goods intended as additions to equipment should give rise to an increase in the output of goods intended to be consumed. From this inherent propensity we can only infer that if general output is increased, i.e. if the quantity, measured in value, of goods in general produced per unit time is increased, then the value of consumer-purchases in unit time will also increase in a certain proportion λ, less than unity, to the increase of general output. If a larger proportion than $1-\lambda$ of the increment of general output is intended by entrepreneurs to constitute a growth of equipment, then stocks of goods ready for consumption will begin to be depleted. *If entrepreneurs are induced by this to increase the output of consumption goods*, then we have the second aspect of the Multiplier principle, in which an extra assumption enables it to explain certain links in a process in time.

Let us illustrate these notions by a simplified model. Suppose that the economy produces only one kind of good, and that this can be either consumed or accumulated. The physical output of the economy at any moment is the physical quantity of this good produced in unit time at that moment. This output is evidently equal to the time-rate of consumption plus the time-rate of change of the

---

[1] The economy's aggregate consumption-spending in unit time is not in strictness a single-valued function of its aggregate income. For any given aggregate income the aggregate consumption is likely to be different with a different *distribution* of that income between the high and low income-brackets. It would be more correct, therefore, to say that aggregate consumption is a function of as many variables as there are individual incomes in the economy. If it is approximately true, however, that the distribution of each given aggregate of incomes is unique, i.e. if for each level of aggregate income there is only one set of individual incomes, the more compact statement involves no loss of accuracy.

[2] This is all that Mr. Keynes requires to postulate to make the Multiplier theorem valid.

accumulated stock. The level of output is the resultant of two sets
of decisions. (1) Entrepreneurs decide what quantity of the good per
unit time they wish to add to their accumulated stock: each makes a
decision referring to his own stock, and the aggregation of these
decisions gives the intended speed of growth I_e of stock as a whole,
from the entrepreneurial side. (2) Income-creators, comprising entrepreneurs, workers, and suppliers of all other means of production,
decide each for himself what proportion of his share of output he
will consume and what proportion he will allow to be accumulated.
The proportion is a function of the absolute size of his share of
output. Thus the proportion in which income-creators as such
desire aggregate output to be divided between consumption and
accumulation is a function of the level of aggregate output. For
any given absolute level E of output, the desires of income-creators
indicate a certain speed I_i of accumulation.[1] It is reasonable to
assume that according to the resultant of the desires of income-
creators $\dfrac{\Delta I_i}{\Delta E} < 1$.

There are two groups of possibilities: (1) the function $I_i = \phi(E)$ or
its inverse $E = f(I_i)$, expressing the interdependence of output and
accumulation according to the desires of income-creators, remains
stable ; (2) the *form* of the above function changes.

Under (1) a change in the level of output can emerge from either:
(i) decisions by entrepreneurs, implying, if they are exactly realized,
that accumulated stock will grow faster or slower in the immediately
ensuing short interval of time than it has in the just completed
short interval; (ii) a change in the aggregate of individual income-
creators' estimates of their incomes (i.e. the absolute sizes of their
shares of output), leading them to adjust their consumption to a
different supposed level of aggregate output, which they believe to
be the actual level.

In case (i) entrepreneurs will at first raise output to a level whose
excess over the old level is equal to the difference which their intentions imply between the new and old speeds of growth of accumulated
stock. But only a proportion $\dfrac{d\phi(E)}{dE}$ of this increment of output will
actually constitute an increment of the speed of accumulation, for

---

[1] The reader will understand that both I_e and I_i are *ex ante* concepts. That is, they
express intentions or expectations, not the emergence of actual recordable values
from moment to moment. They are therefore not necessarily equal.

income-creators as such, to whom the extra output accrues and who have the disposal of it, will by hypothesis use part of it to raise their level of consumption. If entrepreneurs still desire to attain a speed of accumulation I_e, there must be a sufficient increase of aggregate output E to satisfy $E = f(I_i)$ when $I_i = I_e$. This process of adjustment may have effects on the expectations of entrepreneurs and lead to a further increase of I_e, and so on.

In case (ii) the reactions are much less predictable: the actual increase of the time-rate of consumption is likely to induce an increase of output sufficient at least to leave the actual time-rate of accumulation as high as it was initially. This may induce an increase of I_e with further reactions.

Under (2), if initially the speed of accumulation is I_1 and output $E = f(I_1)$, and the form of the latter function then changes to $F(I)$, where $F(I) > f(I)$, it seems likely that the impact effect will be a *reduction of I* to a level I_2 which satisfies $E = F(I_2)$ *at an unchanged level of E*. This will be followed by a growth of E as entrepreneurs try to restore the speed of accumulation to its initial level. Thus, after a time, E may stand at a level $E = F(I_1)$, that is, the new form of the function expressing income-creators' wishes will be in operation with the speed of accumulation back at its initial level. In this case, as with all others, further reactions through the effect on expectations and personal income estimates are likely to follow.

If we now remove the assumption that only one good is produced, output can no longer be measured in physical terms, but must be measured in value, and in a closed economy will have the two components: (1) net speed of improvement of equipment, i.e. the aggregate of those changes in unit time in individuals' valuations of their own plant and inventories, which are due to physical growth or improvement;[1] (2) value per unit time of consumer-purchases. No material difference is made to the theory. An increase in the output of goods intended to become net additions to equipment will induce an increase of consumer-spending, because the workers and

---

[1] Thus if an individual's equipment consists exclusively in a stock of y units of some homogeneous material, each unit having a value x, the speed of change of the total value yx of his equipment will be $\dfrac{d(yx)}{dt} = x\dfrac{dy}{dt} + y\dfrac{dx}{dt}$. We define his contribution to the first component of the economy's output as equal to the first term $x\dfrac{dy}{dt}$, regarding the other as a windfall gain or loss on capital account.

entrepreneurs who produce this extra flow of additions to equipment
will not wish to receive its value entirely in the form of accumulating
wealth but partly in the form of consumption. Only that part of this
flow of additions to equipment whose value they are willing to retain
unspent will constitute a net growth of the economy's equipment.
The remainder will be offset by the depletion of stocks of ready consumers' goods.[1] Further successive increases of output, intended to
arrest and make good this depletion, will each contribute only a part
of itself for this purpose, since those who produce these extra flows
will only accept part of their value in the form of accumulating wealth
and will require in part to be paid with consumers' goods. Hence, the
growth of equipment will not be accelerated by the amount intended
until output has been increased more than was originally regarded
as sufficient for this purpose.

How fast and how far will the level of aggregate output rise ? We
should like to know, for each level of output, by how much this level
would be increased *within each of a number of different periods*, as a
consequence of a given *attempted* increase of its first component.
Perhaps entrepreneurs will go on increasing the economy's output
up to the level where the growth of equipment has been accelerated
to the extent which they initially intended. This is what writers on
the Multiplier principle have hitherto assumed. But it seems to be
based on the implicit assumption that the process of adjusting
aggregate output to this level will leave entrepreneurs' expectations
of the future earnings of equipment unchanged. If when they initially decided to produce more additions to equipment per unit time
they did not expect such a large increase of aggregate output (i.e.
aggregate income), it seems likely that they will decide on a *further*
acceleration of equipment-growth. But if their initial decisions were
based on the expectation of a rapid growth of aggregate output, it is
even possible that the actual increase will disappoint them. In short,
the full elaboration of the Multiplier principle involves a consideration of what will happen to the inducement to invest.

The length of time which must elapse after an attempt by entre-

<hr>

[1] If such stocks are low there may be a tendency for prices of consumers' goods to
be raised. As Mr. Keynes has explained (*General Theory*, pp. 123, 124), this will
change the value of the marginal propensity to consume, partly by causing individuals
with *given* money incomes to postpone some consumption, partly by redistributing
aggregate real income in favour of entrepreneurs whose individual marginal propensi-
ties to consume, in view of their large incomes, are below the average of all individuals.

preneurs to effect a given acceleration of equipment-growth, before
output as a whole reaches any given level, does not depend purely on
how entrepreneurs respond to an increase of sales per unit time to
consumers. The notion of an individual's propensity to consume
means that the amount he now decides to spend on consumption in
a short interval stretching forward from the present moment is a
function of the net output in this interval of himself and his property,
according to his present expectations. If other people are intending to
spend more in this interval than they did in the just-completed
interval on such services as he or his property supply, his expectations
may underestimate his income. When the interval in question has
elapsed, he may become aware that his *ex ante* estimate fell short of
what has actually accrued to him, and in such a case he may set his
income estimate for the next ensuing interval higher than he did for
the one which has just elapsed. But this process of successive adjust-
ments of income estimates, in which each individual's income estimate made at one moment influences those which other individuals
will make of their own incomes at subsequent moments, occupies
time. For example, the impact on the earnings of companies of a
change in the time-rate of spending of some individuals will only
affect the spending of dividend-receivers after a considerable interval
of time. Thus the successive adjustment of income expectations is a
part of the explanation why an attempt to accelerate equipment-
growth starts a process of continuing change occupying time.

The conception of the Multiplier principle set out above in no way
conflicts with Mr. Keynes' exposition.[1] The Multiplier is the inverse
of the ratio of an increment of the speed of equipment-growth to the
accompanying increment of output, the time-interval of measurement being taken as short as we like. The two increments will in
general both be smaller if we measure over a shorter interval, but
there is no reason to expect that their *ratio* will be materially affected.
The Multiplier is therefore a ratio which has some particular value

---

[1] 'In general, however, we have to take account of the case where the initiative
comes from an increase in the output of the capital-goods industries which was not
fully foreseen. It is obvious that an initiative of this description only produces its
full effect on employment over a period of time. I have found, however, in discussion that this obvious fact often gives rise to some confusion between the logical
theory of the multiplier, which holds good continuously, without time-lag, at all
moments of time, and the consequences of an expansion in the capital-goods industries which take gradual effect, subject to time-lag and only after an interval.'
The General Theory of Employment, Interest and Money, p. 122.

at every moment of time. A *period* of time must elapse between the moment when the output of goods not intended for immediate sale to consumers is increased, and the development of an equal acceleration of the net growth of equipment, with its corresponding increase of output as a whole.

The lag in the propagation of a stimulus to output as a whole arising from an attempt to accelerate the growth of equipment is not the only important consequence of the fact that the income relevant to consumption-decisions is income *ex ante*, an estimate which is necessarily based on the *previous*, not the current, consumption-decisions of others. For this implies that the level which aggregate income will actually attain over a short interval stretching forward from the present moment, according to the estimate which it will be possible to make at the end of this interval, will depend largely on what individuals *expect*, at the beginning of the interval, that their incomes will be. Movements of output can be initiated by the adoption of sanguine or cautious expectations of their incomes by individuals.

In our simplified model above we have lastly considered a change in the *form* of the function expressing aggregate consumption as a function of aggregate income. Apart from the behaviour of the Stock Exchange, whose influence can be subsumed under the causes of changes in income-expectations, the most usual influence which might change the form of the function is perhaps the *speed* of change of income-expectations, i.e. the extent to which the expected income of one period differs from what was expected to be the income of the just-completed period. An individual cannot instantly adjust his consumption-scheme to a very large change in his income.

Hitherto we have considered a closed economy, in which net output has two components.[1] The output of an open economy has a third component, namely, the excess of the value of its exports over that of its imports (including in these categories services but not claims). That part of its exports to which there corresponds an equal value of imports is already comprised in our second component: for imports *in themselves* make possible consumption without either current production of goods *or* depletion of equipment, and if there were no exports at all, we should have to exclude from output (of the region being considered) an amount of consumption equal

[1] Cf. p. 138 above.

to the value of its imports. If the value of exports exceeds that of imports, then something is being produced in the region to which there corresponds neither consumption within the region nor growth of the equipment of the region. It will be shown, on the assumption that no part of this excess represents net payment of interest to foreigners, that this third component is entirely on the same footing as, and may be added to, our first component.

In the first place, this flow (the excess in unit time of exports over imports) satisfies the desire of some suppliers of productive services to receive the value of these services in the form of durable equipment or titles to the earnings of equipment, rather than in immediate consumption. Neglecting any effect on exchange-rates between currencies and the repercussions of that effect, let us consider what will happen in the following cases of a change in the value per unit time of goods and services exported, which is uncompensated by any change in the value per unit time of goods and services imported, or of a corresponding uncompensated change in the import-flow: (i) an increase in exports; (ii) a decrease in exports; (iii) an increase in imports; (iv) a decrease in imports. Let s be the excess of the value of what we export in unit time over the value of what we import in unit time.

(i) In so far as this increased excess of exports is not provided for by a diminution in the speed of growth of home equipment, extra workers, equipment, and entrepreneurial services must be engaged in producing this extra flow of excess exports. The suppliers of these extra flows of productive services will wish to receive the value of them partly in consumption: but, by hypothesis, no part of their own output, nor imports corresponding to it, is available for them to consume. Until extra consumable output is forthcoming, they will cause a continuing shrinkage of stocks of ready consumables. The taking into employment of extra resources hitherto unemployed will only arrest this shrinkage to the extent that the newly employed workers and others are willing to be paid with claims on foreigners: to the extent that they demand consumption, they will consume the extra output which they themselves are producing. The extra force of labour and equipment taken into employment to provide the consumption, say A, demanded by the producers of the extra un-balanced exports, must therefore be of such a size that the part of their payment which they are willing to receive in the form of claims on assets abroad, is equal to A. The Multiplier principle works in exactly the same way when the increment of unconsumed[1] output goes abroad as when it stays at home.

(ii) In so far as the output Δs which foreigners have ceased to buy does not continue to be produced as an addition to home equipment, total output[2] will be reduced by some amount $k_R\,\Delta s$, where k_R corresponds to, *but is not necessarily equal to,* the ratio of the *increment* of total output which would be associated with an *increment* Δs of the unconsumed component of output. For, if when total output is high, the economy's marginal propensity to consume is low, this means that its members all taken together are not very eager, in case of an increase of that output, to add to their consumption. Accordingly they will be correspondingly *less reluctant*, if their total output be slightly reduced when it is at a high level, to *reduce* their consumption. Thus, if at high levels of total output an increment ΔI of the non-consumed component will be associated with an increment $\Delta C = (k-1)\Delta I$ of the consumed component; then a *decrement* ΔI will be associated with a decrement $\Delta C = (k_R-1)\Delta I$, where $k_R > k$.[3]

When the economy's output is high we should therefore expect the reduction of output associated with a given *decrease* of the export surplus, to be numerically larger than the increment of output associated, at the same high level of output, with an equal *increase* of the export surplus. Correspondingly, when total output is low, and the economy's marginal propensity to consume consequently high, any increment of output will consist largely in extra consumption, any decrement of output will consist largely in a decrement of net equipment-growth.

(iii) A decrease of the quantity consumed per unit time of home-produced goods, associated with an equal increase of the quantity consumed per unit time of imports, in so far as it results in a decrease in the output of goods intended for home consumption, and not in a piling-up of stocks of these goods, is exactly on the same footing as case (ii), and the 'reverse-multiplier' effect will work in the same way.

(iv) A decrease of the import-flow, not associated with a decrease either of the export-flow *or* of consumption, implies an increase of

---

[1] i.e. not consumed at home.   [2] i.e. of the open economy.
[3] See G. L. S. Shackle, *Expectations, Investment, and Income*, chap. vii. Oxford University Press, 1938.

the non-consumed component of output which will develop according to the Multiplier principle as depletion of stocks of ready consumables is arrested by an increase of output.

The main points put forward in this note are as follows.

1. It is entirely untrue that the Multiplier principle involves any confusion between *ex post* and *ex ante* concepts.

2. The Multiplier itself is a ratio obtained immediately from the marginal propensity to consume. By itself this ratio cannot tell us how fast or by how much the level of output will change as a consequence of an attempt to change the speed of growth of equipment. For this we need also to know what will happen to the inducement to invest as output (i.e. aggregate income) begins to change.

3. The consumption per unit time which an individual decides on is a function of his income *ex ante*. His expectations may be sanguine or cautious. If a large proportion of individuals are sanguine or cautious in their income expectations, the level of aggregate income actually emerging, i.e. aggregate income *ex post*, will move in the direction tending to justify these expectations. Hence income-expectations are capable of initiating a process of growth or decline of output.

4. The form of the function connecting an individual's consumption-spending with his income may become different immediately after a very large, swift, and unexpected change in his income, and will only gradually be restored to the form applicable to gradual changes of his income.

5. In an open economy, the excess of the value of exports of goods and services over that of imports of goods and services is on the same footing with regard to the propensity to consume as that part of home output which constitutes a net growth of home equipment.

6. At any one level of output the proportions in which a marginal *increment* of output will be distributed between consumption and accumulation are likely to be different from those in which a marginal *decrement* of output will be distributed between reduced consumption and reduced speed of accumulation.

THE ECONOMIC JOURNAL

MARCH, 1946

INTEREST-RATES AND THE PACE OF INVESTMENT

IT was until recent years an accepted doctrine that changes of interest-rates powerfully influence the pace at which enterprisers, all taken together, extend or improve their equipment. But this opinion has lately been challenged by the testimony of enterprisers themselves, given in response to systematic enquiry. Some simple developments of theory can, I think, resolve the apparent contradiction, and this it is the purpose of this article to attempt.

The rationale of the doctrine is simple. A piece of equipment is bought because the buyer hopes that its use will at some future time bring in sums of money exceeding those which he will have concurrently to pay out in order to use the equipment, and that the net amounts by which the gross receipts exceed the associated outgoings will together be rather more than equal, when allowance has been made for their futurity, and for his doubt as to the correctness of his estimate of their size, to the immediate purchase price of the equipment. Let x years be the futurity of one such net amount or " net return " whose size he estimates as c; and let 100 r per cent. per annum be the rate of interest which can be had and must be paid on cash now lent for x years, where due payment of interest and principal is treated as certain. Then the equivalent in spot cash of a sum due in x years, if its size were known exactly and for certain to be c, would be $P = c(1 + r)^{-x} = ce^{-\rho x}$. But in fact c is only an estimate or conjecture, and in order to allow for his doubt of its correctness the enterpriser must multiply it by a second coefficient. This doubt will differ in degree for different values of x, and the second coefficient must therefore be written $s = s(x)$. Thus the equivalent of c in *cash free from doubt or deferment* will be $p = cs(x)e^{-\rho x}$. Since the enterpriser need not run his plant at a loss, we can assume that c is non-negative for all x, and if we assume also that ρ stands at one and the same level for all x, we have for the value he sets on an instrument which he has in mind to buy

$$v = \int_0^\infty c(x)s(x)e^{-\rho x}dx.$$

$c(x)$ may be looked upon, if we will, as that specific guess or estimate (regarding the size of the net return whose futurity is x) which has more to be said for it than any other guess *in the light of the enterpriser's existing knowledge*; this estimated size is then multiplied by a coefficient $s(x)$, which will usually be less than unity, to bring into the reckoning the enterpriser's awareness of the insufficiency of his knowledge. The distinction between these two influences on the size of the sum of money which, if it could be looked forward to with certainty, would be equivalent in the enterpriser's mind to his misty prospect of the net return which the instrument will yield at a date x years hence, is blurred and imprecise. Under which heading, for example, are we to put his general awareness of the inventiveness of mankind, which, though no smallest sign may yet appear of any invention which would render the proposed investment obsolete, yet warns him that this obsolescence is possible or even likely? It is on such ground as this that I prefer an altogether different construction, for which, however, I have not yet been able to obtain sufficient critical attention to justify its use here.

One further matter must detain us for a moment. We have spoken, by implication, of the coefficient $e^{-\rho x}$, by which each net return $c(x)$ is to be multiplied, as an allowance for "futurity." Below we shall sometimes call this allowance "time-discounting" and refer to ρ as the rate of "pure" interest. These phrases mean no more than that, because interest greater than zero can be obtained on loans which are regarded as free from risk of default, a future sum c is the equivalent of a present sum smaller than c, when the due receipt of both is *undoubted*. Since this reason for discounting *given* future sums is entirely independent of any question of *doubt concerning the size* of such sums, we need a term to distinguish the former reason, and accordingly use the phrases we have mentioned. Interest on loans free from risk of default is compensation for sacrifice of liquidity; compensation, that is to say, for accepting the possibility that the market value of the "paper" received as evidence of the loan will fall, not through any fear of default, but through a change in the terms on which loans can be obtained. This is a risk of a sort entirely different from that concerning the eventual size of payments to be received in the future; and it is a matter with which we are not concerned, for our problem concerns the *effects*, and not the *causes*, of pure interest-rates.

Let u be the purchase price of an instrument of the kind the enterpriser has it in mind to buy, and y, which we will treat as continuously variable, be the quantity of such instruments ordered by all enterprisers in a unit of time. Then the conditions of production of such instruments being given, we have $u = u(y)$, and the pace of investment in instruments of this type, before allowance is made for concurrent depreciation of those already in existence, is $z = uy$ per unit of time. On account of their differing beliefs about the course of its future net returns (the form of $c = c(x)$), different enterprisers at any one time will assign different values to such an instrument. If these different valuations are arranged in descending sequence, it can plausibly be suggested that the orders placed for such instruments in any one unit of time will go just so far down this list that the price u, which will be higher the larger the number y of orders concurrently placed, is just equal to the least sanguine valuation which actually yields an order. Let us then mean by v the least sanguine of current valuations which actually results in an order, and accordingly assume that at all times $u = v$. We can then write $y = y(v)$. We are now concerned with three elasticities:

that of v with respect to ρ, namely $\eta_{v\rho} = \dfrac{dv}{d\rho}\dfrac{\rho}{v}$,

that of y with respect to $u = v$, namely $\eta_{yv} = \dfrac{dy}{dv}\dfrac{v}{y}$,

that of $z = uy = vy$ with respect to ρ, namely

$$\eta_{z\rho} = \frac{dz}{d\rho}\frac{\rho}{z} = \frac{d(vy)}{d\rho}\frac{\rho}{vy}.$$

We have :

$$\frac{d(vy)}{d\rho}\frac{\rho}{vy} = \left(\frac{dv}{d\rho}y + \frac{dy}{d\rho}v\right)\frac{\rho}{vy} = \frac{dv}{d\rho}\frac{\rho}{v} + \frac{dy}{d\rho}\frac{\rho}{y} = \eta_{v\rho} + \eta_{y\rho}$$

$$= \frac{dv}{d\rho}\frac{\rho}{v} + \frac{dy}{dv}\frac{v}{y}\cdot\frac{dv}{d\rho}\frac{\rho}{v} = \eta_{v\rho}(1 + \eta_{yv}).$$

If we prefer to define the pace of gross investment in instruments of a given kind as the *quantity* of them produced in a unit of time, rather than as the money-value of this quantity—that is to say, as y rather than as uy—then we have

$$\eta_{y\rho} = \frac{dy}{d\rho}\frac{\rho}{y} = \frac{dy}{dv}\frac{v}{y}\cdot\frac{dv}{d\rho}\frac{\rho}{v} = \eta_{yv}\,\eta_{v\rho}.$$

Thus under our assumptions the elasticity, with respect to the interest-rate, of the pace of gross investment in a given kind of instrument, whichever of the two definitions of this pace we adopt, is directly proportional to the elasticity, with respect to the interest-rate, of the least sanguine current valuation of such instruments which yields a decision to invest. Since, as we shall immediately show, a fall in the interest-rate will raise all valuations, some of which were previously extra-marginal—that is, lower down the list than the least sanguine one which yielded an order—may be raised above the margin, and the pace of gross investment in instruments of this type will thus be increased. Since the same will be true of instruments of all kinds, a fall in the rate of interest, not counteracted by any simultaneous other change, must be expected to increase the pace of gross investment in the system as a whole, and, if the only concurrent increase in the pace of depreciation of the whole existing capital equipment of the system is that arising from the increase of gross investment, there will also result an increase in the pace of net investment. It remains, in order to establish a presumption in favour of the doctrine that interest-rates influence the pace of investment, to show that they influence the values which are set on equipment. Let us suppose at first that an enterpriser treats the net amounts which will be earned by some instrument which he has it in mind to buy as known exactly and for certain; and see how under various assumptions as to the distribution over future time of these net amounts, the value which he sets upon the instrument will vary when the interest-rate is varied.

The simplest of these assumptions is that the instrument will yield its entire net return C at a single instant of a known futurity of x years. Then its value will be $v = Ce^{-\rho x}$, and the proportionate change in this value due to a given proportionate change in ρ is

$$\frac{dv}{d\rho}\frac{\rho}{v} = -\rho x.$$

This elasticity increases numerically in direct proportion to the futurity x of the net return, and the proportion in question is itself equal to the interest-rate. In so far, therefore, as the expected net returns from a capital instrument are concentrated near some one future date, its value will be more sensitive to given proportionate changes in the interest-rate, the more distant the date, and the higher the interest-rate itself. A rather more realistic assumption is that the instrument will yield returns, net of all running expense including that for repairs and renewals sufficient to maintain it in perfect condition, at a constant time-rate for ever. Then if this time-rate is c we have :

$$v = c\int_{0}^{\infty} e^{-\rho x}dx = \frac{c}{\rho},$$

so that if a new level of the interest-rate is $\frac{1}{k}$ times the old one, the new value of the instrument will be k times the old one. Could we, for example, reduce the appropriate interest-rate from 3% per annum to 2% per annum, the value of an instrument expected to yield uniform net returns in perpetuity would be multiplied by $\frac{3}{2}$, raised, that is to say, from 33 c approximately, or " 33 years' purchase," to 50 c, or " fifty years' purchase." The supply-curve $y(u)$ of such instruments would have to be extremely inelastic (a condition quite the opposite of that which prevails in a slump) if such a rise of value were not to result in a large proportionate rise in the number of such instruments produced in a unit of time. For small changes we can express the matter in terms of elasticities. We have $\frac{dv}{d\rho} = -\frac{c}{\rho^2}$ and $\eta_{v\rho} = \frac{dv}{d\rho'}\frac{\rho}{v} = -1$. The elasticity of the quantity of the instruments produced in a

TABLE I

L	$\frac{\Delta v}{v_1}$ for $\Delta\rho = 0\cdot03-0\cdot04.$ 1.	$\frac{\Delta v}{v_1}$ for $\Delta\rho = 0\cdot02-0\cdot03.$ 2.	$\frac{\Delta v}{v_1}/\frac{\Delta\rho}{\rho_1}$ for $\Delta\rho = 0\cdot03-0\cdot04.$ 3.	$\frac{\Delta v}{v_1}/\frac{\Delta\rho}{\rho_1}$ for $\Delta\rho = 0\cdot02-0\cdot03.$ 4.
5	0·025	0·025	0·10	0·08
10	0·048	0·049	0·19	0·15
20	0·092	0·096	0·37	0·29
40	0·167	0·182	0·67	0·55
80	0·264	0·316	1·06	0·95

unit of time with respect to the interest-rate is $\eta_{y\rho} = \eta_{yv}\,\eta_{v\rho}$. Even, then, if η_{yv}, the elasticity of supply, is no more than $+1$, a given small proportionate change $\frac{\Delta\rho}{\rho}$ in the rate of interest will produce an equal proportionate change, of opposite sign, in the pace of price-deflated gross investment in the instruments.

The most realistic simple assumption is, however, that the instrument is expected to yield uniform net returns for some finite number of years and then be abandoned. If the expected useful life is L we have :

$$v = c\int_0^L e^{-\rho x}dx = \frac{c}{\rho}(1 - e^{-\rho L}).$$

In the accompanying table (Table I) column 1 shows $\frac{\Delta v}{v_1}$, where Δv is the difference $v_2 - v_1$ produced in v by a change from $\rho = 4\%$ per annum to $\rho = 3\%$ per annum, v_1 corresponds to the first and v_2 to the second of these values of ρ, and the useful life

L is taken successively at 5, 10, 20, 40, and 80 years.   Column 2 shows the same for an interest-rate changing from 3% to 2% per annum.   Column 3 shows the quasi-elasticities $\dfrac{\Delta v}{v_1}\Big/\dfrac{\Delta\rho}{\rho_1}$, where $\Delta\rho = \rho_2 - \rho_1$, $\rho_1 = 4\%$ per annum, $\rho_2 = 3\%$ per annum; and column 4 similarly corresponds to column 2.

In this table we see, for example, that a fall in the rate of interest from a level of 4% per annum to one of 3% per annum raises the value of the instrument, when this is expected to yield net returns of a constant amount per year for L years and afterwards nothing, by 5% if L is 10, by 9% if L is 20, by $16\frac{1}{2}\%$ if L is 40, and by $26\frac{1}{2}\%$ if L is 80.   It is clear that the *percentage* by which the value of a durable instrument is raised by a given reduction of the interest-rate—that is, the sensitivity of the value to such changes—is a strongly increasing function of the expected revenue-earning life.

There is, then, a case for supposing that interest-rates should influence the pace of investment.   Let us turn now to the testimony of enterprisers themselves.

A very full account of the method and results of the questionnaire enquiry, conducted by the Oxford Economists' Research Group in 1939, is given by Mr. P. W. S. Andrews in *Oxford Economic Papers* No. 3, to which the reader is referred.   The results are summarised thus by Mr. R. S. Sayers in the same issue :

> " About one-quarter of the business men gave some answer to the questionnaire.   Of those who replied, about three-quarters stated that the terms (in the broad sense) on which loans could be obtained had not affected their decisions to add to or maintain either fixed or working capital.   One-quarter of those replying (about 6% of those asked) gave some kind of affirmative answer.
>
> " In assessing the significance of these results [Mr. Sayers proceeds] it is necessary to consider firstly whether the 25% who replied constituted a fair sample, for our purpose, of the whole.   Why, in fact, did the other 75% throw the questionnaire into the waste-paper basket ? . . . My own guess is that most of the firms were, as a result of their own experience, not convinced that borrowing terms make much difference to their decisions.   If this guess is the right one, we must obviously work on the assumption that the proportion of business men conscious of the effectiveness of borrowing terms must be much lower than one quarter, though it may be rather more than 6%."

What considerations can we have omitted from the theory stated above, to account for its leading to conclusions that the facts do not seem to support ?   A hint is provided by some of the comments which accompanied the business men's answers.   The following comments of six of them seem specially illuminating :

> A. " Any profit or advantage expected from expenditure on plant or repairs, or from varying the quantity of stock [1] held, has greatly out-

---

[1] *I.e.*, stock-piles of materials or products.

weighed the cost of borrowing or the income receivable by depositing surplus funds with bankers."

B. "If the estimated advantage from a projected extension is jeopardised by a 1% difference in interest, it hardly seems justifiable anyhow."

C. "We are not generally affected by the cost of borrowing money and rates of interest, because we do not come to a decision to spend money on extensions unless or until we can see it will really be profitable to do so. The interest either paid on money borrowed on overdraft or earned as interest would generally speaking be small compared to the earning power on any such expenditure."

D. "Difficult to imagine a position in which interest-rates could have any appreciable effect compared with taxation, on plans for extension. Have for some time been considering laying down small amount of extra plant, but the proposition, which includes a considerable risk, can be attractive only if 50% return on capital value [1] is considered possible. Unless we get 33%, any extension is out of the question."

E. "If expenditure on new craft [2] were to be influenced by the cost of borrowing, the profit on the building project would be very much too low to render it a normal commercial risk."

F. "Expenditure on plant extensions has been made only when the trend of business has shown this to be desirable. Question of financing, and rate of interest, has not affected it, as unless anticipated return were far in excess of such cost, the projects would not have proceeded to decision stage."

These comments all speak of an expected or estimated "profit," "return," or "earning power" which must greatly exceed the cost of borrowing if the investment in question is to be made. The reason for this requirement appears in the references, in comments D and E, to *risk*. We said at the beginning of this article that an enterpriser must allow for his doubt concerning the correctness of his estimates of future net returns by multiplying each by a coefficient whose size will depend on the futurity of the net return in question: but we then, by assumption, excluded this doubt. Let us re-introduce into our expression for v a coefficient $s = s(x)$, and see what effect is produced by assigning different forms to this function. Let us first suppose this form to be such that s has the same value for all values of x; in other words, that the enterpriser makes the same allowance for doubt in regard to every instalment of net returns no matter what its futurity. In this case no difference whatever will be made to the sensitiveness of v with respect to ρ—that is, to the elasticity $\eta_{v\rho}$. For if

$$v = sc \int_0^L e^{-\rho x} dx$$

we have : $$\frac{dv}{d\rho} \frac{\rho}{v} = \{e^{-\rho L}(\rho L + 1) - 1\}/(1 - e^{-\rho L})\rho,$$

which is independent of s. It is not, then, a matter of indifference what form is assigned to $s = s(x)$, if we wish it to account for the meagreness of entrepreneurial reactions to the interest-

---

[1] *I.e.*, capital *cost*.

[2] Ships.

rate. We may assume, perhaps, that $s < 1$ for all x; and let us put $s = \dfrac{1}{q}$. Surely the allowance for doubt will be better able to reduce the leverage of the interest-rate, if q is relatively large for those instalments of net return *whose present value* (when no allowance is made for doubt) *changes by the largest amount* when the interest-rate changes? To discover some form of $s = s(x)$ which will make the allowance for doubt the solution of our paradox, we must discover which these instalments are.

When a reduction of the interest-rate raises the value of a capital-good whose earnings are expected to be uniform for a finite number of years and afterwards nothing, it is not the earnings of the *nearest* future years which contribute most to the total gain of value; nor is it always the most distant. Let u be the present value of an element of net returns due at an instant x years hence, the size c of this element being treated as known for certain; and writing $u = u(\rho, x) = ce^{-\rho x}$ let us study the

quantity $\dfrac{\partial \left(\dfrac{\partial u}{\partial \rho} \right)}{\partial x} = (\rho x - 1)ce^{-\rho x}$. $\dfrac{\partial u}{\partial \rho}$ will have a stationary value

where $\dfrac{\partial \left(\dfrac{\partial u}{\partial \rho} \right)}{\partial x} = 0$, and the only finite solution of $(\rho x - 1)ce^{-\rho x} = 0$

is $x = \dfrac{1}{\rho}$. We have also $\dfrac{\partial^2 \left(\dfrac{\partial u}{\partial \rho} \right)}{\partial x^2} = \rho ce^{-\rho x}(2 - \rho x)$, which at $x = \dfrac{1}{\rho}$

is positive. Thus $x = \dfrac{1}{\rho}$ gives a *minimum* of $\dfrac{\partial u}{\partial \rho}$. Since what we wish to study is a *fall* in ρ, this minimum is for our purpose a *maximum*. If then, for example, $\rho = 0.03$ we shall find that the *largest contribution* to the total gain in value of the instrument, caused by a given (small) fall of ρ, is made by those instalments of net return which are due at dates of a futurity round about $x = \dfrac{1}{\rho} = 33$ years; or if $\rho = 0.02$, by those of a futurity about $x = 50$ years.

The distribution of the total gain in the value of an instrument, due to a fall in the interest-rate, over the different periods in the assumed life of the instrument, is illustrated in Table II, where, however, for sharper contrast we have used a large instead of a small change of ρ, with the consequence of displacing somewhat the date of maximum effect. We again consider the effect of pure time-discounting alone on the value of a prospective series of net returns whose sizes are taken as known for certain. Here column 1 shows the value, discounted to some one point of time standing for " the present," of the assumed net earnings of an instrument in successive future decades of its total life of 80 years, the time-rate of these earnings being supposed constant throughout and the rate of interest ρ being 4% per annum. Each figure in this column, that is to say, is an evaluation of

$$v_m = c \int_A^B e^{-\rho x} dx = \frac{c}{\rho} (e^{-\rho A} - e^{-\rho B})$$

where we put A successively equal to 0, 10, . . ., 70 years, and B correspondingly equal to 10, 20 30, . . ., 80 years. Column 2 shows the same for $\rho = 2\%$ per annum. Column 3 is a com-

TABLE II

Decade.	Present value, in terms of "years' purchase," of net returns in each decade.		Percentage of total value of instrument attributable to the net returns of each decade.		Excess of column 2 over column 1.	Percentage of the total *gain* in value attributable to each decade.	Column 6 cumulated.	
	$\rho=0\cdot04.$	$\rho=0\cdot02.$	$\rho=0\cdot04.$	$\rho=0\cdot02.$				
	1.	2.	3.	4.	5.	6.	7.	
1	8·24	9·06	34·5	22·6	0·82	5·0	5·0	100·0
2	5·52	7·42	23·2	18·7	1·90	12·0	17·0	95·2
3	3·70	6·07	15·4	15·3	2·37	15·0	32·0	83·2
4	2·48	4·97	10·3	12·5	2·49	15·7	47·7	68·2
5	1·68	4·07	7·1	10·2	2·39	15·0	62·7	52·5
6	1·12	3·33	4·8	8·3	2·21	14·0	76·7	37·5
7	0·75	2·73	3·2	6·8	1·98	12·5	89·2	23·5
8	0·50	2·23	2·1	5·6	1·73	11·0	100·0	11·0
Total	24·00 (approx.)	40·00 (approx.)	100·0	100·0	16·00 (approx.)	100·0		

panion to column 1, and shows what percentage of the total value of the instrument is attributable to each future decade of its life, and column 4 is a similar companion to column 2. Column 5 shows the excess of each figure in column 2 over the corresponding figure in column 1; it shows, that is to say, that part of the total *gain* in the value of the instrument which is attributable to each decade of its life. Column 6 shows what percentage each figure in column 5 represents of the total of the figures in column 5—that is, what percentage of the total gain in value is attributable to each decade. In column 7 the figures in column 6 are cumulated, so that, for example, by looking at the figure in column 7 opposite decade 4, we can see what percentage of the total gain in value, due to a change from $\rho = 4\%$ per annum to $\rho = 2\%$ per annum, is attributable to the first half of the instrument's life.

Now let us suppose that the instrument's life is of 40 instead of 80 years. The relevant figures from Table II, columns 1, 2, and 5, are reproduced below as Table III. Here the first two columns again show the present value in terms of " years' purchase " of the earnings of each decade, for interest-rates respectively of 4% and 2% per annum, while column 3 shows the excess of each figure in column 2 over the corresponding figure in column 1; it shows, that is to say, that part of the total gain in the value of the instrument which is attributable to each decade :

TABLE III

Decade.	Present value, in terms of " years' purchase," of net returns in each decade.		Excess of column 2 over column 1.
	$\rho = 0.04$. 1.	$\rho = 0.02$. 2.	3.
1	8·24	9·06	0·82
2	5·52	7·42	1·90
3	3·70	6·07	2·37
4	2·48	4·97	2·49
Totals	20·00 (approx.)	27·50 (approx.)	7·50 (approx.)

From this table it can be seen, for example, that when the value of the instrument is raised from 20 to 27·5 years' purchase, by means of a reduction of the interest-rate from 4% per annum to 2% per annum, ⅔ of this gain of 7·5 years' purchase is attributable to the more distant half of the instrument's life, the period *beginning* 20 years hence. Again, if we had considered a life of only three decades (neglecting the fourth row of the table), nearly half of the total gain of 5 years' purchase would have been attributable to the last third of the useful life.

Let us compare these results with those of Table I. There we found that the value of an instrument is more sensitive to changes of interest-rates *the farther into the future its assumed revenue-earning career extends.* If this career is assumed to be very short—say of only 5 or 10 years—the value responds very little even to quite a large change in the interest-rate. But the length of this career is by no means a matter of mere physical durability. The most frequent reason for assuming *ex ante* that an instrument's useful life will be short is that its earning-power seems liable to vanish, at some unpredictable date, through inventions of new methods and changes of demand. If each future year is regarded as holding some given numerical chance of such a change, or as contributing something to a gradual change, then if we take in enough future years the obsolescence of the instrument by the end of that time becomes virtually certain. Alternatively, we can say that the more distant the future date we look at, the more worthless is any guess as to what the market and other conditions will then be, and the more worthless, therefore, and the more heavily to be discounted for doubt, is any guess as to the earnings at that time of any complex and specialised instrument. Thus a limit is set by uncertainty to the useful life which it is sensible to assume.

In accordance with this argument,[1] let us suppose that the impact (*i.e.*, the reciprocal of *s*) of the enterpriser's allowance for doubt increases exponentially with the distance into the future of the date he has in mind, so that $s(x) = e^{-hx}$. This is not only reasonable *a priori*, but is in fact what every theorist does who speaks of a *marginal rate of risk* conceived as analogous to the rate of risk-free [2] interest, and often, indeed, added to the latter in order that the sum of these two rates may be equated to the marginal efficiency of capital under any of its synonyms.[3] Then writing $R = h + \rho$ we have :

$$v = c\int_0^L s(x)e^{-\rho x}dx = c\int_0^L e^{-Rx}dx = \frac{c}{R}(1 - e^{-RL}).$$

An indication of the numerical value which, for illustration and experiment, may be assigned to *R*, is given us in one of the comments quoted above, where an enterpriser spoke (in comment D) of a proposition which could be attractive " only if 50% return on capital value [4] is considered possible. Unless we get

---

[1] And with our suggestion that allowance for doubt will be most able to reduce the power of changes in interest-rates to stimulate or depress investment, if the impact of this allowance (supposing *s* to be less than 1 for all *x*) is heavy upon those instalments of return which, in case of a change of *ρ*, make the largest contribution to the increase or decrease of *v*.

[2] By " risk-free " or " pure " interest we mean interest free from risk of *default*, not free from the risks entailed by *illiquidity*. See page 2 above.

[3] " Rate of return over cost " (Irving Fisher); " marginal efficiency of capital " (Lord Keynes); " internal rate of return " (K. E. Boulding); " prospective rate of profit " (M. Kalecki). All of these mean an exponent *μ* such that the value of the instrument, $v = \int^\infty c(x)e^{-\mu x}dx$, is equal to *u* its purchase price.

[4] " Capital cost " must be meant : but if we suppose this enterpriser's valuation to be the marginal one, it will be equal to capital cost.

33% [the enterpriser proceeds] any extension is out of the question." Let us suppose at first that, so far as physical durability is concerned, the net return c is calculated after sufficient allowance for repairs and renewals to maintain the technical efficiency of the instrument indefinitely; and that the whole risk of obsolescence is allowed for in the component h of $R = h + \rho$. Taking the enterpriser's remarks to mean that the lower figure gave a value for the instrument which made it marginal in the circumstances of the case, we have as the value relevant to our elasticity calculations:

$$v = c \int_0^\infty e^{-Rx} dx = \frac{c}{R} = \frac{c}{h + \rho},$$

so that $$\eta_{v\rho} = \frac{dv}{d\rho} \frac{\rho}{v} = -\frac{\rho}{R},$$

and if, for example, $\rho = 0.03$, then $\eta_{v\rho} = -0.09$.

In this case, therefore, a change in the risk-free interest-rate from, say, a level of 3% per annum to one of 2% per annum would raise the (formerly) marginal valuation of the instrument by about 3%. Had there been no allowance for doubt (had the marginal rate of risk been zero), the percentage increase in v due to this fall in ρ would have been 50%. It begins to be clear that we have got hold of a solid clue to the meagre powers of the interest-rate as a stimulator of some forms of investment.

A marginal rate of risk as high as $h = R - \rho = 30\%$ per annum may be exceptionally high. Moreover, it may be that the " return on capital value " of 33% should be interpreted not as R, but as $\frac{c}{v}$: for the former, even when considered as the magnitude which becomes equal to the marginal efficiency of capital when u is equal to v, is a rather sophisticated notion. So long as the useful life is taken as unlimited, R and $\frac{c}{v}$ are the same; for if $v = \frac{c}{R}(1 - e^{-RL})$ so that $R = \frac{c}{v}(1 - e^{-RL})$, then

$R \longrightarrow \frac{c}{v}$ as $L \longrightarrow \infty$.

An appreciable divergence appears between R and $\frac{c}{v}$ when RL is small, for then the factor $(1 - e^{-RL})$ becomes appreciably less than 1. Thus for any given value of R a sufficiently small value of L will make $R \Big/ \frac{c}{v}$ small. But even if h is only 15% per annum—that is, half what we have assumed above—so that

$R = 18\%$ per annum, the ratio $R\big/\dfrac{c}{v}$ is already 0·835 for L no greater than 10; and with so short a useful life as this, a change in the rate of pure interest from $\rho = 3\%$ per annum to $\rho = 2\%$ per annum, even with a zero marginal rate of risk, would change v by only 0·037 or, say, $3\frac{3}{4}\%$. Thus if the "return on capital value" which an enterpriser takes as his minimum requirement is of the order of 10 or 15% per annum, then whether this figure means R or $\dfrac{c}{v}$, the value of the instrument will be insensitive to even very large proportionate changes in the rate of pure interest : for if, on the ground of the absence of positive contrary signs, the revenue-earning life of the instrument is assumed to be long, allowance for doubt will render negligible the net returns of all but a few years immediately ahead; while if it is assumed to be short, the influence of the rate of pure interest is weak even without any allowance for doubt.

TABLE IV

5-year period.	Present value, in terms of "years' purchase," of the net returns in each 5-year period.		Percentage of total value of instrument attributable to the net returns of each 5-year period.	
	$R = 33\%$ per annum.	$R = 18\%$ per annum.	$R = 33\%$ per annum.	$R = 18\%$ per annum.
1	2·424	3·294	80·8	61·0
2	0·466	1·339	15·6	24·8
3	0·089	0·544	3·0	10·1
4	0·017	0·221	0·6	4·1
Total	2·996	5·398	100·0	100·0

This part of our argument is illustrated in the accompanying Tables IV and V. In Table IV, column 1 shows the value, discounted both for deferment and doubt at a combined rate $R = h + \rho = 33\%$ per annum, of the net returns in successive future 5-year periods of the instrument's assumed useful life of 20 years, these net returns (which, in common with the useful life itself, are estimates made in the light of the knowledge available to the enterpriser at his " present moment ") being supposed constant throughout. Column 2 shows the same for $R = 18\%$ per annum. Column 3 is a companion to column 1 and shows what percentage of the total value of the instrument is attributable to each future 5-year period of its life, and column 4 is a similar companion to column 2. Table IV uses 5-year periods, instead of the decades of Table II, because with such numerically large exponents the present values of net returns decrease so rapidly with increasing futurity.

In Table V, column 1 shows the percentages by which the value of an instrument, assumed to produce uniform net returns for 5, 10, 20, and 40 years respectively, is increased by a reduction of the rate of pure interest ρ from 3% per annum to 2% per annum when the marginal rate of risk h is 30% per annum; column 2 shows the same for $h = 15\%$ per annum, and column 3 the same for $h = 0$.

From Table V it will be seen that even with a marginal rate of risk as low, in comparison with those suggested in comment D, as 15% per annum, a reduction of the rate of pure interest by as much as one-third may increase the value of an instrument expected to be used for 40 years by only some 6%. If no allowance needed to be made for uncertainty, such a reduction of the rate of pure interest could increase the value of this

TABLE V

$\Delta v = v_2 - v_1$, where v_1 corresponds to $\rho = 0.03$, v_2 corresponds to $\rho = 0.02$.

$L.$	$\dfrac{\Delta v}{v_1}$ for $h = 0.30$.	$\dfrac{\Delta v}{v_1}$ for $h = 0.15$.	$\dfrac{\Delta v}{v_1}$ for $h = 0$.
5	0·019	0·022	0·025
10	0·027	0·037	0·049
20	0·030	0·052	0·096
40	0·031	0·059	0·182

instrument by 18%. Now, there must surely be at any time in the minds of the enterprisers a larger number of contingent investment plans each having a value lying within 18% of its cost than there are of such plans each having a value lying within 6% of its cost. If so, allowance for doubt, when this allowance takes the form and degree we have supposed, greatly reduces the sensitiveness of investment to given reductions of the rate of pure interest.

We have shown that allowance for the *hazards* which beset the prospective earning career of many forms of equipment can easily render ineffective, as a stimulator of investment in these forms of equipment, even a large proportionate change of the rate of pure interest. If the problem we are trying to solve is held to consist of the question " What factor severely restricts the influence of interest-rates on the pace of investment? ", we answer that this factor is the allowance for doubt. But if our problem is cast in the form " Why is it that enterprisers deny,

in the main, that interest-rate changes *have ever* affected their
investment-decisions ? ", then there is an additional explanation.
It is this latter question which is posed by the replies to the Oxford
questionnaire.

When a man takes a decision on any matter whatever, he
tacitly or unconsciously takes into account a great range of circumstances which are all relevant, in the sense that if any one of
them were materially different his decision might be different.
But a very large proportion of these circumstances are simply
taken for granted, and conscious thought and attention are concentrated on those elements of the problem which are either
incompletely and doubtfully known, or else which are liable to
rapid change on a scale which affects the issue. The very fact
that he is engaged in making a decision shows that something in
the relevant circumstances has changed, and, before beginning
his consideration of the issue, he must list in his mind all such
changes which have occurred since the problem last occupied
him. *These* will then seem to be the efficient causes of his
decision. When he is afterwards asked how his decision was
reached, he will make no reference to all those aspects which
merely seemed to provide a stable frame for the play of the active
factors : elements which, without necessarily remaining perfectly
constant, had shown *proportionate* changes (on which the degree
of contrast, and the power to attract attention, depend) too
small to be noticed.

Let us call a reduction of an interest-rate from, *e.g.*, 4% per
annum to 3% per annum (or from 5 to 4, or from 2 to 1), a *unit
reduction* of the rate. Then the largest fall in the yield of British
Consols which occurred between any two successive years in the
period 1870–1913 was of 0·15 unit, while a fall, between two
successive years, of 0·33 unit or more occurred only three times
in the eighteen years 1919–36. Turning back to the case where
L tends to infinity, so that

$$v = c\int_0^\infty e^{-Rx}dx = \frac{c}{R} \text{ and } \eta_{v\rho} = -\frac{\rho}{R} = -\frac{\rho}{h+\rho},$$

let us again put $h = 0·30$, $\rho = 0·03$, $R = h + p = 0·33$; and in
the light of the figures just given regarding historical *speeds of
change* of ρ, let us consider a change in ρ of 0·33 *unit*—namely,
from a level of $3\frac{1}{3}$% per annum to one of 3% per annum. This
change in ρ will imply a change in R from $33\frac{1}{3}$% per annum to
33% per annum—that is, a proportionate change $\dfrac{\Delta R}{R} = 0·01$,

and since $v = \dfrac{c}{R}$, such a change in ρ, the rate of pure interest,
will raise the marginal valuation of the instrument by about
one-hundredth. If the elasticity of supply of the instruments in
question were as much as 5, still a drop from $3\frac{1}{3}\%$ per annum
to 3% per annum in ρ, the rate of pure interest, would give a
percentage increase in the pace of gross investment in such
instruments of no more than

$$\frac{\Delta\rho}{\rho}\eta_{z\rho} = \frac{\Delta\rho}{\rho}\eta_{r\rho}(1 + \eta_{yv}) = 0\cdot11 \times 0\cdot09(1 + 5) = 6\% ;$$

or if we prefer price-deflated gross investment

$$\frac{\Delta\rho}{\rho}\eta_{y\rho} = \frac{\Delta\rho}{\rho}\eta_{yv}\,\eta_{v\rho} = 0\cdot11 \times 5 \times 0\cdot09 = 5\% ;$$

But are not such calculations rather beside the point in such a
case as this? Is it really to be supposed that an increase of *1%*
in the estimated, or rather the conjectured, value of the instrument will strike out any spark of enthusiasm in the enterpriser's
mind? Will he even trouble himself to revise his estimates at
all on account of such changes as have ordinarily occurred in
recent decades, in the long-term rate of pure interest? And we
must then ask: even if such an increase in value should be
noticed, and even acted upon, by a few enterprisers, *how many*
would there be, even over the whole range of industry, who had
in mind at any one time a project which was sub-marginal *by
only 1%*?

In this article I have endeavoured to show—

(*a*) the rationale of the belief that interest-rate changes
influence the pace of investment;

(*b*) that this influence must certainly be strong on the
pace of investment in instruments of those kinds which men
believe can be depended on to continue earning net returns
for many decades after they are constructed;

(*c*) that the strength of the influence of interest-rates on
the pace of investment in those kinds of equipment which
are subject to the hazards of invention and fashion can be
rendered negligible by an allowance, of a size such as enterprisers themselves imply that they adopt, for doubt concerning the correctness of the " best guess " they can make,
on available knowledge, as to the size of future net returns
from such equipment; provided the *form* of this allowance
is that of a rate used for discounting in the same manner as

the interest-rate; or is some other strongly-increasing function of futurity;

(d) that *historically* the movements of the long-term interest-rate in Britain have seldom been rapid or abrupt enough to constitute appreciable changes of circumstance, or to engage the enterprisers' conscious attention as such.

It may be well to repeat, in conclusion, that where, as with houses, doubt concerning future net returns is small, there is nothing in what we have said which contests the belief that the interest-rate can powerfully affect the demand-price and thus the pace of investment in a given type of instrument.

G. L. S. SHACKLE

London.

Part IV

THE PHILOSOPHY OF ECONOMICS

GENERAL THOUGHT-SCHEMES
AND THE ECONOMIST

WE are prisoners of ideas. Before we can act in regard to any thing, we must be able to think about that thing, before we can think about it we must recognize it or conceive its nature, to recognize or have a conception of something is to classify it, is to give it a place in some scheme of thought, such schemes of thought are supplied to us ready made by our environment, our education, our social intercourse. Thus for the most part we can think, and can shape our conduct, only in accord with certain stereotypes. Imagination itself, the characteristic and most supremely human faculty, is perhaps no more than the composition of mosaics with *tesserae* that experience, personal and ancestral, has supplied.

If such be accepted, some questions present themselves. Most fundamental, most important to our human self-esteem, is the question whether we can ever break out of our prison. Can we at times invent new thoughts, thoughts of new kinds, can reason transcend itself to make new structures of reasoning? Greater and less, addition and subtraction, earlier and later, cause and effect, knowledge and ignorance, permanence and evolution; is everything that we can think, every thought that we can have, no more than a shuffling together of these elements and elements like them, into patterns which have been eternally possible, merely waiting to be realized? This is the most interesting question; but in so far as I hope to touch on it at all, I can do so only in discussing one aspect of a different and humbler question, namely, that of the mutual compatibility of our established stereotypes of thought, the inter-communication, as it were, of the various cells of our prison.

If I were asked: What is Science? I would answer: Science is classification. It involves, of course, the whole art and business of inventing the classes of entities and that of establishing their inter-sections, in fact, the whole business of imagining, of creating,

179

the scheme of classification which can take care of all the possibilities of nature and society, in so far as these possibilities manifest themselves in repetition. It is repetition which allows of science. When men try to make history into a science, they do so by seeking repetitiveness in the phases of growth and decline of civilizations, or of technologies, or of business cycles, or of ' growth '. What is an explanation of some phenomenon? It consists in saying ' *That* belongs *here* '. Suppose I feel a sudden sharp pain in my arm. Am I worried? No, because I have observed a small yellow creature crawling on my arm. I file the pain at once under ' wasp stings '. It is ' explained '. This classification intersects with, and is indeed contained within, another pigeon-hole labelled ' Injuries not usually serious '. All this amounts to knowledge, and this knowledge has been achieved by classification.

It is cross-classification which principally gives us knowledge, for then we find associations between one state of affairs and another, we discern structure in our surroundings. If one of two frequently associated states seems each time to precede the other, we are tempted to call it a *cause* of the other state. This temptation may be re-inforced if we can show that the operation of this ' cause ' is merely a special type of a much wider class of instances where something analogous happens. Structure, however, is a more general idea than cause, and does not depend on it. Structure is mathematically expressed by the idea of function, the idea of a rule which restricts in some specific way the sets of measurements which we compose into vectors or points and the sets of such vectors or points which we compose into curves, surfaces and other varieties. In examining the mutual compatibility of the thought-schemes which, by whatever agency, impose themselves upon us, it seems appropriate to begin with function and cause.

Suppose we have seven kinds of phenomena A, B, ... , G, and that we use these letters as labels of the rows of a rectangular array of ' empty boxes '. And suppose T, U, ... , Z, are seven other kinds of phenomena which we use as labels of the columns of the same rectangular array. If observation shows us only instances which we can file into the boxes AT, BU, CV, DW, EX, FY, or GZ, and that the observable world appears to leave the other boxes empty, we have already a piece of cross-classificatory knowledge, we have a restrictive pattern by which certain phenomena appear to be regularly and exclusively associated, we have a glimpse of structure. The 'kinds of phenomena' A, B, ... need not be widely diverse in qualitative character. Instead, they may be merely different members of some class of measurements defined by its unified subject-matter, they may, that is to say, be different numerical values of some variable. If the other list of phenomena, T, U, ... , are also merely different items in a class of actual or conceivable measurements, the pattern displayed by our rectangular array will be a function in the mathematician's sense, it will restrict the pairs or sets of values, one from each of a list of variables, which it allows, or we can say more briefly, it will define a class of vectors or points.

Now the word 'cause' suggests activity, change, event, followed by some other such change or event which would not have happened if the former event, or something equivalent, had not occurred. It is obvious that the idea of function is quite different from this. If we have a circle of known radius, we can calculate its circumference to as good an approximation as we like. But here there is no event, except our act of measuring the circle, it would be quite out of touch with ordinary usage to say that the radius of the circle 'causes' the circumference to be such and such, for why should we not say that the circumference causes the radius to be such-and-such? However abstract its mathematical origins or the modern analyst's interpretation of it, the idea of function is plainly invaluable in describing the structure of our physical world. A mathematician would be prepared to assume, at least for the sake of argument, that the whole cosmos and everything that goes on in it could in principle, and if we had 'room and time enough' be described, stated and set down as a function, $F \equiv 0$. But if everything were thus accounted for, in a complete inter-locking of all phenomena, what room would there be for any notion of 'cause'? The idea of a function totally describing the whole nature and history of the cosmos, past and future, would not be that of a mathematical machine tool into which we can put raw data and get out finished conclusions, for plainly there would be no question of choosing what data to put in: the only answer the function would give us is: The cosmos is like this; or even: The cosmos is this. To use the notion of 'cause

8   GENERAL THOUGHT-SCHEMES AND THE ECONOMIST

and effect' seems to imply an absence of all-pervading determinism in the cosmos. Except in so far as the 'cause and effect' locution is merely a way of directing attention to certain aspects or portions of the total, inter-locking structure of things, of singling out particular features of this structure, this way of speaking seems to imply that there are *sources* of trains of events, sources in somewhat the physicist's sense of the word when he speaks of 'sources' and 'sinks' of energy in some region or system. If all causes are themselves determinately and precisely caused, we are in a complete determinist universe where nothing can happen differently from what it does.

Is it useful, then, to give a more substantial meaning to 'cause', to make it mean something characterizing the world itself and not merely our method of examining that world? When we elect, as economists among other investigators do, to single out two, or very few, phenomena at a time and examine their mutual influences and interactions against a supposedly fixed and passive background of other things, then we are using one of the characteristic and indispensable methods of science, the experimental method or something as close to it as social scientists can get. It is surely legitimate in such a procedure, if we find that by bringing about phenomenon A we can in the right circumstances always produce B, but that we cannot produce A by bringing about B, to call A in these circumstances the 'cause' of B. But here we have our clue. We spoke of 'bringing about' phenomenon A. If we look upon this 'bringing about' as in the strict sense an initiative of our own, something itself 'uncaused', then we are thinking of the physical world as equipped with countless levers available for human beings to manipulate and so produce effects which they may expect and desire. We are regarding the world, in its state at any moment, as an incomplete system, one whose immediately future behaviour depends on the way in which data or impulses not deducible in character or quantity from the past of the system, are going to be fed into it *ex nihilo* by human agency.

Now you may well feel that to set apart from each other in this way, to regard as subject to quite different modes of being, the human and the non-human world, is too much to accept. Consciousness, it may be held, does not imply enfranchisement from the

' laws of nature '. But if so, are we not in a purely determinist world, where it must be doubted whether the economist's peculiar concentration on what he calls ' choice ' can be justified? Why bother with 'choice' when choice is merely subservience to necessity? Why call it choice, when we merely go the way our chains compel?

What, then, is the economist's basic pre-supposition about the world he studies? His purpose is to understand it scientifically. A scientific explanation, I have ventured, however recklessly, to suggest, is in essence an act of rather complex classification. We sort things into kinds, and as long as our classificatory scheme holds out, and offers us the necessary pigeon-hole, we are happy enough. I even tried to persuade you that mathematical analysis itself can be looked on in this light. The economist, then, finds that particular box in his scheme, where the class ' reductions of price ' intersects the class ' extensions of demand ' filling up very rapidly as he files his observations. From this fact, if he is an empiricist, he draws a so-called ' law '. Another box collects the cases where large and rapid increases in the quantity of money have been accompanied by rising prices, and shows, perhaps, more instances than the box where a rising general price-level intersects with a constant or falling stock of money. (These are crude illustrations, not meant to stand up to detailed criticism; I well know the trouble that statisticians or econometricians have had, even with multiple correlation methods, in sorting out their observations so as to make theoretical sense.) Then the theoretician takes over. He proposes ideas, such as that of diminishing marginal rates of substitution, which enable us to enclose our observed phenomena in still wider and more general classes, giving us a greater sense of explanatory power and of the unity and coherence of the social and economic organism or mechanism. And all this time the economist is relying upon repetitiveness, upon a basic uniformity in the texture of economic life. How, then, is he going to explain invention, development, evolution, irreversible change?

The problem whether science can explain evolutionary, one-way changes seems to me a fundamentally important one. I have already referred to the example of human history in the conventional sense. Those historians, such as Spengler and Toynbee, who have tried to scientificize history have had to resort to repetitiveness. Their

10   GENERAL THOUGHT-SCHEMES AND THE ECONOMIST

latest recruit is Mr. Walt Rostow of the *Five Stages of Economic Growth*. But even he has to admit one stupendous anomaly, or at any rate, one great question that no appeal to repetitiveness can answer. How did the very first ' take-off into self-sustained growth ', the original and British one, happen? In the biological sciences, evolution is accounted for by a mechanism or several distinct mechanisms. But at least one of these has a very interesting essential feature, whose implications are quite startling once you have thought about them. It depends upon *random* change. Irreversible changes occur in the transmissible detailed design of some living creature. A particular specimen differs from anything that can be accounted for by its ancestry, yet this modification is passed on to its off-spring. When the off-spring of such random mutants find themselves, by reason of this change, specially well equipped to cope with some available environment, they thrive, multiply and oust their less well adapted rivals. Thus forest-dwelling apes get on well with their long arms, which are the reason, not the result, of their adoption of the forest habitat. *Homo* self-styled *sapiens* has prospered by his erect posture, which enabled him to grasp things with his hands now freed from their duty as feet, to inspect these things closely on all sides with a long leisurely stare of curiosity, to throw them around, as toys, as weapons, as tools . . . . He began to think about them, he began to think about things *such as* them, he remembered what he had done and sought to do a like thing again . . . . A *like* thing? This was to classify, to conceive abstract ideas. Concept-making man had come. And the secret of all this, we are told, is *random* genetic mutation.

So history is random? This is at least an escape from ' history is determined from the beginning of time '. Economic theory in recent years has taken quite definitely (I do not know whether to say ' deliberately ' : there were no committee-meetings about it) a particular turning, has adopted a particular policy, in response to the challenge of this past fifty years of war, revolution, depression and general social upheaval. It was plainly necessary to have theories going beyond the mere explanation of a state of general, perfect and fully-informed adjustment, where within an unchanging institutional and political environment it was supposed that the inborn tastes and the given skills and possessions of all the very various members of the society would be accommodated to each other ' optimally ', so that when each person had perfect and there-fore equal knowledge of the circumstances, potential and actual, which faced him, and also had equal freedom, he would elect that course of action best serving his own interests; serve them best, that is, given that everyone else would similarly serve his own interests. This equilibrium scheme of thought was, so far as it went, a miracle of efficiency and incisive explanatory power. But it did not explain change, and so, of itself, it could do nothing to explain history. So the economists had to think again. They saw, first of all, the business cycle; that splendidly repetitive phenomenon which nevertheless described events and not mere situations. Business cycle theories began by being very makeshift affairs. A business cycle consists of a number of phases, so for each phase we will have an explanation, was the first approach. Nowadays we have business cycle machines, models which by their very design are bound to respond to any impulse or shock by producing oscillations. The precise behaviour of such a machine depends solely on two classes of data: first, its own detailed design, expressed in equations which bind functionally together events which are supposed to occur at different dates; and secondly, the exact force of the shock from outside the machine which throws it out of its equilibrium state or path of steady, e.g. exponential, movement. Slight changes in the parameters of the equations may make all the difference to the kind of oscillation, damped or anti-damped, that the machine produces, but these parameters are, in a sense, the sole expression, within the model, of all the psychic, social, political and institutional influences that govern people's response to particular economic circumstances. For the unreality of perfect all-pervasive relevant knowledge, supposed to be possessed by all the members of the society and to include simultaneous knowledge about each others' thoughts, we have substituted the artificiality of mechanism, behaviour which can be described without any mention of thought, choice, decision. Whether it adopts an equilibrium model or a cyclical one, economic theory seems resolved to treat economic conduct as mere response. But if we have no other principle than mere consistent response to the existent circumstances we are in a perfectly determinist hypo-thetical world. There seem to be two ways of escape. We can

12   GENERAL THOUGHT-SCHEMES AND THE ECONOMIST

appeal to some fundamental randomness in things, manifested for example in genetic mutation and actually arising in sub-atomic structure. Or we can suppose that human thought is more than mere response.

There is an arresting contrast between the unquestioning sense of personal, originative, history-making power afforded us by any private act, however humble, of decision, and the passivity, the mere mechanical subservience or mathematical determinism implicit in the attempts we make as scholars to unravel the driving motives and shaping circumstances of the deeds of other people. For each of us his own decision, surrounded as it is by compelling circumstance, by weighty considerations, moral pressures, desires, tastes, habits and the whole authority of social life, yet seems to have a central freedom, a void to be filled by a new spring of initiative in our own mind. Decision, when it is the real and living act emerging into our own private consciousness, seems to us to come in some degree *ex nihilo*. Yet we look upon ourselves as rational, as trying to respond to circumstances, to do our best with the situation presented to us, to make what we can of the materials given to us. How can these two attitudes, these two meanings ascribed to human action, be mutually reconciled? Do we make history or merely enact it? Do we speak parts written for us or spontaneously improvise them ourselves?

Decision is choice, but choice amongst what? Not amongst actual experiences depending upon stimuli from without or our own motor responses, for when you are actually experiencing or physically doing something, it is too late to reject it in favour of something else. Choice is amongst imagined experiences. And when a man summons up an array of imaginations, how does he know what action-course will actualize any one such picture? Or when, instead, he reviews his rival available acts, how does he know what outcome to attach to each? He does not and cannot know. But can he perhaps make a list of all possible consequences of each rival available act, and thus call to his aid all the apparatus of the theory of distributive probability? Even in a fundamentally random universe, statistics might rescue him. But not in a universe of ultimately creative thought. If a thought can contain an element undeducible from any record of the thinker's past no matter how perfect, by any logical process no matter how powerful, then in principle no list can ever be made which can be known to be complete, of the distinct outcomes which a decision-maker might invent or imagine for any action-course open to him. If so, distributive probability can have no application to his problem of choice amongst actions. For probabilities can only be meaningfully assigned to the items of a complete list of contingencies, or to the intervals of a variable whose meaning is in stable dependence on such a list.

There are many interpretations of the word probability, many different prescriptions for assigning probabilities to contingencies and for using the resulting distribution for practical guidance in action. The common factor in all these ideas is contained in the word distribution. The notion of probability depends upon the combined presence (i) of an exhaustive list of possible outcomes of some carefully specified type of performance or trial, and (ii) of some procedure or argument for assigning to each item in this list a share of a fixed total, usually taken to be the number one, representing the certainty, implicit in the exhaustiveness of the list, that one or other of the listed results must occur.

The distributive procedure depends in the last analysis on dividing the whole field of possibilities into elements each of which is on the same footing, in the matter of claiming a share of ' probability ', as each of the others, so that these elements are equi-probable. Then any outcome, whose realization consists in the realization of any one of several elements, will be assigned the total of the probabilities of all those elements. What we are here to mean by ' on the same footing ' is one of the central semantic problems of probability theory, but it can be practically resolved either *a priori*, as by claiming, for example, that the die with its six faces is symmetrical and therefore we have no reason to regard one face as more probable than another, or *a posteriori*, by examining the statistical record of a ' large number ' of trials. What seems to me plain is that none of these ideas or procedures would make sense unless we were able to assume a given field of possibilities. *A priori* assignment of probabilities requires us to know enough about the contingencies to assure ourselves of their symmetry. Statistics may absolve us from knowing about ultimately ' individual ' contingencies by giving us information about the frequency of ' outcomes ' which can claim realiza-

14   GENERAL THOUGHT-SCHEMES AND THE ECONOMIST

tion in the case of realization of any one of several contingencies. But statistics will evidently not tell a meaningful story unless the universe which is being sampled stays the same universe. When we imagine a universe of thoughts, and elect to suppose that new thoughts can pour into this universe *ex nihilo*, we have not got a stable basis for statistical probability.

Economic theory faces a basic dilemma, which it was Keynes's chief contribution to begin to make explicit. The aim of a science is coherence. It must take for granted a number of undefinables, ideas of which it gives no account but merely names them and possibly points to examples of them. These things may be undefined only within the bounds of the particular science itself, finding their descriptions and explanations in terms of another science; or they may be the ultimate undefined terms of mathematics, such as 'successor'. Given these elements, the science seeks to compose from them a structure reducible to the application of comparatively few principles. Thus, granted only the right to leave certain items undefined, the science hopes to be able to analyse completely any situation which comes within its scope. For a science concerned with human conduct, with human choice of action, this means that every action, or event composed of actions, must be accountable as the upshot of specifiable circumstances or pressures, it must be exhibited as the inevitable outcome of a pre-existing combination of factors. But what becomes, in this case, of a human capacity, if we believe in it, for unpredictable thoughts? What becomes of imagination, invention, social evolution? Economics, it seems, can try to be a science like chemistry, or it can try to explain the life of human beings, but not both.

What human beings do depends on what they know. If, under 'know', we include all their beliefs, assumptions and conjectures, and everything which enters into their description of the state and nature of the world, we shall have expressed in that sentence what it is which mainly prevents economics from being scientific in the way that chemistry or mechanics are. For it is intensely difficult, within a theory simple enough to deserve the name, to show exactly how and with what success people can find out, not only about a passive environment, but about each other's contemporary intentions and about each other's state of knowledge, which last presents us evidently with the problem of an infinite regress. These difficulties have not been properly recognized by economists. The whole brilliant, incisive and all-inclusive neo-classical theory of value, brought to perfection by Walras and Pareto, Wicksteed and Wicksell about the turn of the present century, depended on the astounding assumption that people know everything relevant to their choices. The question what this knowledge must consist of and how it is to be obtained is cut out by an Alexandrine sword-stroke of superb efficiency: the notion of general equilibrium. General equilibrium, when we look at it as a solution to the problem of knowledge, turns out to mean that people exchange conditional promises of action, only finally committing themselves to specific action when the system of these conditionals has been solved as a whole to indicate for each person the action that he prefers given that everyone else elects and performs that particular action which the solution prescribes for him. And how is it conceivable that such a system, of indescribable complexity, can be solved? So simply, the requisite knowledge for each person, though nominally it includes all the detailed actions of ' other people ' in making, buying and selling goods, really amounts to no more than the *prices* of these goods; and these prices are determined on that extremely powerful if not absolutely accurate computer, the market.

The greatest paradox which the idea of knowledge brings into economic theory is that of knowledge as a commodity. How much is it worth while to pay for knowledge? No one can know until he has acquired the knowledge, and before then he will have had to pay for it, by way of the costs of a research programme or the purchase of a secret or, more prosaically, the purchase of an entertainment, a visit to the theatre, a copy of a novel or of a newspaper. Who knows what he will get for the fivepenny price of *The Times*? Who would buy *The Times* if he knew precisely, completely and for certain what was in it? Economics is the study of how men seek to cope with two of the great basic, inescapable conditions of life: scarcity, or lack of means; and uncertainty, or lack of knowledge. But economic theory cannot bring lack of knowledge under the same sort of analysis as lack of material means. The possession or the non-possession of knowledge alters everything. An equilibrium analysis of the role of knowledge as a commodity is a contradiction

16   GENERAL THOUGHT-SCHEMES AND THE ECONOMIST

in terms.   Equilibrium copes with scarcity on the assumption that
the problem of knowledge is solved.

But general equilibrium with all its splendour and incomparable
intellectual efficiency, reducing everything to the logic of maximiza-
tion, only describes a momentary world.   The world of change,
evolution and invention is quite beyond its scope.   What, then, of
prediction?   Is not the power to predict said to be the mark and
test of science?   In what sense and degree can economics claim to
be predictive?

But first, in what sense can other sciences claim to be predictive?
We have to make an absolutely vital though very obvious distinction
between prediction and prophecy.   Scientific predictions, those
statements which are implied by some theory and which therefore
serve to test it, are conditional statements.   They say: If such and
such a set of circumstances is brought about, or found somewhere
to exist, these will be accompanied or followed in time by such and
such other circumstances.   The predictions of science are merely a
mode of its description of nature.   A theory begins with ' a minimal
description of what is '.   This minimal description, treated as a
set of axioms, logically implies a volume of other general propositions and particular assertions.   If we find that these latter are
falsified under practical test or observation, the theory must be
modified or replaced with another.   To make a scientific prediction
is to suggest what will be the completion of a picture which is already
partly filled in, it is not to say what picture is going to appear on a
blank canvas.   A scientific prediction starts with *if*.   Now to suggest
the future course of human events can only resemble scientific
prediction if the described events are to arise out of a known configuration of desires, beliefs, intentions and resources, and such
knowledge, if it can ever be possessed by anyone, can at the utmost
refer only to the present.   Prediction of human events can be
scientific only if it refers to the immediate future.

Prediction of how human beings are about to act in the most
immediate future, prediction of very short range indeed, might
claim a formal respectability if it were conceivable that the tensions
and intentions of society and individuals at the present moment
could be known in detail, and if it were claimed that those new
thoughts, whose coming to birth we have invoked as a release from

determinism, would take some time to have any marked public effect on affairs. There is perhaps a more strange possibility. If we regard the more cataclysmic social events as the sudden bursting of restraint by latent forces which have built themselves up gradually over many years, we can conceive that the character, configuration and strength of these forces might be discerned as they came into being, so that the shape, but not the date, of the eventual upheaval might be descried. To have a name for this conception, the perceived pattern of latent social or economic forces which have gathered strength and only await some ' signal ', some event which should reveal the partisans to each other and tip the scale of impatience, I have elsewhere suggested the word ' rig '. The power to discern the ' rig ' and the readiness to effect an orderly and quiet release of its pressures is the mark of political maturity. If such pre-vision had any reality, it would still be in effect a short-range prediction, for at most it could hope only to describe the immediate sequel to the release of the latent forces. Since that release might result from any one of an infinity of different sorts of accident, the date of this release would remain utterly unforeseeable. All this does little to advance the claims of economic or political ' science ' to be scientific in the manner of the natural sciences. Do they really wish to make that claim? To do so is to make nonsense of our practical, intuitive, unselfconscious interpretation of our own most serious individual feelings. It implies that the absorbed thought and pressing anxiety which mark our efforts to reach a decision in some important matter are mere side-effects of the operations of a fateful mechanism, perhaps necessary to the working of this mechanism but quite deceptive in the burden they seem to place on the individual conscience and capacity. Decisions can be anguishing. But does, or need, a machine feel anguish? If the cosmos is a vast computer programmed from the beginning of time, what need is there for consciousness itself? But if consciousness is the vehicle of a true creative activity, an ultimate source of events unimplied by what has gone before, then we can understand its purpose.

It may seem to you that I have strayed from my brief or terms of reference. Many economists would impatiently reject or deride the preoccupations I have suggested to you. But I believe them

18   GENERAL THOUGHT-SCHEMES AND THE ECONOMIST

to be important.   How can economics be a success, a practically effective illuminant of history's ever-untrodden road, unless its ambitions conform with the realities of the human condition? What can economic theory really hope to give us by way of practical tools?

I want to suggest to you the notion of the stereotype.   The ordinary business of living from hour to hour involves countless repetitions of a great number of diverse kinds of drill.   By a drill I mean a settled procedure, from the elementary act of turning a light-switch to the sophisticated following-out of a cooking recipe. In each such drill we have a sequence of operations and a more-or-less confidently expected result.   Without these drills and our un-questioning reliance on their efficiency we could never keep up with the ceaseless and relentless demands of life.   These drills are small spotlighted areas in the vast dark stage of the environment.   What would be the good of turning a light switch, if there did not exist the tremendous organization and instrumentation of the Central Electricity Generating Board and the Grid?   What would be the good of posting a letter if the Post Office were not there to take charge of it?   We do not have to know how one Board generates and other Boards distribute electricity, or how the automatic ex-changes enable our telephone call to get through, in order to press the technological frame of life into service.   There is an orderliness in our surroundings which we rely on, only needing to understand a fairly small part of the whole process which gives effect to our wishes.   Each of us builds the unique structure of his or her personal existence out of countless stereotyped patterns of action.   The letter you compose is unique, unparalleled, strictly matchless.   But it uses language, the most marvellous of stereotypes in the contrast between its infinite flexibility, subtlety and power, and its rigid forms of word shape, vocabulary and grammar.   If, now, stereotypes or drills play so large a part in our small-scale business of personal living, is it not likely that they are the heart of the matter in the larger-scale business of public policy?   For it is stereotypes that economic theory in the first place provides.

Alfred Marshall's ' bit at a time ' method does not do all that is required of theory.   It is liable to mislead us in such matters as the theory of employment, where it tempts us to use the familiar demand-

and-supply analysis that we apply to a single consumable, and to assume that the supply curve and the demand curve can be drawn independently of each other. When the thing being dealt in is labour, a rise in the price cannot fail to alter the society's income and thus its demand for commodities and thus its demand for labour, so that a movement along one curve requires us to re-draw the other. Again, in fiscal theory, it will not do to consider the effects of taxation separately from those of government expenditure. I would say, indeed, that the most important lesson to be learned from economics is the universal inter-dependence of all economic variables. The test of a natural-born economist is whether this idea is the ever-present, tacitly and unquestioningly accepted background to all his economic thinking. Yet Marshall's method is the proper basis for our work. It shows in concrete detail how things happen. It provides the essential stereotypes: the supply-curve and all that can be read into it and extracted from it; the mode of growth of firms and industries; the relation of demand to price. Marshall gives us the pieces to handle, and an intimate familiarity with these pieces is as vital as a grasp of the Grand Design that Walras or that Keynes conceived, and it is as indispensable as those studies of comprehensive consistency or coherence which are nowadays so prominent under the names of ' indicative over-all planning ' or ' the Social Accounting Matrix '. These powerful schematizations and projections ultimately rest on an understanding of the stereotypes: the consumption-function, the Multiplier, the propensity to import, the Accelerator, the full employment ceiling, the capital-output ratio, liquidity preference, the price and income elasticities of demand, the interest-elasticity of investment, and so forth.

There is one more general idea, with its special economic embodiment, that I would like to use as my conclusion. It is this very idea of coherence that I have just referred to. Although I have stressed stereotypes or models of simple action-and-consequence configurations or of repetitive associations of circumstance, there remains the vital truth that these are but tiles composing the great mosaic picture of society's business as a whole. This total picture, in order to be convincing and beautiful, must itself be a coherent unity where everything fits together without loose ends. The method of ensuring this is a kind of accounting, called Social

20   GENERAL THOUGHT-SCHEMES AND THE ECONOMIST

Accounting, which, in its most modern, elegant, efficient and powerful form, makes use of a branch of mathematics called matrix algebra.   The use it makes of this is chiefly notational, and indeed the manipulative aspect is fortunately nowadays taken care of by the electronic computer.   The social accounting matrix is the visible embodiment of coherence in a general economic scheme, for each entry in the table plays a double role, showing by its position both the source and the destination of the *valutum* concerned.   This scheme has evolved from the brilliant invention of input-output analysis by Wassily Leontief in the early 1930's, whereby he showed how the detailed response required of a complex productive web of industries supplying and drawing upon each other, when the final ' bill of goods ' to be delivered as the end-product of this productive machine was changed in a specified way, could be calculated, as it were, at one stroke (even though that ' stroke ' consisted in the solution of a great system of equations, or the inversion of a very large matrix).   It is, I believe, in the development of these comprehensive ' schemes of coherence ', embracing the whole economy and yet, like a great microscope, able to resolve an astonishing degree of detail, that economics has the best hope of justifying itself as a tool of the human mind able to match, though not to imitate, the achievements of the natural sciences.

ECONOMICS AND SINCERITY

By G. L. S. SHACKLE

WHAT does an economist mean when he says, regarding such-and-such a theory, 'I believe it' or 'I do not believe it'? Can he formulate a single, precise, and unambiguous test which will confer on any theory that passes it the right to be used without misgiving for all and every one of the professional duties laid on the economist? Ought he to impose on himself a code which, if there is some theory that he disbelieves, would forbid him to base policy recommendations on it, to teach it, or even to use it in his own thinking? What are the particular kinds of temptation to which the economist is exposed, and in what, precisely, does the successful rejection of these temptations consist, and what kinds of self-denial does it involve?

When all life's questions are answered for any one of us, life itself will surely have ceased to hold for him any interest or purpose. Are we then to say that so long as a man finds a theory interesting he does not yet believe in it? And if we constrict the notion of belief to this extreme degree, are we therefore to forbid him to act upon, teach, or think with any theory that he still finds interesting? An absurd and artificial dilemma, perhaps you will say. But if it be once admitted that a theory which we take invariably, absolutely, and unquestioningly for granted, and which we regard ourselves as having explored to the uttermost so that all its implications, and the consequences of acting on it, are known, could have no power of stimulating thought and indeed would be incapable of being any longer the object of thought, it follows of necessity that all the theories which have any active role in an economist's mental life and in his work must be ones that he can still cast doubt upon, can question and suspect, can feel to be incompletely worked out, and to hold unknown possibilities for good or evil when used as the basis of policy. To use only what we perfectly believe is therefore practically and essentially impossible. If to base advice upon, to teach, and to spend time in thinking about, things that we do not perfectly believe is morally wrong, the economist must shut up shop, must resign from his life-work and cease, as such, to exist. In what sense and in what degree, then, are we justified in using theories that we do not fully believe?

The very attempt to define an ideal and perfect degree of belief, in the sense of a willingness to commit ourselves wholly and unreservedly to some theory, to accept the consequences of applying it in any and every set of circumstances, shows that the concept is useless as a test of a theory's fitness to be used and taught. Perfect belief in this sense would require the perfect theory, able to interpret every situation, to predict the consequences of every course of action, to fit perfectly as a component mechanism into

2   ECONOMICS AND SINCERITY

the great engine of human knowledge and link up economics with psychology, technology, anthropology, history, politics, ethics, and philosophy without loose ends. To call such a conception a theory is almost a contradiction in terms. Let us then ask what are the essential and inevitable limitations of theories in general; what is their true nature and proper purpose; in what respects they can be superior or inferior; and whether there are any absolute tests, or any tests adapted to circumstances, which will tell us whether or when a given theory may be honourably invoked or must be repudiated.

In making a theory we begin by *selecting* some features from amongst all those that the world seems to present. Deliberate rejection and neglect of a part of reality is, then, part of the process of theory-making, and at the very start we have an immense disparity between the simple and poor pile of materials out of which the theory will be built, and the measureless wealth and complexity of detail afforded by whatever part of the field of phenomena we may have marked out for our operations. Now our chief guide in making this basic and all-important selection is tradition and historical accident, or, at best, the intuitive genius of one or two men living in a remote time when, superficially, human circumstances were vastly different. Why does the economist repudiate any suggestion that he should become an engineer, a chemist, or an expert in agriculture ? Why does he say that technology is none of his business ? Does not the wealth of nations intimately depend on these very kinds of knowledge, and the growth of that wealth upon advances in them? Who drew this frontier where it stands today ? Economics is not a natural science, pure or applied, but a human science, you will say. Why then does the economist say that psychology is none of his business ? Do we say that economics is concerned with men's preferences, choices, hopes, fears, beliefs, decisions, imaginings, motives, behaviour, and yet say that the inner truths about the working of their minds are none of our business ? When a man chooses in the market-place, he is a fit object of study by the economist, but not when he chooses in the polling-booth. Ethics is not for the economist: economic man must play his queer game according to the rules, not presume to discuss them. The rules, indeed, are changed for him from time to time ; sometimes he is rationed, sometimes not ; sometimes he is exhorted to exercise patriotic restraint, at other times to exercise patriotic abandon ; sometimes to save, sometimes to spend ; it is very confusing for him when the rules are changed in the middle of the game, and all the good habits carefully conditioned into him from his youth turn out to be bad habits, and then perhaps good habits again, just when he has conquered them. But the economist must only allow himself a side-glance at the springs of that history-in-the-making which necessitates all this. Who drew *these* frontiers where they stand today ?

But does it matter if the materials for the theory are chosen according to an ancient and an arbitrary canon ? Indeed it does, for these materials have got to be built up into a machine that will work, a pattern that will make sense. We may remember the disaster that overtook the Sleeping Princess in the fairy-tale, simply because her parents had forgotten to invite to the christening party one of the most powerful fairies. If our selection of materials for a theory leaves out of account some powerful factor, all our plans based on that theory are liable at any moment to go astray. Sooner or later the princess will prick her finger ; the trifling accident, unnoticed at the time of its occurrence, will set off a train of consequences which our inadequate theory has not warned us to be on the look-out for.

Let us sum up this first stage of our argument. Economics is a field of study enclosed within arbitrary boundaries. These boundaries are not part of the nature of things. No doubt after 175 years we can say that they correspond to a consensus of powerful minds. If the physiocrats failed to set economics off on a different path it was, perhaps, because its actual path was the true highway. Nevertheless these boundaries are artificial. Is there any natural discontinuity between a man's economic motives and conduct on the one hand, and, on the other, his conduct as politician, scientist, philosopher, poet, lover, or mystic ? It is fair to ask, I think, whether the builders of economic theories are not in these days unduly conservative and somewhat tradition-bound in their choice of materials.

Having chosen his materials, the theorist proceeds to fashion from them a variety of structural members, a collection of ideas or concepts with which to build his theory. The economist has thus carved out such things as perfect competition, general equilibrium, the stationary state, marginal productivity, liquidity preference, the enterpriser or taker of decisions in face of uncertainty, and so forth. Each of these is designed to reflect some feature of what the economist observes, and does reflect it more or less faithfully. But now there is a second process of selection to be gone through. Like the misguided amateur of horology who has taken his watch to pieces, the economist finds that even in his restricted box of tricks there are far more pieces than he can contrive any use for in any one attempt at reconstruction. Some of the concepts are mutually incompatible and some are seeming duplicates with recondite but essential differences. Must we then admit that we can construct a number of entirely different models to explain one and the same world ? Like a small boy who has thrown his cricket ball through a window, the economic theorist offers a variety of mutually contradictory explanations. I think it can justly be contended that modern economic theory does not show one picture but many highly contrasted ones, maintaining none the less that they are all likenesses of the same reality.

4   ECONOMICS AND SINCERITY

If, when he button-holed the Wedding Guest, the Ancient Mariner had propounded the question 'What is a theory?' perhaps his harassed victim might have answered, 'Well, it's something that tells you what to expect in the circumstances; when things happen that weren't happening before, a theory makes you feel you are still in a familiar world; a theory tells you what to do to get desired results.' And I think this answer, considering the adverse conditions in which the *viva* was conducted, might at least have earned a pass mark. Seen in this light, a theory looks extremely practical. It is plainly the most essential of all tools for dealing successfully with one's environment in space and time. Yet in another light a theory has nothing to do with reality. It is an abstract deductive system, perfectly exemplified by a modern version of Euclid. Here we start with some words or other symbols which we do not define. We then make a number of statements about the ways in which these undefined things can be related to each other, taking care that these *postulates* are not mutually contradictory. Then we proceed to draw out the logical implications of this set of postulates, we work out, that is, what the postulates say *in effect*, beyond what they say patently and explicitly. Now suppose we can find amongst the phenomena we observe in the external world some that seem to be related to each other in the ways that the undefined entities are assumed in our abstract deductive system to be related to each other, and suppose we assume that this structure of relations between phenomena is invariant. Then we must conclude that all the theorems which are true of the undefined entities in our abstract system are also true of the observed phenomena of reality. What we have done is to assume a structural identity between the two patterns: the logical pattern of ideas in our abstract system, and the association, concurrent or in temporal sequence, of certain selected types of events in the external world. Now it is a common experience to find that amongst our friends Harry resembles John, and John resembles Alfred, but Alfred does not seem at all to resemble Harry. The reason is evidently that while, for example, Harry and John are alike in features and colouring, John and Alfred are alike in voice and manner. We cannot hope to find an abstract structure simple enough to give us a feeling of imaginative grasp and familiarity, and yet comprehensive and subtle enough to account for the limitless variety of detailed pattern in the unrolling tapestry of historical events. We have to choose between theories each of which accounts for some features and not others. To see what sort of consequences this has, let us consider some of the types into which economic theories fall.

There are many different cabinets each with its own set of pigeon-holes amongst which we can distribute economic theories. There is the cabinet which divides them into *general* theories and *particular* theories. But we must be careful. The word 'general' can here mean either of two quite different things. It may mean that, within some context of thought (perhaps very limited), all possible types of situation have been provided for. This is what it means in the title 'The General Theory of Employment, Interest, and Money'. Or it can mean that the theory to which it is applied is one where everything in the whole economic world is explicitly admitted, and shown, to depend on everything else. This is how we are using the word when we say that Walras constructed a theory of 'general equilibrium'. It is in this second sense that 'general' theories stand over against 'particular' theories. Each kind has its own dangers. A particular theory builds an insulating wall round a small piece of the economic system and declares that nothing which happens inside that wall shall be deemed able to set up waves which can pass outwards through that wall and, being reflected or even amplified by contact with what lies outside, to come back through the wall and affect what is going on inside it. Thus, for example, we often regard the supply conditions and the demand-conditions for a particular commodity as independent of each other. We justify this in either of two ways. We may say: 'Only a very minute percentage of those who demand this commodity are also those whose services help to supply it, and whose incomes, in consequence, depend partly on how much of it is sold in unit time, and at what price.' Or we may say: 'Those who are demanding this commodity *today* will not, by offering higher prices and buying larger quantities of it, be able thus to affect their own incomes until *tomorrow*. Thus *today* demand and supply in this market are independent of each other.' Now the former argument is very well for such particular commodities as do not bulk large in any one person's budget. For them clearly the incomes of its suppliers will be in total only a small fraction of that total of incomes whose variations could shift the demand curve for the commodity. But it will never do to apply it to the market for labour, as those theorists used to do who thought that a fall in money wages would cause more people to be given employment. When we are tempted (often with ample justification) to use a *particular* theory, we ought to make sure that the insulating wall does not enclose so large an area that jangling and disturbing echoes will come back from what lies *within* the wall. General theories, on the other hand, may make the solution of special problems so difficult that thought is paralysed and we are prevented from reaching some valid conclusions. It has been said that the economist, by too drastic use of simplifying assumptions, 'may fail to see the wood because he has cut down most of the trees'. General theories, by contrast, tell us too little about too much.

Another cabinet devides economic theories into static and dynamic. A static theory describes a state of affairs which, once attained, nobody would have any incentive to alter. It is a conception which owes much more to physical analogies than to psychological insight. Nobody, so far as I know, has yet written that chapter in the history of economic thought which would explain how *equilibrium* came to be a technical term of our subject and would trace the part this word has played and the meanings it has borne in our literature. But perhaps it is not too fanciful to suppose that the immense prestige and ascendancy in men's minds which mechanics, and in particular celestial mechanics, came to possess during the seventeenth, eighteenth, and nineteenth centuries must have suggested to economists the search for some simple and all-inclusive principle to explain the structure of their world. Impressed first of all by the physical constraints which nature and geography imposed on the satisfaction of men's abiding needs, they turned then to those needs themselves, and in the opposition between desire and scarcity they perceived the principle of *balance*, of the ultimate compromise which nobody could alter to his advantage. Implicit in the idea of equilibrium is that of stability, an inherent tendency of things to recover their 'balance of power' adjustment if any change in the governing conditions, the bounty or parsimony of nature and men's own desires and knowledge and institutional arrangements, disturbs it. Now to say that things have a tendency to *recover* an equilibrium is to say that they have a tendency to *seek* one: if the notion of stable equilibrium truly fits some aspect of reality, we have an explanation not only of rest but of movement. Economists have indeed sometimes come to believe that a tendency towards an equilibrium is part of the nature of every economic system, and that in seeking to explain movement, that is, why the system occupies a different situation at the end of each successive unit time-interval, we need only discover what shift in the governing conditions has made a movement necessary, and what it is that prevents the adaptation to this shift from being instantaneous. But once it is admitted that adaptation need not always be instantaneous, we have brought in the idea of time-lags between events and their consequences. And this idea is dynamite for the believers in a universal tendency to equilibrium.

Beginning, perhaps, with Wicksell and his rocking-horse analogy, some economists, most notably Professor Frisch, have sought inspiration in the behaviour of physical systems with quite different results from those of the equilibrium theorists. They have looked at mechanical and electrical systems whose natural and inherent response to an impulse is to *oscillate*. The time-lag is the key which unlocks this door and permits the economist to play with wave-motions of every kind. And what may well amaze him is the simplicity of the assumptions that suffice to provide us with damped, undamped, or anti-damped oscillations by a slight adjustment in the numerical value of one coefficient. Functional connexions of the simplest and most obvious kind are all we need assume, provided the connexion is between variables at different dates. But if small changes in the numerical values of parameters can so radically affect the behaviour of the system, is it not of prime importance to find out what are the actual values of such parameters in existing economic system ?

Economics in the older-fashioned sense finds itself nowadays rather in the position of a legitimate monarch of retiring disposition who finds his authority challenged by the dynamic personality and boundless ambitions of a young brother, newly grown up and of somewhat doubtful pedigree. Econometrics, if we date its birth from the founding of the Econometric Society in 1930, is now twenty-two years old, and claims the throne by its descent from economics, mathematics, and statistics. To an avowed legitimist this seems an inflated claim. As for the application of *mathematics* to economics, what of Cournot, Marshall, Wicksell, Edgeworth, and Fisher, to say nothing of Walras and Pareto ? As for *statistics*, what of Tooke, Newmarch, Stamp, and Sir Arthur Bowley ? What, we might ask, is there new in econometrics except its name, which attains, as it were, the second degree of portmanteaux-ism by eliminating one of its essential *m*'s: surely it should be ECO/*NOMO*/METRICS, or better, perhaps, metro-economics? However, this insinuation is not fair. There *is* something new in econometrics ; something that is not to be found in mathematical economics in the sense of Marshall's Appendixes, nor in economic statistics as understood by the great compilers of the past. Mathematical economics is the expression, in rather general analytical forms, of hypotheses concerning the essential structure of the economic organism and the drawing of inferences from it. We are content to write $y = f(x)$ without specifying the precise sequence of operations denoted by the symbol $f(\ )$. But the econometrician is *not* content with this. He wishes to write out in full an equation, not merely with all its parameters explicitly represented by letters, but with actual numerical values assigned to them. And how right he is to want this. Mr. Hicks has reminded us that if the numerical value of the coefficient which expresses the dependence of current net investment on a single earlier change of output is altered from a trifle less to a shade more than some critical value, the result will be altered from stability to explosion. In economics, quantitative as opposed to mere qualitative thinking is essential, and the econometrician is amply justified in seeking to test and to quantify the hypotheses of the qualitative economist (and this term includes the mathematical economist) by reference to recorded facts. Yet the econometrician has suffered painful shocks and disastrous disinflation of his claims. What did he tell us about unemployment in the post-war transition ? Why does he speak pompously of 'incomplete information' when all he means is uncertainty, that familiar spirit who walks with us everywhere ? Does the econometrician realize that his references to 'incomplete information' imply that there can come within human reach and ken something that could properly be called 'complete information'? And does he realize that *omniscience* has not, traditionally, been claimed by mortal man, at any rate in his more sober moments of decent humility? Small wonder that this ὕβρις has sometimes fallen into the pit. For this phrase 'incomplete information' betrays a gross and cardinal error: the belief or supposition that, in real life, a man can ever know whether or not his information is complete. Does there not come to us, upon the echo of this phrase, a faint ripple of Homeric laughter rolling down from Mount Olympus?

The only problems where information can be known to be complete are those of the pure mathematician, the class of problems, that is to say, which we expressly define as being entirely unrelated to the world of external observation. The econometrician is an applied mathematician: for him there never will and never can be information known to be complete. The forms of the functions which he has fitted, with the great labour and an ingenuity which we must all admire, to data supplied by observation, to data, that is to say, about the *past*, cannot be guaranteed to hold in the future. Economics is not physics, it is *psychics*, the study of men with all their capacity for learning and experimenting and inventing and imagining. We are bound to applaud the econometrician for seeking to put numbers in place of letters in the formulae supplied to him by the theoretical economist, but we must warn ourselves that these numbers are not eternal truths.

We have glanced at the nature of theories and considered its bearing on the ethics of employing them. Let us turn for a moment to their genesis. I have nothing to say of the unaccountable spark which fires new thoughts in a man's mind and gives him moments of almost painful excitement. I wish only to consider what happens to a theory when it becomes the common property of the colleagues and pupils of its originator to the third and fourth generation.

What are the merits and the dangers of an oral tradition? It is, I suppose, a sign of greatness in a University faculty or department, or at least a source and sign of prestige and evidence of time-honoured respectability, to be able to claim an oral tradition. The two great examples that spring to mind are those of Cambridge and Vienna. How does an oral tradition come into being? Surely it must be founded by some thinker of superlative achievement who is also an able and assiduous teacher. He must also, no doubt, be fortunate in his pupils, some of whom, if the tradition is to gain influence and momentum, must approach him in intellectual stature. This will assure the doctrine of a sufficiently prolonged vitality and widespread renown for it to become established and respectable, a staple of textbook diet and a yoke under which all future students will have to pass. But more is needed. If the master had no pupils, the doctrine would become part of the literature but would not hang in the sultry air of lecture rooms and impregnate the very furnishings of those where seminars are held. If he had only pupils of high originality the doctrine would be too rapidly transformed and developed to be properly called at any time a tradition. There must be a host of lesser men, able to receive and to impart the doctrine but not to improve it. These will give it stability of form, will make it gradually easier for pupils to understand, will rub off the rough edges of its original formulation, and polish it to become a presentable, civilized item of the teaching economist's stock-in-trade.

Which parts of this process are good and desirable, and which are bad? The bringing to bear on any doctrine of the searching light of able, leisured, well-informed common-room discussion, over many years and by a great number of perfectly disinterested men, must tend to discover weaknesses and elucidate assumptions, to ensure that the assumptions are mutually compatible, to elicit clear definitions and reveal ambiguities, to drive out infelicitous terminology, to refine, simplify, and clarify verbal expression. So much for what happens in the evening. *In vino veritas.* But what of the morning? Then the teachers must teach. They must present the doctrine as something worthy of being studied, grasped, learnt, and acted upon. They are no longer impartial critics but purveyors of a commodity. Moreover, they may feel themselves to be guardians of a tradition. They can permit themselves to offer pious emendations of classical texts, but not to embark on wholesale heresy. Thus the doctrine will tend to become fossilized. Some of its assumptions will cease to be *mere* assumptions in the modern, formal, non-committal sense and become Euclidean 'self-evident truths'. Finally it may be asked: 'why have an *oral* tradition?' Are men too lazy, or too much afraid of criticism, to put their thoughts on paper? Economists ought to be a guild of craftsmen, not a priesthood with mysteries.

I have one more topic to broach concerning the genesis of theories, and it is this: ought those of us who embrace economics as a life-work to feel entitled to specialize to no matter what extreme degree, to concentrate all our powers and affections upon one narrow tract or upon one single kind of work? Is it right that those whose inborn urge and aptitude is teaching (I mean teaching in the strict sense, the art and practice of imparting and eliciting ideas, of sowing thoughts and garnering enthusiasms, of implanting skills and shaping minds) should be encouraged to devote themselves wholly to this, or (to see the matter in a harsher light) should be so burdened with teaching duties that they have no time nor reserves of strength for anything else? Is it right that those whose bent is the gathering, sifting, and sorting of facts and their compilation in orderly array should never be compelled to lift their heads from their holerith cards and let their minds run free upon the philosophy of what they are doing ? Is it right that those whose strong magic is locked up in the hieroglyphs of confluence analysis and factor analysis should never be called upon to explain themselves to us others, so that in fact they would have to explain what they are doing to *themselves* ? Ought theory to compartmentalize itself so that the grower of business-cycle roses never looks over the wall at the vegetable marrows of monetary theory with their vast inflations, or peers sourly at the grapes in that hot-house, the theory of value ? I do not think these exclusivities (for this word I salute *The Times* fourth leader) can be good either morally or intellectually. Can it be good for our moral fibre to be always free to do just what we really enjoy doing ? Ought not teachers sometimes to be given an enforced rest and made to research, and ought not researchers to have thrust upon them at intervals an unwanted holiday and be made to teach ? But whether or not it is good for our characters and our self-respect to be faced sometimes with tasks that do not lie on our chosen track, with the unfamiliar and the formidable, I cannot doubt that it is good for the freshness and the richness of our minds. The professional expert tends to be a man who knows what cannot be done ; the amateur, free from such inhibitions, sometimes just goes and does it.

May I turn now, for the last section of my paper, to the question of how theory should be expressed. One aspect of this is the choice between literary, diagrammatic, and algebraic or analytical modes of thinking and of communication, but a frontal attack on this theme would require a book rather than a paragraph. I can only strike it a glancing blow in pursuing a rather different quarry.

It is the ambition of some economists to establish their subject's claim to be a science. However that may be, the *exposition* of an economic theory is an art, and in art, according to some experts, we are faced with a conflict and a competition between the claims of content and of form. How real is this opposition? Are form and content like guns and butter at present, the one needed to preserve the other but none the less compelled to elbow it out? What is the scarce resource for which they compete? Is it the writer's nervous energy and powers of concentration, or is it, more fundamentally, something to do with the structure of a sentence or the design of a chapter, which structure cannot (so it might be asserted) accommodate at one and the same time the thought in its purest essence and the adornment needed to give it grace and power of fascination ? Let us seek light on this from some analogies. An architect drew attention recently to a surprising contrast, which I will express in my own words in the form of a question: Which was the more beautiful, the Victorian age's imitation gothic buildings encrusted with ornaments and turrets, or its utilitarian suspension-bridges with their cobweb strength ? The *content*, so to speak, of a steel bridge is its strength. What gives it that strength is nothing other than its form. In pure mathematics is it not true that content and form are one ?

Economics is essentially a mathematical subject, for it treats by logic of the relations between quantities. I am far from suggesting that its arguments can only be handled by means of a formal notation using the symbols of algebra or the calculus. Economic theory, mathematical by its very nature, can yet often be best expressed in words. But the verbal statements must then strive to compete, in exactness, lucidity, and economy, with the symbolic statements that could replace them. For the verbal statements too (can we not argue ?) meaning and form are inseparable.

I have listed exactness, lucidity, and economy as the first essentials of expository prose. I do, indeed, think that these three qualities are the ones we ought most to strive for, seeking precision first of all since here in particular the oneness of form and content must reside. A thought can have no *public* existence save in virtue of the way it is expressed. Some of us may think primarily in mental images or form-phantasms, we may possess the power to make the arcs and ogives of our diagrams curl, shift and unbend, shrink and expand, in a verbal silence in the mind, arguing with ourselves purely by means of a visual imagination. But to convey these thoughts to others we must resort in part at least to words, and the shape of our sentences will be taken for the shape of our thoughts. To convey these thoughts at all, however, to get anything across, we must be lucid. People sometimes speak as though precision and clarity were one and the same. This is a mistake. The painful contortions of legal phraseology are necessary and justified because only thus can the framers of laws say exactly that which they mean. These strivings for exactness make the statute book unintelligible to any but a lawyer. Lawyers, however, are driven to these extremities because they are deprived of one powerful device which the theorist can call in aid: *abstraction*. The lawyer must expect to have his meanings 'twisted by knaves to make a trap for fools'. He cannot simplify and select the objects of his discourse by means of definitions. He cannot draw up the rules of his game before he consents to play it. For the theorist it is different. The things referred to in his theories are not men and women of flesh and blood, unsimplified, passionate, cunning, mercurial, devious, incalculable, but are mere chess pieces, their possible moves and powers exactly known. To be both clear and precise at the same time is possible for the theorist, and to fall short in this is to be second-rate. Thirdly, there is economy. The good sentence contains not a wasted word. By this I do not mean that a word should be left out if *nearly* the same meaning could be expressed without it. The subtlest nuances, the most impalpable distinctions, are within the theorist's rights, and he must not be accused of prolixity merely because he has elected to bind elusive thoughts with many verbal strands. Nor need we think that economical prose is necessarily plodding and flat-footed. The athlete's leanness is one secret of his speed.

There is a well-known saying that 'knowledge is power'. It would be at least as true to say that 'language is power'. It is not only the professional spell-binders, the politicians and dictators, the leader-writers, the novelists, the poets, priests, and prophets, for whom a silver tongue is the indispensable vehicle of their magic. We also, humble economists, working, as some think, in the mere kitchen of the palace of culture, are entirely dependent on the power to compress our thoughts into the mould of words.

Have I given you the impression in all this that I think of the economist as a mere dabbler in ideas remote from the realities of life, a spinner of fine webs of thought that break at a touch, a player of meaningless games with symbols, a verbal juggler, and an oracle of more than Delphic ambivalence and obscurity? I did not mean to. The great economists have been moved as surely by a hunger for truth as any natural scientist. Pure curiosity, the desire to know for the sake of knowing, the sheer inner need to understand, is what has impelled them. Like the philosophers, they have been subject to their temptations. They have sometimes fallen in love like Pygmalion with the beauty of their own creations, and allowed elegance the ascendancy over realism. Sometimes they have succumbed to the lure of paradox and made things needlessly difficult in expression. Some economists, lesser than the greatest, have been dazzled by the flash and glitter of their own algebraic swords as they whirled them in the ritual dance of formal analysis. Yet on occasion these sharp tools alone could cleave the Gordian knot, and the list of the greatest economists includes a high proportion who have in some degree been also mathematicians: Cournot, Marshall, Wicksell, Pareto, Edgeworth, Keynes, and Irving Fisher are enough to tell us this.

And finally, what of the economist's right or duty to offer counsel in the practical contingencies of the nation's life? Being sure that he does not know everything, being certain only that nothing is certain, ought he to be silent? The class of economists are like a ship's crew who have been wrecked in a swirling tide-race. Often a man will hear nothing but the roar of the waters in his ears, see nothing but the dim green light. But as he strikes out his head will come sometimes well above water, where for the moment he can see clear about him. At that moment he has the right to shout directions to his fellows, to point the way to safety, even though he may feel sure that next moment he will be again submerged and may then doubt whether after all he has his bearings.

UNIVERSITY OF LIVERPOOL.

Evolutions of Thought in Economics

The evolution of a body of theory can be traced, I think, by means of the questions which, from time to time, it deems important or the essential frame of premises which it accepts. The choice of questions to be penetrated and the scheme-of-things to be assumed will be guided by the history which is being, and has lately been, experienced. The incentive for theory-making is the need to have one's mind at rest. To have some conception of how things hang together is re-assuring. Thus those questions will seem important which cause concern or apprehension. If things seem to have gone wrong, or if the visible state of affairs is different from what had been looked for, explanations will be sought and sequels imagined and their possibility tested in thought. The answers which are suggested for these formulated and unfamiliar questions will have to rest, however, on answers already tacitly accepted to older questions, perhaps more fundamental and even eternal, which few people actively consider, which are present only to especially restless and probing minds. In some historical eras, such basic questions are more easily forgotten than in others. History, that is to say, experience which we ourselves have passed through or which others have recorded, or which we can reconstruct from traces presently before our eyes, is the source of our questions whether of the newly-emerged and pressing kind or of the kind which express the ever-present frame of human existence.

The century which followed the Napoleonic war now seems an extraordinary and almost unique episode in the history of the world. Wars were rare, locally circumscribed, and short. In England, money retained unchanged, or even increased, its purchasing power. There were great technological advances, but they were not, perhaps, too frequent to be accommodated by the change of generations. This tranquil age (as we may call it in comparison with our own) gave to economic affairs some of the constancy or consistency of behaviour seen in the natural world. That natural world could be described by systems of scientific "laws". It could be seen as a vast, steadily work-ing, understandable machine. It was tempting and reasonable to suppose that a similar system of principles could be conceived or discovered for the world of business. This had indeed been the vision of economists from the outset. Quesnay's *Tableau Economique* en-compassed the whole world of production and exchange, illustrated the "division of labour", and showed society as an *organism*, an entity in which the whole depended on each part and each part depended on the whole. Quesnay was physician to Louis XV, and was also in-terested in the principles of farming. Why should not the body politic, human society, find its analogue in the body of flesh and blood? In our day Quesnay's eighteenth century model has been succintly re-expressed in terms of Leontief's input-output analysis.

The essential notion of Quesnay's *Tableau* was the specialisation of different groups of people to different tasks or roles, and the conse-quent need for these groups to exchange their services or their pro-ducts. But a great question was left unanswered, or even unasked. How did it come about that goods and services, in their various kinds, exchanged for each other in particular quantities? This question took on a particular form or application, in which it appeared as the most important and, perhaps we may say, as the most sensitive and emo-tive of all economic questions. For if we can explain why a particular number of hours of some kind of work, or of the service of some natural resource or some machine, exchanges for particular quantities of the means of subsistence or enjoyment, we are on the way to explain why the total annual produce of a society is shared in such and such proportions amongst various groups of its members. This latter question, that of income distribution, is intimately linked with that of the exchange rates, the *prices*, of goods and services in terms of each other.

The question of income distribution, the question how a particu-lar sharing of the total produce comes about, or the question of the principle on which that sharing ought to be made, is the one which loomed largest in the minds of many early economists and may be said, perhaps, to loom largest for ourselves. For the purpose and incentive of every kind of business, every activity of production and exchange, is acquisition, the gaining of the means of survival, comfort and enjoyment. And it is needless to argue that the question how much can be acquired, in this way or that, is an unremitting pre-occupation. Towards the end of the nineteenth century, the puzzle of income distribution seemed at last to find an incisive anwer. The means of that answer was peculiarly interesting. It was an application of the differential calculus, an application which economists call the method of small increments, or the marginal principle. It says that action of a particular kind will be carried to that pitch or scale where a small further step would bring more loss than gain of satisfaction, more drawback than advantage. For example, a house-wife will do best for her family by so distributing the weekly expenditure over various goods that it makes little difference to the family's general comfort whether the final florin goes on tea, butter or electricity, and a bread-winner will prefer such weekly hours of work that an extra hour would tire him more than the proceeds would be worth. When the yearly number of man-hours, of acre-hours and of machine-hours of various kinds are each of them such that one extra unit would only just increase the yearly product by enough to pay its wage, then, if the list of those "factors of production" is complete, and if each of the quantities employed of them is finely sub-divisible, it can be shown that if, for each kind of factor, we multiply its employed number of units by its wage per unit, and add together the resulting total wage bills, the result of this summation will be equal to the total yearly produce. This theorem, which as a mathematical abstraction is due to Euler, provided the clinching element and crowning triumph of the Theory of Value and Distribution, which explained, on a single and simple principle, the prices of goods and services in terms of each other, the mode of allocation of quantities of each means of production to this and that industry, and the mode of sharing the total annual produce of all industries amongst the providers of these means. One further assumption was recognised as needful in order to validate this conception. Perfect competition, so great a multiplicity of such small firms in each industry that no one firm by any change of output within its capacity can affect the price, ensures that an industry's output can be measured indifferently either in physical volume or in value. By this assumption the theoretician is absolved from having to make two theories of distribution, one for a money-using and one for a non-money using economy. When thus completed, it is not surprising that a body of thought of such majestic compass and omnicompetent application, exhibiting such a pervasive unity and simplicity of principle and, in consequence, such arresting intellectual beauty, should have seemed to close the door upon all questions and leave only minor refinements still to be made. It is not even surprising that the economic earthquakes of our century, the sweeping away of the orderly and stable Victorian world, the immense accelerations of technological change and the bewilderment of administrators in face of these events, should in large measure have left the edifice of neo-classical value-theory still standing in so many able minds. That edifice, the conception of General Equilibrium, the expression and effect of general prereconciliation of choices of action, still seems to many the ideal illuminator, the lamp which we need only refine still further and make yet more precise and subtle, for its rays to penetrate everywhere into all corners of our field. The situation is a strange one. The unshakable citadel seems to have become a refuge, waiting for the storm to subside, claiming still a basic validity, garrisoned still by the majority of the profession of economics. Yet even in the nineteenth century, one of the chief architects of the "marginalist" theory of value insisted on its difficulties and deceptions.

In his *Principles of Economics* Alfred Marshall sought, by observing the evolution of English productive and commercial society during a particular historical era, to arrive at some laws of such evolution that should be general and permanent in some degree. It was, he said, the nature and mode of this unending process which economists ought to be concerned with: "The main concern of economics is thus with human beings who are impelled, for good and evil, to change and progress. Fragmentary statical hypotheses are used as temporary auxiliares to dynamical — or rather biological — conceptions: but the central idea of economics, even when its Foundations alone are under discussion, must be that of living force and movement" (Preface to the eighth edition, page XV). With this policy, Marshall founded a Cambridge tradition in economics. Marshall himself was a Wrangler (First Class Honours man) in the Cambridge Mathematical Tripos, so were Ralph Hawtrey and Maynard Keynes. Yet all three of these keen minds cast their thoughts essentially in literary form, all three were lucid, lively and engaging writers who threw a rich mantle of description and suggestion over the bony frame of logic; so did F.Y. Edgeworth and Denis Robertson. Keynes (until the *General Theory*) leads his reader on with a seductive ease of exposition. Denis Robertson showed how economics could be presented with, it has been said, "a heaven-sent lightness of touch". Marshall's own work is pervaded by a deep humane idealism. He drew upon the thought of philosophers, for example, Hegel, Comte and Herbert Spencer. His width of sympathy and open mind exposed him sometimes to a charge of lack of rigour. "Jevons carved in stone, Marshall knitted in wool" Keynes said. It is true that Marshall's urge to unify and nucleify ideas sometimes led him to endow his special terms with a skein of different meanings. The Principle of Continuity set forth in the Preface of the first edition of the *Principles* refers not only to many types of case where it may be tempting, but is not justifiable, to make sharp distinctions between categories, but covers also the mathematical notion of continuously variable quantities and functions. The two meanings which Marshall thus gives to "continuity" seem quite distinct.

Marshall knew that the economic world is one. So is the earth's atmosphere. Yet we know that the atmosphere is always in flux, its effects take time to develop their power and transmit themselves about the earth. Marshall said that time "is the centre of the chief difficulty of almost every economic problem". He spoke frequently of the business man as being impelled and guided in action by what he *expects*. To make the idea of expectation central to the theory of economic action, or the theory of action in the most general sense, is to recognise that time is not a mere space or dimension, it is not a range of locations all of them equally capable of being visited and inspected. Time-to-come is the undiscovered country. Marshall's relatively tranquil era did not often subject the business man to such upheavals as our century has seen: the wiping-out of the value of currencies, the unemployment in Western countries of tens of millions of people, social and political turmoil and undreamt-of technological change. Marshall, therefore, did not greatly emphasise the business man's problem of uncertainty. He refers to the possibility of the capital invested in a business being entirely lost, he speaks continually of the business man's essential task of estimating the costs of production of specific goods and the price which these goods may eventually fetch. The uncertainties of business are implicit in his account, but they are not given high explicit prominence. Yet his book is an account of business as an aspect of life, of the strenuous, exacting human predicament, of the unremitting need for attention, calculation, adaptation. In this his book differs essentially from those which describe an ultimate, or a timeless, state of universal perfect adjustment of everything to everything else. The economic world is one, but to describe it as a general equilibrium does not explain its character of a channel for the surging current of history.

Keynes's stricture on Marshall's style of reasoning does not do justice to the intractable and elusive task which Marshall had set himself. Marshall was a close observer of an evolving industrial and social scene. He sought to draw from this segment of living and contemporary history an insight into the nature and operation of the process of history itself in its economic aspects, the permanent and basic social physiology which it manifested. It is a typical irony of human experience that Keynes himself came to recognise our essential, irremediable ignorance of the content of time-to-come, in all but a very limited range of respects, as the prime character of the business man's environment. Marshall was an exact reasoner where exactness was possible. He was an early user in economic theory of what he called "the methods of the science of small increments", the differential calculus, and had a great admiration for the pioneer of that method in economics, Augustin Cournot, whose great classic book appeared in 1838. Marshall's recommended and adopted policy of thought in economics, his judgement of what is possible in the study of human affairs, is exceedingly interesting in itself. "The economist needs the three great intellectual faculties, perception, imagination and reason: and most of all he needs imagination, to put him on the track of those causes of visible events which are remote or lie below the surface, and of those effects of visible causes, which are remote or lie below the surface". "His main reliance must be on disciplined imagination". (Book I, Chapter iv of the first edition).

A timeless system of general pre-reconciliation of choices has no use for money. The goods and services to be exchanged are things wanted for their own sake, not for the sake of a further and subsequent exchange into something else. There will be no opportunity for further exchanges, and no need for them, for pre-reconciliation of choices enables each participant to obtain that selection of quantities of goods and services which he prefers above all others that he could obtain by free agreement with other participants, given his and their tastes and endowments. It is in a world where we look forward to time-to-come that we need money. Money enables a seller to put off deciding what specific goods, useful in themselves and having particular qualities and capacities (goods *proper*) he will accept in exchange for what he gives. Money is sometimes called a store of value, but value can be stored, conveyed through calendar time, by means of any durable valuable goods. It is sometimes called a medium of exchange. But a *medium* of exchange is only needed because we do not know what there is to be had and where to get it. Money is a medium of *deferment* and of *search*. The shopper who sets out for the market with her full purse is a searcher. Money is needed because at every calendar moment which presents itself, which is the momentary *present*, there is for each of us a lack of knowledge, a lack which, *within that moment*, is irremediable. Keynes defines three motives for holding a stock of money (instead, let us say, of a stock of houses, trees, wine or beautiful paintings). They were the transactions motive, where money is held because of an awareness that payments of indefinite destination and date will soon have to be made; the precautionary motive(but precautions are provisions against unknown contingencies); and the speculative motive, where it is feared that if goods proper, or even a borrower's bonds, were held, these assets might decline in value in terms of ready cash. Any durable goods could serve as a reserve against contingencies, were it not for the speculative danger of a loss of value. The nature and usefulness of money are intimately bound up with the awareness of a lack of knowledge. The world where money is held in stock is the world of uncertainty, the world where we know there is time-to-come but cannot know what it will bring. Those theoreticians who studied a system of universal fully-informed pre-reconciliation of choices, a necessarily timeless world of complete and perfect relevant knowledge, were able, and were obliged, to exclude money from their conception.

The presence and importance of money in the economic scene was, of course, unquestionable. Money served as the unit of account to render the values of all goods capable of immediate mutual comparison. However, the money actually represented by tangible notes or visible book-entries had a life of its own, and this life was described by some writers in a theory separated from that of value. The account thus given of money was, as it were, *hydraulic*. Money moved about, not only in measurable quantities per unit of time, but even, as it were, in labelled consignments which had to pass from one ownership to another in order to perform their service and have their effect. The Quantity Theory of money was encapsulated by Irving Fisher in a formula, $MV = PT$, which, though itself a truism, was capable of yielding insights when some one or other extra condition was assumed. Let us suppose that the only currency in use in some closed economy is banknotes each constituting one unit of money. And suppose there is a law that every recipient of any banknote must at once put his dated signature on the back. Then let M stand for the number (supposedly constant) of banknotes in existence at all dates during some year, (the *money stock*). Let F stand for the total number of signatures on all the banknotes taken together, whose dates fall within that year. (F is then the money flow). Let V stand for F divided by M. V is thus the *velocity of circulation of money*. Let T be the number of parcels of goods changing hands during the year, and let P be the total value of all these parcels divided by their number, so that P is the average value of a parcel. Then the formula MV = PT merely says that the annual value of banknotes paid for goods is identically (i.e. necessarily and by the meaning of terms) equal to the annual value of goods given in exchange for banknotes. Let us now suppose, for example, that M is doubled, while V and T remain unchanged. Then P must have doubled. Or if, for example, V declines while M and T remain constant, P must decline. The obviousness of these conclusions, and the need to ensure that the goods bought with the money-flow MV include all those, and only those, listed under T, do not render the conclusions worthless. But there is an aspect of the Fisher formula which is in essential and sharp contrast with the propositions of value theory. The latter refer directly to the choices and acts of human individuals. The Fisher formula says nothing explicitly about human deliberative conduct. It is, in ostensible meaning, purely mechanical.

The Quantity Theory of Money, which seeks to explain how the average price of goods in general is raised or lowered in comparison with its level at some "base-date" in the past, can be given a form which shows this average (comparative) price level as influenced by human taste and judgement. The "Cambridge" version of the Quantity Theory suggests that an individual, a firm or a corporate authority will pursue some preferred ratio between the flow of money which, as cash receipts and outlays, passes through its hands, on one hand, and the stock of money which it usually keeps in readiness, on the other. The method of this pursuit most readily open to it may be to regulate the size of its outlay. A reduction of the outflow will not necessarily at once reduce the inflow, and thus a larger stock can be built up. Alternatively the individual or firm may be able to borrow extra money, but this recourse will, in the aggregate over all individuals and firms, ultimately encounter a limitation of the banking system's power or willingness to increase the total of its outstanding loans. The linkage between the aggregate stock and the aggregate flow of money can be expressed as a target ratio between these two, in the sense that if all individual and corporate holders of money stocks achieved their own preferred ratios of stock to flow, this target would be the result in the aggregate. We can write $M = kY$, where M is the aggregate of the money stocks held by individuals, etcetera, Y is their aggregate cash flow, and k is the target ratio. This theory (which is capable of many variant refinements) is much closer than the Fisher formula to the reasonings employed by value theory. But it is not wholly at one with them. Perhaps in any subject matter the most potent means of clarification is to formulate some direct question. What question ought to be asked by the monetary theorist? In a remarkable article in *Economica* of 1935, called "A Suggestion for Simplifying the Theory of Money" Sir John Hicks wrote as follows: "What has to be explained is the decision to hold assets in the form of barren money, rather than of interest — or profit-yielding securities. So long as rates of interest are positive, the decision to hold money rather than lend it, or use it to pay off old debts, is apparently an unprofitable one. This, as I see it, is really the central issue in the theory of money". The seed of the answer, Hicks finds, is already present in Keynes's *Treatise on Money*, where the possibility of a preference on the part of some asset-owners for holding bank deposits rather than securities is explained by their bearishness, that is, their fear that the prices of securities may be about to decline in terms of money. This is the beginning of the notion of liquidity-preference. Of the three motives which Keynes discerns for it, it is the transactions-motive, the need to have ready money available in case of impending contingent out-payments, that Hicks especially contributes to. He points out that lending or investing money involves expense and trouble, and that if the amount to be lent is small and the time before it may be needed is short, that trouble and expense will not be sufficiently compensated by the interest, in absolute amount, which will be earned. Keynes had offered no analysis of the transactions-motive, presumably deeming it self-evident. His momentous suggestion was the speculative motive, the true bearishness, the real and massive source of liquidity-preference.

The transformation brought about in economic theory by Lord Keynes was the effect of a bold, brilliant and unfettered intellect, stirred by cataclysmic events and projected into other minds by an electric personality. That personality could shock as well as enchant, it was often used to shatter the complacent reliance on received ideas which seemed to him to be choking the right path of history-in-the-making. He was eager to influence events, but also eager to be the author of novelty and excitement in ideas. In 1921 his *Treatise on Probability*, adopting a suggestion of Leibniz, sought to make probability a branch of logic instead of a branch of actuarial arithmetic. Was probability a key idea for economics? The human predicament which Keynes's probability sought to cope with was, in the end, recognised by him to be unsolvable. It is the dilemma of the human essential, unresolvable condition, that men's knowledge concerns the past, but their decisions, their choices of action and policy, are what create the future. In the final encapsulation of his theory of employment, an article in the *Quarterly Journal of Economics* of February, 1937 ("The General Theory of Unemployment"), he rejected in a few incisive and contemptuous lines the notion that business in its aspect of enterprise and the creation of new productive facilities can be the child of reason fully-informed, of the logical use of sufficient data. In a world of certainty, *enterprise* would be needless and impossible. Let us go beyond Keynes's own statements and say that the world of freedom of origination and the world of calculated certainty clash in essential, fundamental exclusion of each other. If we live in one, we cannot live in the other.

If one term more than any other unites the variant strands of Keynes's thought, it is *liquidity-preference*. The source of this desire is the very Scheme of Things itself, the elemental unknowledge of the content of time-to-come. Men want to have means and powers of action; but they want those means to be protean and apt to all contingencies, the contingencies of a world in a great measure composed of such. Except when it is burning up in a fire of inflation, money is the most liquid of resources. Even to lend it, even when the borrower's honesty and ultimate solvency are trusted to the last degree, involves a danger, a possibility of loss. For when he signs a bond, the borrower promises to pay stated sums at stated dates. If the lender, at some date during the period of those dates, should find himself needing the money he has lent, he cannot claim it from the borrower. He can only sell his bond to a third party. At what price? At the moment when he lends, he cannot know. Nor can he know that the emergency or opportunity which calls for ready money will not arise. To induce a lender to accept this danger, he must be compensated, and the compensation is the interest-rate, the excess of the borrower's promised deferred payments over the sum initially lent to him. In this manner of viewing the act of lending, I am again going beyond Keynes, but not beyond the essence of the speculative motive for holding bank-deposits, ready cash, rather than bonds or investments, unless those securities are to be had at a price low enough to offer good hope of an impending rise.

In liquidity-preference, Keynes drew from the real business scene a suggestion indispensable to his theory of employment. That theory rested on the supposition that the sum which business men in a broad sense intend in the aggregate to spend in some named interval on improving or extending their productive facilities can differ from the sum which, in the aggregate, people at large intend to save in that same interval out of their incomes. But according to prevalent ideas at the time when he was writing, the rate of interest was the price which brought those two sums, investment in equipment on one hand and saving on the other, into equality. If the rate of interest did perform this role and was itself thus determined, how could intended investment and intended saving differ from each other? By ascribing the cause and determination of interest to liquidity-preference instead of to the task of equilibrating saving and investment, Keynes released those two variables from mutual dependence and showed how aggregate effective demand for products of all sorts could fall short of their full-employment supply.

Liquidity-preference is an expression of uncertainty, of the consciousness of unknowledge of history-to-come. That consciousness of unknowledge is the ultimate and simple basis of Keynes's explanation of how involuntary unemployment can exist in face of a supposed tendency for men to pre-reconcile their choices and thus go as far as they can to make them rational. The theory of value, which before Keynes was the core of economic theory, says that a man can always gain all the employment he desires by reducing low enough his claimed share of the product he helps to make. Each extra man of his kind of skill which the employing firm might engage will increase its output (its weekly quantity produced) of the product, but as we pass in review a series of possible numbers of such men that it might employ, these suppositious numbers differing from each other by one man, the differences made to the output, as we go up the steps of the series, will be smaller and smaller. We also suppose that whatever wage, in terms of product, is paid to one employed man, is paid to all. There will be some number of men such that the difference made to the output by one extra man would be equal to the wage paid to each of them. That is the number which it will best pay the firm to employ.

This account of the matter, on its own terms, is valid so long as we assume *that wages are paid in product*. If we suppose them paid in money, all is changed.

The firm must then pay wages in money while the product is in course of being made, and subsequently sell the product. How can it know whether the product which will emerge will sell for enough to pay the related wages? In times of depressed business, every addition to the inventory of product awaiting sale may require a reduction of the price per unit which can be charged. The difference *in terms of money value* which the presence or absence of one man makes may be zero, or negative. Above all, it is *unknown* when the decision to engage an extra man must be taken, or rejected.

Keynes's theory of employment was summarised by himself with devastating force and effect in his article in the *Quarterly Journal of Economics*. In its ultimate astonishing simplicity, it says that unless everything that can be produced at full employment is bought with the income represented by that flow of production, enterprisers, employers, will be left with unsold goods, undesired stocks of products, and will cut down their output and, to that end, the employment that they give. Income-receivers as such, the employed and the employers, do not wish to consume the whole of their money incomes, but save some of it. This desired saving would, at full employment, leave a gap between income and expenditure, that is to say, between the quantity of goods produced in a given interval and the quantity willingly acquired in that interval. This gap must be filled, if full employment is to be tolerable to the employers, by those employers' own expenditure on goods not for consumption but for improvement and extension of productive facilities. Desired saving must be matched by desired enterprise — investment, at any level of employment and output which is to be capable of persisting. But to invest in productive equipment is to be enterprising, enterprise is a march into the undiscovered country, and employers' nerves can fail. This is the Keynesian theory of employment, grounded in the basic Scheme of Things and the nature of mankind.

Much else was done in the 1920's and the 1930's besides the creation of a theory of employment. Piero Sraffa revealed an internal contradiction in the notion of perfect competition. His famous article of 1926 in the *Economic Journal* revived a problem which had occupied Augustin Cournot in his classic *Recherches sur les principes mathématiques de la théorie des richesses* of 1838, and had been dealt with by Marshall in his *Principles*. The result was a theory of mono-polistic, or imperfect competition, chiefly the work of Sir Roy Harrod, Edward Chamberlin and Joan Robinson. The Austrian (Böhm-Bawerk's) theory of capital was wrought afresh by Professor Hayek. In a brilliant fusing of the real industrial organism pictured as a whole, its statistical description, and the tracing of the ripples which are propagated through this organism by a change in the pattern of consumers' demand, using a tool of matrix algebra, Wassily Leontief invented input-output analysis, to which the electronic computer has brought immense possibilities of practical application. Sir Roy Harrod gave in the last of those years a first sketch of a theory of growth based on the notion of the capital-to-output ratio, and this same conception was invented, simultaneously and independently, by Evsey Domar. Those were years of brilliant theoretical fertility, still expressed in literary forms rich with suggestive subtlety and depth.

Aldeburgh

                                        G.L.S. Shackle

WHAT MAKES AN ECONOMIST?

TO BE A complete economist, a man need only be
a mathematician, a philosopher, a psychologist, an
anthropologist, a historian, a geographer, and a
student of politics; a master of prose exposition; and a
man of the world with experience of practical business
and finance, an understanding of the problems of
administration, and a good knowledge of four or five
foreign languages. All this in addition, of course, to
familiarity with the economic literature itself. This
list should, I think, dispose at once of the idea that
there are, or ever have been, any complete economists,
and we can proceed to the practical question of what
arrangements are likely to provide us with men who
will feel not wholly confounded when an important
economic decision confronts them.

Thoroughness in attacking this problem requires us,
I think, to start by considering the nature of theoretical
knowledge in general, then the character and the
scope of economic theory in particular. Having seen
what kind of intellectual tasks the economist is required to perform with what material, we can hope to
discern the kind of aptitudes and attainments that
will give a schoolboy or girl the promise of doing well
in economics, and advise his schoolmaster about what
the pupil should do with his years in the VIth Form at
school if he decides thus early to look forward to a
university degree in economics. To the end of
persuading some boys and girls of high ability to look
at this possibility, we can show what claims economics
can make as a cultivation of the mind and as a background for the administrator and the statesman. And
at last we can ask what ingredients the University
itself should pour into the mould thus provided by
nature and the schoolmaster.

The business of creating theoretical knowledge consists in describing structures which repeat themselves. Here I use the word *structure* to name the very essence of all knowledge beyond the mere memory of direct impressions from our surroundings. It is our common experience that such impressions are classifiable. To each class we give a name, and then we arrange these names in patterns, linguistic, geometrical, pictorial, and so on, to indicate that impressions belonging to certain classes occur, in some sense, 'together', in logical, spatial, or temporal-sequential association. The suggestion that some particular associations are repetitive or, we may say, invariant, is called a law or a theory. The paleontologist finds a bone of a certain shape, and his theory tells him that search in the locality will reward him with other bones, of whose sizes and shapes he has a mental image. Here we have structure in a very concrete and obvious form, that of a skeleton. The chemist weighs the water displaced by a piece of some solid, then weighs this piece. The ratio of the two numbers he gets puts him in mind of a whole group of impressions of various classes, colour, softness, ease of melting, and so on, suggested by a theory summed up in the word 'lead'. The medical man notes his own headache and the dryness of his skin, and decides that it will be five days before he can work again: influenza is his name for a structure of impressions involving duration. I need not give more examples. We manage our lives on the assumption that under the infinitely various and changeful combinations of particular sights, sounds, scents, savours, and sensations there is a dependable repetitiveness. This kind of invariance of structure is the subject-matter and necessary pre-supposition of all theory.

You will have noticed that, if what I say is true, the materials which compose these structures are words, symbols, or images, and not things which nature gives

2

us direct and ready-made. Some of these words are the names of classes of our impressions of nature, such as length, weight, colour; or of crystallised patterns of such impressions, such as gold, flame, man. Some of them are the names not of patterns of receivable impressions but of ghosts or fictions which play a somewhat analogous part in our thinking; gravity and aether for the physicist, gene for the biologist, and so on. Lastly some words are names of different ways in which our impressions of nature, or our constructs from those impressions, can be *related*, the ideas of spatial or temporal relative location, of equality or of greater than or less than, of logical equivalence or definition, and perhaps, more hazardously and elusively, of cause and effect. The phenomena, the classes or the patterns of impressions, having been distinguished, and the possible relations between them conceived, how do we know what relations to postulate between given phenomena? How are the essential shapes of our theoretical structures determined? From the infinite variety of possible shapes the choosing of a few to be tried and used is an act of imaginative and even artistic commitment of a kind which is as near as mortal man can get to ultimate creation.

Some of us may recall the words with which Victorian children were admonished to tell the truth:

> Oh what a tangled web we weave
> When first we practise to deceive.

Any statement, whether we believe it to be true or false, carries implications far beyond what it explicitly says. What it says in so many words may not obviously conflict with some other statement which we accept. But when one or other of these statements is unravelled and interpreted and allowed as it were to grow from the acorn to the oak, so that some of what is latent in it is displayed, then we may find that the two statements in fact contradict each other. When we draw consequences from a set of premises we add nothing

3

to what is already in the premises but merely make what is there more visible and thus easier to compare with other statements. If the agreement is unsatisfactory, we may decide to modify our premises and see, by drawing out the fresh consequences that our new assumptions yield, whether the coherence of our whole system of statements is thereby improved. Thus we seek progressively to satisfy one criterion of a good theory. Now this work of spreading out the content of a statement, of drawing out inferences from a set of premises, is the whole business of logic or mathematics. It is, as we all know, in its higher flights a business demanding very special aptitudes and rare kinds of insight, as well as intensive practice and much knowledge of certain stylised or crystallised forms of thinking, the formal mathematical methods which relieve our memories of part of the weight of long concatenations of argument. This exploration and mutual confrontation of hypotheses is as much a part of theory-making as the invention of the explicit hypotheses themselves.

The building-up of a body of theoretical knowledge calls then for two kinds of intellectual capacity and effort. One of these is imaginative or as we may say creatively selective, and thus creative in a primary and radical sense; the other is analytical or logical, and thus creative only in a secondary, a corrective or completive sense. There is no doubt in my mind that the majority of highly gifted men are specially endowed in one or other of these ways and not in both; when a man has both powers in superlative degree we have an Einstein or a Keynes. The only point I would make here is that we must not suppose analytical power alone is sufficient to make a great theorist. Many men have studied economics whose capacity for handling mathematical tools was by no means inferior to that of Keynes; but they did not produce the Keynesian revolution.

4

From this glance at the nature of theoretical knowledge in general let me pass to the character of economics in particular.

Explanation is the relating of the unfamiliar to the familiar. The essence and prime purpose of theory or explanation is to show that a large collection of seemingly diverse and unrelated appearances is in truth merely a large number of different views of the same thing, and that thing itself from some viewpoints familiar. Thus, explanation seeks in a sense to reduce the mysterious to the prosaic, and diversity to unity. Now science as a whole will never be able to start its explanations from nothing and carry them through the whole of human experience. A part of that experience must be treated as belonging so essentially to the very nature of human consciousness that men feel no need for any truth interior to these direct intuitions. Science as a unity must of course seek the minimum such basis and on it build up all else step by connected step into a coherent picture of the whole cosmos and of human life. But it would plainly defeat the whole purpose of the division of science into distinct disciplines, if each of these attempted to go right down to the minimum intuitional basis. The chemist assumes that you know what he means by weight and volume, and for an explanation of these refers you to the physicist. The biologist assumes that you know what he means by carbon, hydrogen, and oxygen, and for an explanation of these refers you to the chemist. The economist assumes that you know what he means by hunger and by fertility, and for an explantion of these refers you to the biologist. So there arises the question of the best place for the frontier between one discipline and each of the others, and this is peculiarly troublesome in the case of economics.

Some of you may remember a verse by Edward Clerihew Bentley which explains the difference between geography and biography:

5

Geography (it says) is about maps
But biography is about chaps.

I doubt whether a geographer would accept the suggestion here that geography is not a human science; it is very largely concerned with human activities. But far more so is economics. Economics is entirely concerned with men's doings and arrangements, their wants and their means of satisfying them, their hopes and fears, beliefs, ambitions, conflicts of interest, their valuations and decisions, their governments and their material well-being. Economics emphatically is about chaps.

Many men have attempted to say in a sentence or a paragraph what economics is about; it is better, in my view, to begin by saying that economics is about human nature, human conduct, and human institutions, and then to say which parts of this huge field the economist is willing to leave to others. Nevertheless he must set up his flag at some particular spot in order to show the kind of ground he wishes to regard as his own; and I think there is still good reason for saying that this spot must be the market-place. Men's conduct and decisions can be influenced in many ways; by threats of violence or duress, by the firing of their spirit and imagination by rhetoric or by example, by the preacher's eloquence and the teacher's toil, or by the blandishments of lovers; but the simplest and most reliable, the commonest and the easiest is to offer them something *in exchange* for what they are required to give or do; and the market-place, in the wide and rather abstract sense in which, of course, I am now using this word, is where exchanges of all kinds take place.

It is by coming together in the market-place that men are able to be *economical*, in the ordinary sense of that word. For it is there that they can find out what other men are most keenly anxious to obtain. If by a *given* sacrifice of ease and leisure I can produce any one of half-a-dozen different things, I shall do best

6

for myself by producing the one that other men most eagerly desire; for that thing, of all the half-dozen, will elicit from them the most effort and sacrifice on my behalf; and thus by studying their interest I shall serve my own, and get the most possible satisfaction in return for a specified amount of effort; and that is precisely what we mean by 'economy'.

If this market mechanism plays a less predominant part to-day than it did forty years ago in answering the questions: How much work of this kind and of that shall be done? How much shall be produced of this stuff and of that? and: In what proportions shall each of these products be shared out amongst those who contributed in one way or another to their making? yet even to-day in western countries it does most of the work of answering those questions, which express between them the core of what is agreed to be the subject-matter of economics. If, then, the economist takes up his stand in the market-place, he is correctly indicating where his interests start from. But they will lead him far afield. What he is watching there is human conduct, and questions will arise in his mind about human motives and human nature. Economists have sometimes come to believe that they can get little help, in understanding the economic aspect of men's actions, from the psychologist. Such a feeling cries out for the most searching examination, since it is on the face of it absurd. This attitude has indeed, in my view, been rendered completely untenable by the development of economic theory itself in the past 20 years. I do not suggest that the fault is all on the side of the economist. Whether the psychologists can meet our needs I am not yet sure, but that we have needs that they ought to meet I am quite certain. Economics is concerned, solely concerned, with some of the manifestations of human nature, and psychology is the science of human nature. Somewhere at the heart of this estrangement there is a mistake which we

7

must try to find. At any rate it is plain that on one side economics has a frontier with psychology, or rather, that there lies between them a no-man's-land crying out to be explored and appropriated, that we might call economic psychics. Here, in my view, interest should centre on the workings of the individual mind rather than on the total behaviour of huge human aggregates. We need, for example, to understand the processes of forming expectations and making decisions. The famous question of the form of the Keynesian consumption-function rests upon foundations of individual psychology which no one so far has seen fit to explore as a psychologist. By what kind of psychic test does a man detect just that stage in the day's work at which the fruits of a further half-hour's effort will not quite compensate him for that effort? What scheme of incentives would make him postpone that judgment? A long list of other such questions will occur to every economist. Here indeed is a ripe field for imaginative research, if only the economists will haul up their iron curtain out of sight and seek appropriate help.

I said a moment ago that the market mechanism is no longer the only means by which the practical questions are answered: How much of this and of that shall be produced, by what means, and for whom? But since the manner in which these matters are decided is still the prime concern of the economist, he must study whatever it is that has partly ousted the market from this function. In western countries the individual, nominally and ultimately at least, can still make his contribution to the answering of those questions, but nowadays there is much that he can no longer influence by a continuous direct pressure in the market, where the smallest details of his preferences could be signalled to his suppliers and make themselves felt; there is much that he can only affect at long intervals, in an exceedingly crude and uncertain way,

8

by means of the electoral vote that he can cast for one big bundle of ill-defined, ill-assorted, and changeable policies or another. The whole question of government: its nature, purpose, justification, and detailed working, the source of the authority exercised by statesmen, the basis of society's claim to the individual's acquiescence in its decrees, the justice and admissible scope of the administrator's interference in his life; all this, in a country where the central government takes away from the citizens some two-fifths of their income and spends it on their behalf, must loom large on the economist's horizon, and it is plain that just beyond another part of the boundary of his subject there lies political theory. But a very large part of the whole study of government activities is actually inside his province, and perhaps we are already well on the way to that situation where the Government, rather than the consumer or the enterpriser, will be the economic agent to which the economist will direct most of his attention. The revolutionary change which has come about since 1939 in the relation between the importance, in the economic field, of those impersonal market forces of competition which were the main concern of economists until the thirties, and the importance of those radically different mechanisms by which the inarticulate purposes of a people are channelled and rendered explicit stage by stage via the polling-booth, the parliament, the cabinet-room, and the Whitehall department, has not yet had time to revolutionise our text-books. Still less has there been any recognition in them of that other but closely related revolution whereby the international exchange of goods has become a game for governments, a field for all the arts of diplomacy, negotiation and bargaining, calling for a combination of the talents of the chess-master and the poker-player. It may surprise those of my audience who are not economists to be told that one of the most

9

important and radically novel contributions to economic theory that appeared in the past 10 years was called The Theory of Games and Economic Behaviour. No longer can economic theory be called the pure logic of choice. It is many things besides, and this book has brought into it the pure logic of strategy in the widest sense of that term.

The study of government is the study of institutions, and there are other human institutions, in all three senses of organisations, of practices, and of social inventions or devices, which profoundly influence the character and largely govern the outward forms of the economic process. The most fundamentally important of these is perhaps the device of money, in all its manifold aspects. The history of the evolution of money, I could almost venture to suggest, is a strand in the history of the growth of civilisation second in importance only to that of language. Money began as a commodity, and has ended as a system of recording transactions and bringing every act of purchase and sale, of borrowing and lending, of working and producing and consuming, that takes place anywhere in the whole world at any time, into some degree of relation with every other such act. In its tremendous power and radical simplicity this tool of human advancement, money in its basic meaning and role of an accounting system, ranks surely next to the alphabet itself. If, then, such things as money and monetary habits, and all the intricate machinery which has been built on them, are part of the very fibre of man's civilised existence and are things of gradual and painful growth from primitive beginnings, ought not the economist to call in the anthropologist, the student of cultures and social machinery in a general sense, to aid him to understand these things?

Economics is concerned with man; with man as a creature capable of thoughts and feelings, of likes and dislikes, of hopes and fears, of invention and imagination. But, perhaps you will say, all this, no doubt, is what makes him human and distinguishes him from the brute creation; yet he is an animal, and in the last resort his life is conditioned and his survival determined by biological factors; his needs are bodily needs. What has economics to say of hunger, of the body's need for warmth and shelter, of the capabilities of muscles, of the physiological basis of fatigue? Are not these things relevant? The economist will agree that they are, but he will enter a caveat. The sum of human happiness is not arrived at by adding up calories and kilowatts, not reckoning working hours per week. There are people, I am told (I find it hard to believe) who can see nothing in the dancing flames upon the hearth, whose hearts, if they have any, are warmed as well by a hot-water pipe as by all Prometheus' magic. To them, no doubt, an open fire is so many therms per hour wastefully supplied. To the economist the question how most *heat* can be obtained from a given quantity of fuel is irrelevant. He is only concerned to know how most *happiness* can be obtained from it. This happiness may be derived from bodily warmth, or from spiritual comfort and inspiration. Man is the measure of all things. Every object and occurrence that has economic significance derives it wholly from the relation of this object or event to man's desires and beliefs and valuations. Thus although, beyond yet another frontier of economics, there lie engineering, chemistry, agricultural science, and all the gamut of technology, these things are not in themselves the economist's concern. The frontier here is clear and definite. This does not mean, of course, that the economist can dispense with *facts* from the technologist; on the contrary, before he can make economic statements of fact about particular industries in particular places, or give practical advice, he will need such facts in great quantity and detail.

11

There are yet two more directions in which the economist can look out from his own territory over that of other specialists, and here the frontier is again in doubt. For here he sees geography and history, one partly and the other wholly concerned with man himself. Whenever the economist is asked to give practical advice in the affairs of a nation or an industry, his thoughts will turn at once to his friend the geographer, without whose help he himself, *qua* economist, can say little to the point. All the physical and many of the human factors which should guide the location of industry are matters for the geographer. As for the frontier with history, there is a whole province in dispute. I have the impression that in the past the historians neglected it to their loss, and that it is the economists who on the whole have shown themselves apt to become historians, rather than the historians who have readily put on the spectacles of the economist. But from whatever source, economic history in Britain has gathered to itself a learned and ardent band of specialists, who reckon nothing impossible in their effort to recreate our past manner of life, and who will soon, I think, establish this branch of knowledge as an autonomous discipline.

As a necessary background for my problem: What kind of man or woman, with what aptitudes, interests, and training, is likely to find in some aspect of economics a congenial study, an equipment for a career, and perhaps a field for original work: I have tried to survey very briefly the ground that economics calls its own and the ground of other disciplines whose aid the economist needs or whose findings he must treat as data. Against this background, let me try now to set the scene of the selection and training of an economist, as it seems to me that these things should be done.

If a schoolmaster, tossing one night on his sleepless bed, were suddenly to realise that his insomnia was due to the pangs of conscience arising from his never having tried to prepare any pupils to become economists, or even given the matter a moment's thought, what advice should we give him in his effort to repair this omission? What tests, actual or within his own mind, ought he to apply to those of his pupils who had just completed their Vth Form studies and so were now free to specialise, to see if they were likely to do well in economics? What qualities or performances ought he to look for, when scrutinising their results in examinations? Above all, what ought he now to encourage them to do with their last year or two at school? Ought they to begin the actual study of economics? Or are familiar themes the best for practising with that master-tool of all our thinking, that greatest organ of intellectual expression ever yet evolved, the English tongue? Ought they to be still sharpening their mathematical tools, or already trying, in an unfamiliar, subtle, and treacherous subject-matter, to apply them? And, finally, if his decision is that he himself will not open to them the books of economics, but will yet tell them that such a subject exists, what account of it ought he to give? Ought he to make it seem easy or difficult? Are some notions of it indispensable furniture of every cultivated person's mind or is it decorative but useless embroidery on the practical man's knowledge of the world? Can it be a vehicle of intellectual excitement and beauty, like pure mathematics, or is it only something that will help you to get a job?

The economist, like the teacher of nearly all other subjects, must open his heart to two kinds of pupil. He will, of course, hope to find sometimes the quiet flame of an enquiring mind, the true contemplative, even the bold seeker of adventures of the spirit who one day will be able to say to himself

libera per vacuum posui vestigia princeps

But for the most part he must be content with those

who will accept an economics course as an interesting
way of learning how to build and exhibit arguments
of their own, to test and perhaps demolish those of
others, to interpret and make sense of a complex
mass of facts, to see through the casuistry of special
pleaders and the verbiage of propagandists; and a
means of practising these arts in that context of life
in which their own professional careers as business
executives, Civil Servants, administrators, accoun-
tants, or lawyers will be laid. There are, I think, two
things that he can reasonably ask the schoolmaster to
do. First, to bear economics in mind as a possible
eventual outlet for the outstanding intellectual all-
rounder with some leaning towards the arts rather
than the natural science side. The boy who finds
mathematics fascinating without, perhaps, marching
through the school course with that instinctive and
professional certainty that would mark him as an
out-and-out mathematician; who betrays a con-
noisseurship of words and a delight in language, a
gift for expression in English and a sufficient pleasure
in the classical languages to awaken thoughts of
scholarships, without really promising to become a
Porson's prizeman; who can find in every chapter of
the history book the universal and eternal problems of
man's dependence on his fellow men side by side with
his rivalry and conflict with them, and can see with
the historian's eye the age-long empirical struggle to
reconcile self-interest and enlightened compassion;
who delights in maps and finds them, perhaps, more
interesting than test-tubes; this is the potential
real economist. Secondly, I ask the schoolmaster to
realise that to-day our economics classrooms are filled
with some of the best brains amongst the University's
whole student membership. Ours is not the Department where he can find secluded corners for those who
are all-rounders in a different sense, and who, having
never shown the slightest aptitude for anything what-

234 Time, Expectations and Uncertainty in Economics

ever, are equally well fitted for all professions, and (I suspect him of sometimes having thought) might just as well become economists as anything else. A few such did on rare occasions in the past infiltrate the economics classrooms by a process that you, schoolmaster, will easily understand. They had shown their distaste for all the subjects studied at school, plainly they must try something else. But what is there? 'Ah', you said to yourself 'economics; besides, I have heard that it's a soft option'. You left us to secure our good students for ourselves. All your more responsive pupils had been good at something in particular; at French, perhaps, and if they felt they had already spent enough years upon that, still it would be natural now to try Spanish or Italian; or it seemed the obvious thing to go on with the history or the geography which your own enthusiasm had rendered absorbing. Thus many of your better pupils came to the University already pre-empted, in their own minds, by one or other of the regular school subjects, or allied subjects. To-day, when the practical questions on which economists are supposed to give advice are so prominent in our national life, economics has by the end of school-days already secured a footing in many of the most enterprising minds amongst school-leavers. Our duty is all the plainer, therefore, not to let our subject be looked on as one where exact and rigorous thinking is a pedantry. Send to us, then, schoolmaster, as in recent years you have done, a share of your best pupils. Send us those whom, fifty or sixty years ago, when the range of university subjects was so much narrower, you would have been in doubt whether to advise to read classics or mathematics, and whose minds have something of the fineness and urbanity that a joy in Greek and its philosophers implies.

So much for the question what kind of young man or woman has the best hope of shining in economics.

15

Now, what is the best use for the specialist years at school, what should be done in the VIth Form? This is, I think, only a question of expediency and not of principle. But to answer it we must consider a question that perhaps should have come earlier in this lecture. It is all very well to ask ourselves what kind of person can give most to economics, but we ought also to ask what economics can give to those who devote to it one or five or six of the years of their youth. In short, why study economics?

First, because as an ocean on which to practise the art of intellectual navigation, economics has fathomless virtues. It presents every kind of difficulty which any scientific study can throw up; the area to be charted is so immense and covers so many mysterious deeps that there can be no end to the work, however many may engage in it. Once he is launched upon this sea, a man's life work, if he be of the true scholarly temper, spreads away before him to his life's horizon. Some have found their way across this ocean by a patient following of the coastline from one set of landmarks to another, never having to grapple with more than a small part of the whole problem at any one time. These were the Marshallians, working in the tradition of the great English empiricists who distrusted vast structures reared upon a single supposedly all-conquering idea, and preferred a construction in the English spirit of trial and error, of many supports and a variety of building methods. Others, if I may return to my metaphor of navigation, believed, like Walras, that they had found a star to guide them across the ocean in one swoop. In the equi-marginal principle, embodied in a system of simultaneous equations, they believed they had found a key to unlock the whole economic universe and explain everything. Their system was very beautiful, as well it might be, since it made in effect the tremendous assumption that every economic

236 Time, Expectations and Uncertainty in Economics

decision is a choice between perfectly apprehended alternatives. In their world, man knows what he is doing. But though it may seem absurd to explain human conduct in abstraction from human ignorance and fallibility, the so-called General Equilibrium theory invented by Walras and developed by Pareto is one of the greatest creations of economists. It made unmistakeably clear once for all that the whole economic world is *interdependent*. The ocean to which I have been comparing our economic world is an apt metaphor in yet another sense. We may think of every individual, every firm, and every government as a boat upon the surface of this ocean. Every movement made by any boat will set up waves which, after a shorter or longer time-lag, will affect much or little every other boat on the ocean. This conception of complete and all-embracing human inter-dependence is not one, I think, which occurs naturally to an unsophisticated mind. Yet what understanding of man's lot in this world, and of his own personal situation in a deeper sense, can any human being claim who has not grasped it?

Thus I claim for the study of economics two chief merits: First, that it is difficult, not, however, in the way that some parts of mathematics are difficult, because their proofs involve a tremendous concatenation of logical steps, but in the sense that the subject-matter of economics is elusive, subtle, and complex to an extreme degree, because it is, in the last resort, the unsearchable heart of man. Mathematics, maybe, teaches men to scale intellectual crags, where each ledge or handhold can only serve if it is part of a chain or ladder of such ledges; but economics teaches men to walk upon quicksands or to find ways to overleap them. Now this call for resourceful and daring inventiveness in the manufacture of concepts to reason about is very well indeed for those who are already well-practised in reasoning about ready-made

familiar things which, although just as truly fictive as
the notions of the economist, appear to be drawn more
directly from observation. But to pile this added
difficulty of finding the straw on top of the more
ordinary labour of intellectual brick-making is, I
think, too much to ask of those who are still at school.
And for the second merit of economics; this is, that it
teaches men who are about to embrace some policy or
course of action, to bear in the back of their minds the
warning that this step will affect, much or little and
sooner or later, everything in the economic universe;
this again, I think, is an idea more acceptable and
assimilable by somewhat mature minds. Thus it is
my own feeling that the schoolmaster, having seen
with all his care and energy to the sharpening of the
tools of thought and expression, should be content to
see them exercised upon the natural sciences, and,
except for geography, should leave the human sciences
to the student's University years with their better
opportunities for free and leisured meditation and
their, perhaps, more developed scepticism.

And so to the University course in economics. The
first task of the University teacher of any liberal art is
surely to persuade his students that the most important
things he will put before them are questions and not
answers. He is going to put up for them a scaffolding,
and leave them to build within it. He has to persuade
them that they have not come to the University to
learn as it were by heart things which are already
hard-and-fast and cut-and-dried, but to watch and
perhaps to help in a process, the driving of a causeway
which will be made gradually firmer by the traffic of
many minds. The ordinary student can perhaps
contribute little to this except by striving to say
clearly what are the, to him, unsatisfactory things, the
gaps and puzzles, and the incantations that hide some
secret he does not share. But this he can only do by
thinking, and once he has begun to do that with a

feeling of freedom and a sense of independent experiment and exploration, he is already a worthy member of the class.

You may have wondered why I traded so much upon your patience with a long discussion of what economics is about and what subjects lie next it in the great fabric of human knowledge. Economics is like a country of the plain, lacking sharp natural frontiers within which it could pursue a self-contained existence, and the greater versatility that this calls for in its citizens, who, because of the constant intellectual traffic with their neighbours, have to be able as it were to speak several languages, poses a serious problem for the designer of the syllabus. There is one problem in particular, which has been a cloud of steadily growing blackness upon our horizon for many years. This is the question of how far, and how, economists should become mathematically literate. No one nowadays would deny that economics is an essentially mathematical subject, even in the old-fashioned sense of mathematics as a discipline concerned always in some way with quantities, for the business of economics also is to reason about quantities. But this is far from saying that all economists should equip themselves to use the formal notations of algebra, the differential and integral calculus, matrices, the theory of sets, and so on. There is much to be said for acquiring some mathematical insight and technical competence, for as 'he moves easiest who has learned to dance,' the pedestrian tasks of the economist will be performed with all the more grace and efficiency if he has practised something demanding a formal elegance of procedure, while the ready-made tools of thought which mathematics provides will save him as much trouble as a vacuum cleaner saves the modern housewife. But let him beware of putting his vacuum cleaner on the mantelpiece as an ornament. The kinds of mathematics that economists use are humble and utilitarian, seldom of a sort to arouse the thrilled interest of the mathematician. However, the mathematically trained economist is exposed to a more subtle and far more serious danger than that of mere barbarity in the presentation of his argument. This arises from the domination of applied mathematics in the past by classical dynamics. The world which we explore in that well-known chapter on the dynamics of a particle is a wholly deterministic, predestinatory world, where, and this is the nub of the matter, there is no real or significant distinction between past and future. The astronomer feels as certain that a total eclipse of the sun will be visible in Cornwall in 1999 as he does that a total eclipse was visible in Birmingham in 1927. But the writer of the textbook of classical particle dynamics feels more certain even than the astronomer; he feels *absolutely* certain just where his particle will be at any given instant, for he has excluded *by assumption* every possible accident which could interfere with its career. Can the economist reasonably analyse the conduct of men and women, on the supposition that those men and women believe themselves to know for sure all the relevant consequences of their actions? It is a cardinal fact of human life that we do not know the future, we cannot calculate the consequences of our actions but only guess them. A world without uncertainty would be an utterly inhuman world, of a character which we cannot imagine, and which some have very plausibly suggested is actually logically impossible to conceive and self-contradictory. The assumption of perfect foresight makes nonsense of economics, and yet it is so natural and obvious an assumption for the economist trained in classsical dynamics (as some great economists have been) that some have sometimes actually made it *unconsciously*. Now, of course, the physicist of to-day has greatly modified the views that his grandfather held in the nineteenth century, about the nature of determinism in the physical world. Let me quote to you a passage from a recent article in the *Times Literary Supplement.**

> 'Do not the "social scientists"—the psychologists, political scientists, sociologists, and *par excellence* the now almost completely symbolical, formal, and econometrical economists —groan and travail for a nineteenth century certainty of "laws", two generations late, just when the most advanced physical scientists are rounding the bend towards chance, uncertainty, and all fortuitousness?'

I am delighted, as some of you will understand, to hear someone telling the economists, in effect, that they should regard uncertainty as the very nerve and essence of their subject, or great parts of it. I myself have been telling them so for a dozen years and more. My only doubt about the statement I have quoted is whether our friends the natural scientists are in truth as far round the bend as the anonymous writer says. The Heisenberg uncertainty principle, even as interpreted by Sir James Jeans, does not, I think, involve for physics anything which can be easily recognised to resemble the consequences that human ignorance of the future has for economics.

Indeed, habits of thought derived from statistical procedures, or from the statistical interpretations of determinism to which the 'uncertainty principle' has driven the modern physicist, can be as dangerous for the economist as the outlook unconsciously induced by classical mechanics. Statistical methods are a means to increase *knowledge*, not a means for analysing or describing men's feelings and conduct in face of true, irreducible uncertainty, which can be ascribed in the last resort, if to nothing else, then to the ultimate impossibility of their ever knowing whether or not, in any particular case, they have all the relevant information. The econometricians have invited rebuke by publicly declaring that only the present crudity of their

* September 5th, 1952, front-page article.

21

techniques (which they will improve) prevents them from telling us in advance what future months and years will bring. There are great scientific tasks for econometrics to perform, but to confound science with prophecy is an unworthy blunder.

Let me, then, try to state briefly my own faith in the matter. Mathematics must be the servant of economics and not its master. The kinds of mathematics required (statistics apart) are relatively workaday ones, and when the occasional cry is heard that some particular branch of economics calls for some new branch of mathematics to be invented, we must not think that even if this appeal is gloriously answered by the mathematicians, anything will be fundamentally changed. The important and practical questions are, first, whether the modest equipment of mathematical conceptions and methods which is all that most economists have time or good reason for aspiring to, should be taught to them by mathematics teachers quite separately from their course in economics, or whether this instruction should be infiltrated into the economics course itself so that mathematical notions and their economic applications and illustrations are inseparably interwoven; and, secondly, if we opt for a separate course in mathematics for economists, whether this should precede the main attack on economic theory, as a necessary preparation for it, or whether the need for mathematical equipment should be allowed to arise in the students' minds as they grapple with their economics course, and should be satisfied by a series of mathematics lectures very carefully dovetailed into those on economics so that each need is met as it arises.

To require students who abandoned algebra two or three or five years ago and have never heard of the calculus, to embark suddenly on an intensive year's cold-blooded instruction in these things, before they are allowed a glimpse of the need for them in economics, is, it seems to me, as though one should ask a man to swallow a tablespoonful of coffee-berries and then pour a cupful of hot water down on top of them in the hope that the two ingredients will somehow get appropriately mixed up in his inside. Half the difficulty in teaching the art of manipulating symbols to those who are not natural symbol-riggers is that it seems to them a purposeless game whose rules cannot be understood. If, in spite of your best efforts, you are always off-side for no reason that is ever made clear in a game where the goal-posts are invisible, you are bound to lose interest in the affair. It is in order to make the goal-posts visible that I think we should interweave the two courses, letting the need for some mathematical notions arise in the economic context and satisfying it on the spot. We need a text-book, and it should be a book of economics which insinuates mathematics, not a book of mathematics illustrated from economics.

And now, Mr. Chairman, and ladies and gentlemen, I have discussed the aptitudes and interests, the types of personality, the aims and objectives, the methods of selection and of training, the syllabuses and curricula, that contribute to the making of an economist. There is one thing I have not mentioned. The good economist is like a bottle of wine. He must begin by having the luck to be laid down, as it were, in a vintage year, when he himself and his class companions are the high-quality stuff in which ideas and theories ferment and discourse sparkles in a glow of golden light. But this is not enough. He must mature. And you may think, if you like, that perhaps your Brunner Professor of Economic Science is not altogether disinterested when he expresses the hope that an economist improves with keeping, and will be worth imbibing even in his old age.

A Bibliography of the Works of G. L. S. Shackle

1933

'Some Notes on Monetary Theories of the Trade Cycle', *Review of Economic Studies*, Vol. 1 No. 1, October 1933, pp. 27–38.

1936

'The Breakdown of the Boom: A Possible Mechanism', *Economica* (New Series), Vol. 3 No. 12, November 1936, pp. 423–435.

1937

'Dynamics of the Crisis: A Suggestion', *Review of Economic Studies*, Vol. 4 No. 11, February 1937, pp. 108–122.

1938

a. *Expectations, Investment and Income*, Oxford University Press, 1938, pp. 119.
b. 'An Index of Real Turnover, 1919–36', *Oxford Economic Papers*, No. 1, pp. 32–52 (with E. H. Phelps Brown)
c. 'British Economic Fluctuations 1924–38', *Oxford Economic Papers*, No. 2, pp. 98–134 (with E. H. Phelps Brown)

1939

a. 'The Multiplier in Closed and Open Systems', *Oxford Economic Papers*, No. 2, May 1939, pp. 135–144.
b. 'Expectations and Employment', *Economic Journal*, Vol. 49 No. 195, September 1939, pp. 442–452.

1940

a. 'The Nature of the Inducement to Invest', *Review of Economic Studies*, Vol. 8 No. 22, October 1940, pp. 44–48.
b. 'A Reply to Professor Hart', *Review of Economic Studies*, Vol. 8 No. 22, pp. 54–57.

1941

'A Means of Promoting Investment', *Economic Journal*, Vol. 51 Nos. 202, 203, June, September 1941, pp. 249–260.

1942

'A Theory of Investment Decisions', *Oxford Economic Papers*, No. 6, April 1942, pp. 77–94.

1943

'The Expectational Dynamics of the Individual', *Economica* (New Series), Vol. 10 No. 38, May 1943, pp. 99–129.

1945

a. 'Myrdal's Analysis of Monetary Equilibrium', *Oxford Economic Papers*, No. 7, March 1945, pp. 47–66.
b. 'An Analysis of Speculative Choice', *Economica* (New Series), Vol. 12 No. 43, February 1945, pp. 10–21.

1946

'Interest-rates and the Pace of Investment', *Economic Journal*, Vol. 56 No. 221, March 1946, pp. 1–17.

1947

'The Deflative or Inflative Tendency of Government Receipts and Disbursements', *Oxford Economic Papers*, No. 8, November 1947, pp. 46–64.

1949

a. *Expectation in Economics*, Cambridge, The University Press, 1949, pp. x + 146.
b. 'The Nature of Interest Rates', *Oxford Economic Papers* (New Series), Vol. 1 No. 1, January 1949, pp. 100–120.
c. 'Measuring Industry's Output', *Accounting Research*, Vol. 1 No. 2, July, pp. 1–11.
d. 'Some Theoretical Aspects of Payment by Results' (in English and Italian) *Economia Internazionale*, Vol. 2 No. 4, November 1949, pp. 841–853.
e. Part III of a symposium on 'Expectations in Economics', *Economica* (New Series), Vol. 16 No. 64, November 1949, pp. 343–346.

f. 'A Non-Additive Measure of Uncertainty', *Review of Economic Studies*, Vol. 17 No. 42, 1949–1950, pp. 70–74.
g. 'Probability and Uncertainty', *Metroeconomica*, Vol. 1 No. 3, December 1949, pp. 161–173.

1950

'Three Versions of the φ-surface: Some Notes for a Comparison', *Review of Economic Studies*, Vol. 18 No. 46, 1950–1951, pp. 119–122.

1951

a. 'Twenty Years On: A Survey of the Theory of the Multiplier', *Economic Journal*, Vol. 61 No. 242, June 1951, pp. 241–260.
b. 'The Nature and Role of Profit', *Metroeconomica*, Vol. 3, December 1951, pp. 101–107.
c. 'Interest-rates as an Instrument of Economic Policy', *Liverpool Trade Review*, Vol. 50 No. 12, December 1951, pp. 355–358.

1952

a. *Expectation in Economics* (second edition), Cambridge, The University Press 1952, pp xvi + 144,
b. *Mathematics at the Fireside*, Cambridge, The University Press, 1952, pp. xii + 156,
c. 'On the Meaning and Measure of Uncertainty, Part I', *Metroeconomica*, Vol. 4 No. 3, December 1952, pp. 87–104.

1953

a. 'Economics and Sincerity', *Oxford Economic Papers* (New Series), Vol. 5 No. 1, March 1953, pp. 1–12.
b. 'A Chart of Economic Theory', *Metroeconomica*, Vol. 5 No. 1, April 1953, pp. 1–10.
c. 'The Logic of Surprise', *Economica* (New Series), Vol. 20 No. 78, May 1953, pp. 112–117.
d. *What Makes an Economist*, Liverpool, Liverpool University Press, 1953, pp. 1–23.
e. 'On the Meaning and Measure of Uncertainty, Part II', *Metroeconomica*, Vol. 5 No. 3, December 1953, pp. 97–115.
f. 'The Economist's View of Profit', *The Company Accountant*, N. S., 26 June 1953, pp. 8–13.

1954

a. (Edited with C. F. Carter and G. P. Meridith), *Uncertainty and Business Decisions*, Liverpool. The University Press.
b. 'Expectations in Economics', Chapter IX in (a) above.
c. 'Final Comment', pp. 100–102 in (a) above.
d. 'Foreword to the English Translation', pp. 5–13, Wicksell, K., *Value, Capital and Rent*, translated by S. F. Forwen, London, George Allen and Unwin, 1954, reprinted, New York, Augustus M. Kelly 1970.
e. 'Bank Rate and the Modernisation of Industry', *The Bankers Magazine*, Vol. 177 No. 1323, June 1954, pp. 553–556.
f. 'The Complex Nature of Time as a Concept in Economics', *Economia Internazionale*, Vol. 7 No. 4, November 1954, pp. 743–757.
g. 'Professor Kierstead's Theory of Profit', *Economic Journal*, Vol. 64, 1954, p. 116.
h. 'The Liberal Tradition in Economics', *The Banker's Magazine*, December (Review article on L. Robbins, *The Economist in the Twentieth Century and other Lecturers in Political Economy (1954)*.)

1955

a. *Uncertainty in Economics and Other Reflections*, Cambridge, The University Press, 1955, pp. xv + 267.
b. 'Business Men on Business Decisions', *Scottish Journal of Political Economy*, Vol. 2 No. 1, February 1955, pp. 32–46.
c. 'Expectations, Income and Profit', *Economisk Tidkrift*, Vol. 57 No. 4, December 1955, pp. 215–235.
d. 'The Nature of Inflation', *The Company Accountant*, N.S., 41, Conference Number, 1955, pp. 13–21.

1956

a. 'Expectations and Cardinality', *Economic Journal*, Vol. 66 No. 262, June 1956, pp. 159–162.
b. 'Marshallian and Paretian Stems', *Metroeconomica*, Vol. 8 No. 3, December 1956, pp. 159–162.

1957

a. (Editor with C. F. Carter and G. P. Meridith), *Uncertainty and Business Decisions*, second revised and enlarged edition, Liverpool at the University Press.

b. (With G. Gould), 'Odds, Possibility and Plausibility in Shackle's Theory of Decision: A Discussion', *The Economic Journal*, Vol. 67, p. 659.
c. 'The Nature of the Bargaining Process', pp. 292–314, in Diunlop, J. T. (Ed.) *The Theory of Wage Determination*, London, Macmillan and Co., 1957.
d. 'Foreword to the English Translation', pp. xiii-xvi, of Fossati, E., *The Theory of General Static Equilibrium*, Oxford, Basil Blackwell, edited and final translation by G. L. S. Shackle.
d. 'Foreword' to Frowen, S. F. and Hillman H. C. (Eds.), *Economic Issues*.

1958

a. *Time in Economics*, Amsterdam, North Holland, pp. III.
b. (Editor), *A New Prospect of Economics*, Liverpool, Liverpool University Press, 1958.
c. 'What is Economics', in (b) above.
d. 'What is Theory', in (b) above.
e. 'The Tool-box of the Economist', in (a) above.
f. 'Expectation and Liquidity', pp. 30–44, in Bowman, M. J. (Ed.), *Expectations, Uncertainty and Behaviour*, New York, Social Science Research Council, 1958.
g. 'The Economist's Model of Man', *Occupational Psychology*, Vol. 32 No. 3, July 1958, pp. 191–196.
h. 'Decisions in Face of Uncertainty: Some Criticisms and Extensions of a Theory', *De Economist*, No. 10, October 1958, pp. 673–686.

1959

a. *Economics for Pleasure*, Cambridge, The University Press.
b. 'Time and Thought', *British Journal for the Philosophy of Science*, Vol. 9 No. 36, 1959, pp. 285–298.
c. 'Brief Testament', *Weltwirtschaftliches Archiv*, Vol. 82.

1960

'Business and Uncertainty', *The Banker's Magazine*, Vol. 189, 1392, March 1960, pp. 209–213.

1961

a. *Decision, Order and Time in Human Affairs*, Cambridge, The University Press, pp. xxvi + 330.

b. 'Time, Nature and Decision', pp. 299–310 in H. Hegland, (Ed.), *Money, Growth and Methodology*, Lund, C. W. K. Gleerup.

c. 'Incertezza e profitti', *Mercurio*, Vol. 4 No. 2, February 1961, pp. 13–17.

d. 'Recent Theories Concerning the Nature and Role of Interest', *Economic Journal*, Vol. 71, June 1961, pp. 209–254.

e. 'Keynes and the Nature of Human Affairs', *Weltwirtschaftliches Archiv*, Vol. 87 No. 1, 1961, pp. 93–110.

f. 'The Ruin of Economy', *Kyklos*, Vol. 14 No. 4, 1961, pp. 482–496.

1962

a. 'Decision oet Incertitude', *Futuribles* (Bulletin SEDES, No. 813, Supplement No. 26), 1 March 1962, pp. 43–48.

b. 'L'eclissi della < <Grande Teoria> >', *Mercurio*, Vol. 5 No. 10, October 1962, pp. 9–14.

c. 'Descrizione dello Stato di Incertezza', *La Scuola in Azione*, Vol. 21 No. 1, 17 September 1962, pp. 59–77.

d. 'Battles Long Ago', *Weltwirtschaftliches Archiv*, Vol. 89. (Review Article of Kaldor, *Essays on Value and Distribution* (1960).)

e. 'The Stages of Economic Growth', *Political Studies*, Vol. 10. (Review Article on W. W. Rostow's work of the same title (1960).)

f. 'Values and Intentions', *Kyklos*, Vol. 15. (Review Article on J. N. Findlay, book of the same title (1961).)

g. *Para comprender la economia* (Spanish language edition of *Economics for Pleasure*), Mexico-Buenos Aires, Fondo de Cultura Economica, pp. 326.

1963

a. 'I tre significanti del tempo nella trattazione economia marshalliana', *Rivista Internazionale di Scienze Economiche a Commerciali*, Vol. 10 No. 1, January 1963, pp. 38–52, 95.

b. 'Theory and the Business Man', *Scientific Business*, Vol. 1 No. 1, May 1963, pp. 5–11.

c. 'L'équilibre: étude de sa signification et des ses limites'. *Cahiers de l'Institut de Science Economique Appliquée: Les cahiers Franco-italiens*, Serie BA, No. 2, Février 1963, pp. 59–77.

d. 'General Thought-Schemes and the Economist', *Woolwich Economic Paper*, No. 2, 3 March 1963, pp. 1–20.

1964

a. 'The Hedgehog and the Fox', *The Indian Journal of Economics*, Vol. XLIV, No. 175, April 1964, pp. 241–255.

b. *Analise Economica ao Alacance de Todus* (Portuguese language edition of *Economics for Pleasure*), Rio de Janeiro, AGIR, pp. 261.
c. *Economio* (Dutch language edition of *Economics for Pleasure*), Utrecht-Antwerpen, Prisma-Boeken, pp. 288.

1965

a. *A Scheme of Economic Theory*, Cambridge, The University Press, pp. xi + 209.
b. 'The Interest Elasticity of Investment', pp. 894, in F. H. Hahn and F. P. R. Brechling (Eds.), *The Theory of Interest Rates*, London, Macmillan and Co.
c. *A la découverte des mécanismes de l'économie moderne* (French edition of *Economics for Pleasure*), Paris, Dunod, pp. 237.

1966

a. *The Nature of Economic Thought: Selected Papers 1955–64*, Cambridge, The University Press, pp. xiv + 322.
b. 'Policy, Poetry and Success', *The Advancement of Science*, Vol. 23, No. III, September 1966, pp. 265–273.
c. 'Policy, Poetry and Success', *The Economic Journal*, Vol. 76, 1966, pp. 755.
d. *Para comprender la economia* (Spanish language edition of *Economics for Pleasure*), Primera Reimpresión.
e. *Capire L'economica* (Italian language edition of *Economics for Pleasure*), Milano, Fetrinelli, pp. 220.
f. *Decisions, orden y tiempo en las activadades humanas* (Spanish language edition *Decision, Order and Time in Human Affairs*), Madrid, Editorial Tecnicos, pp. 300.

1967

a. *The Years of High Theory: Invention and Tradition in Economic Thought, 1926–1939*, Cambridge, The University Press, pp. vii + 328.
b. 'On the Nature of Profit', *Woolwich Economic Papers*, No. 13, July 1967, pp. 1–26.
c. *Time in Economics* (second printing), Amsterdam, North Holland, p. 111.
d. *Les Mathematiques au Coin du Feu* (French language edition of *Mathematics at the Fireside*), Paris, Dunod, pp. xi + 171.
e. *Décision, Déterminisme et Temps* (French language edition of

Decision, Order and Time in Human Affairs), Paris, Dunod, pp. xiv + 266.

1968

a. 'Economic Expectations', pp. 389–395, in D. L. Sills (Ed.,) *International Encyclopaedia of the Social Sciences*.
b. *Expectations, Investment and Income* (second edition), Oxford, Clarendon Press, pp. xxxvi + 130.
c. *Economics for Pleasure* (second edition), Cambridge, The University Press, pp. viii + 280.
d. *Uncertainty in Economics and Other Reflections* (Library Edition), Cambridge, The University Press, pp. xv + 267.
e. (Editor), *On the Nature of Business Success*, Liverpool, Liverpool University Press.
f. 'Policy Poetry and Success', pp. 3–18, in (e) above.
g. Foreword, pp. vii-x, A. Coddington, *Theories of the Bargaining Process*, London, George Allen and Unwin.

1969

a. *Decision, Order and Time in Human Affairs* (second edition), Cambridge, The University Press, pp. xvi + 330.
b. 'Theory and the Business Man', pp. 1–14, in A. M. Boum (Ed.), *Studies in Accounting for Management Decision*, London, McGraw-Hill.
c. 'Introduction', pp. 13–18, in T. L. Smyth (Ed.), *Essays in Modern Economic Development*, London, Duckworth.
d. 'Policy, Poetry and Success', pp. 101–117, in R. L. Smyth (Ed.), *Essays in Modern Economic Development*, London, Duckworth.
e. *Nationalökonomie für Manger* (German language edition of *Economics for Pleasure*), Munchen, Management Buchclub, pp. 251.
f. *Ekonomika pro potesini* (Czech language edition of *Economics for Pleasure*), Praha, Mala Moderni Encyklopedie, pp. 269.
g. *Um Esquema de Teoria Economica* (Portuguese language edition of *A Scheme of Economic Theory*), Rio de Janeiro, Zahar Editores, pp. 206.
h. *La naturaleza del pensamiento económico* (Spanish language edition of *The Nature of Economic Thought*), Mexico, Fondo de Cultura Economica, pp. 318.

1970

Expectation, Enterprise and Profit, London, George Allen and Unwin, pp. 160.

1971

a.   'Discussion Paper on Robert Clower: Theoretical Foundations of Monetary Policy', pp. 32–34, in G. Clayton, J. C. Gilbert and R. Sedgewick (Eds.), *Monetary Theory and Monetary Policy in the 1970's*, Oxford, Oxford University Press.
b.   *Economics for Pleasure* (second paperback edition), Cambridge, The University Press, pp. viii + 280.

1972

Epistemics and Economics: A Critique of Economic Doctrines, Cambridge, The University Press, pp. xviii + 482.

1973

a.   *An Economic Querist*, Cambridge, The University Press, pp. viii + 135.
b.   'Marginalism: The Harvest', pp. 321–336, in R. D. Collison Black, A. W. Coats and C. D. W. Goodwin (Eds.), *The Martinal Revolution in Economics*, Durham North Carolina, Duke University Press.
c.   'Keynes and Today's Establishment in Economic Theory: A View', *Journal of Economic Literature*, Vol. 11, pp. 516–519.

1974

a.   *Keynesian Kaleidics*, Edinburgh, The University Press, pp. vi + 92.
b.   'Decision: The Human Predicament', pp. 1–10, in D. M. Lamberton (Ed.), *The Information Revolution*, Philadelphia, The American Academy of Political and Social Science.

1975

Para comprender la económia (Spanish language edition of *Economics for Pleasure*), Segunda reimpresión.

1976

a.   'News from Sweden', pp. 10–19, in M. Richards (Ed.), *Population, Factor Movements and Economic Development*, Cardiff, University of Wales Press.
b.   *Perspective empresariales y beneficio* (Spanish language edition of *Expectation, Enterprise and Profit*), Barcelona, oikas-tau, p. 218.

c.   'Time and Choice', Keynes lecture in economics, 1976, in *Proceedings of the British Academy*, Vol. LXII, London, Oxford University Press for the British Academy, pp. 309–329.

1977

'New Tracks for Economic Theory', pp. 23–37, in S. Weintraub (Ed.), *Modern Economic Thought*, Philadelphia, University of Pennsylvania Press.

1978

'Time, Choice and Uncertainty', pp. 47–55, in T. Carlstein, D. Parkes and N. Thrift (Eds.), *Timing Space or Spacing Time, Vol. 1: Making Sense of Time*, London, Edward Arnold.

1979

a.   *Imagination and the Nature of Choice*, Edinburgh, The University Press, pp. x + 159.
b.   'On Hicks's Causality in Economics', *Greek Economic Review*, Vol. 1, pp. 43–55.
c.   *Capire l'economia* (Italian language edition of *Economics for Pleasure*), Fourth Printing, Milano, Fetrinelli, pp. 220.
d.   'Imagination, Formalism and Choice', pp. 19–31, in M. J. Rizzo (Ed.), *Time, Uncertainty and Disequilibrium*, Lexington, Massachusetts, D. C. Heath and Co.

1980

a.   'Imagination, Unknowledge and Choice', *Greek Economic Review*, Vol. 2 No. 2, 1980, pp. 95–110.
b.   'Evolution of Thought in Economics', *Banca Nazionale Del Lavoro, Quarterly Review*, March, pp. 15–27.

1981

'F. A. Hayek', pp. 234–261, in D. P. O'Brien and J. R. Presley (Eds.), *Pioneers of Modern Economics in Britain*, London, The Macmillan Press.

1982

a.   'Sir John Hicks's 'IS-LM: An Explanation': A Comment', *Journal of Post-Keynesian Economics*, Vol. 4 No. 3, 1982, pp. 435–438.

b.   'Means and Meaning in Economic Theory', *Scottish Journal of Political Economy*, Vol. 29 No. 3, 1982, pp. 223–234.

c.   'Comment', *Journal of Post-Keynesian Economics*, Vol. 5 No. 2, pp. 180–181.

d.   'Cantillon far ahead of his Time', pp. 765–779, in *Homenaje a Lucas Beltran*, Madrid, Editorial Moneda y Credito.

e.   'Foreword', pp. vii, viii, in R. F. Hebert and A. N. Link, *The Entrepreneur*, New York, Praeger Publishers.

1983

a.   'The Romantic Mountain and the Classic Lake: Alan Coddington's *Keynesian Economics*', *Journal of Post-Keynesian Economics*, Vol. 6 No. 2, pp. 241–257.

b.   'Levels of Simplicity in Keynes's Theory of Money and Employment', *South African Journal of Economics*, Vol. 51 No. 3, pp. 357–367.

c.   'A Student's Pilgrimage', *Banca Nazionale del Lavoro Quarterly Review*, No. 145, pp. 108–116.

d.   'Decisions, Process and the Market', *Journal of Economic Studies*, Vol. 10 No. 3, pp. 56–66.

e.   'The Bounds of Unknowledge', pp. 28–37, in J. Wiseman (Ed.), *Beyond Positive Economics?*, London and Basingstoke, The Macmillan Press.

f.   *The Years of High Theory: Invention and Tradition in Economic Thought, 1926–1939*, Cambridge Paperback Library, Cambridge, The University Press, pp. viii + 328.

1984

a.   'Comment on the paper by Randall Bausor and Malcolm Rutherford', *Journal of Post-Keynesian Economics*, Vol. 6 No. 3, pp. 388–393.

b.   'Foreword', p. xi, xii, in A. H. Shand, *The Capitalist Alternative: An Introduction to neo-Austrian Economics*, Brighton, Wheatsheaf Books.

c.   'To Cope with Time', pp. 69–79, in F. H. Stephen (Ed.), *Firms, Organization and Labour: Approaches to the Economics of Work Organization*, London and Basingstoke, The Macmillan Press.

1985

a.   'Keynes the Meeting-Point of History and Thought', in F. Poudon (et. al), *Les Écrits de Keynes* (Paris, Dunod), pp. 19–23.

b.   'Controlling Industrial Economies', *Kyklos*, Vol. 38 No. 1, pp. 120–122 (Review Article of S. F. Frowen (Ed.), *Controlling Industrial Economics: Essays in Honour of C. T. Saunders* (1983).)

1986

a.   'Markets, Entrepreneurs and Liberty', *History of Economic Thought Newsletter*, No. 36, Spring (Review Article on W. D. Leekie book of the same title).
b.   'The Origination of Choice', in I. M. Kirzner (Ed.), *Subjectivism, Intelligibility and Economic Understanding: Essays in Honour of Ludwig M. Lackman* (London, Macmillan).

1988

'Treatise, Theory and Time', in Rubio de Urquia (Ed.), *La Herencia de Keynes* (Madrid, Alianca Editorial).

1989

Business, Time and Thought (Collected Essays 1964–1988), Edited by S. F. Frowen, London, Macmillan.

Notes

1.   Book Reviews have only been included where they are either explicitly or tacitly Review Articles.
2.   The contents of Professor Shackle's three papers – previously Collections of Essays consist of the following papers listed above:
   Uncertainty in Economics (1955): 1939(a); 1945(a); 1946(a); 1947; 1949(b), (d), (e) and (f); 1950; 1951(a) and (b); 1952(c); and 1953, all papers.
   The Nature of Economic Thought (1966): 1955(b) and (d); 1958(g); 1959(c); 1960; 1961(b), (d), (e) and (f); 1962, all papers. To these Professor Shackle added four hitherto unpublished papers.
   Business, Time and Thought (1989): 1976(a); 1977; 1979(b); 1981; 1982(a), (b) and (d); 1983(a), (b), (c) and (e). To these one previously unpublished paper was added.

Name Index

Akerman, J. 14(n.1)
Andrews, P. W. S. 165
Armstrong, W. E. 84–5, 88–9

Böhm-Bawerk, E. von 219
Boulding, K. E. 170(n.3)

Carter, C. F. 14(n.1), 85, 89
Chamberlin, E. H. 219
Comte, A. 210
Cournot, A. 201, 206, 212, 218

Descartes, R. 26, 34
Domar, E. D. 102n, 219

Edgeworth, F. Y. 201, 206, 210
Ellsberg, D. 86–7
Euler, L. 209

Fisher, I. 170(n.3), 201, 206, 213–15
Frisch, R. 84(n.1), 200

Gallie, W. B. 14(n.1)
Gödel, K. 34

Harrod, R. 219
Hart, A. G. 103(n.3)
Hawtrey, R. G. 148, 210
Hayek, F. A. von
    and capital theory 219
    and the individual 51, 102n, 103(n.1),
        123(n.1)
    and monetary theory 138–43, 148
Hegel, G. W. F. 210
Hicks, J. R. 201, 215

Jeans, J. H. 240
Jevons, W. S. 86–7, 211

Kahn, R. F. 123(n.1), 124
Kalecki, M. 170(n.3)
Keirstead, B. 14(n.1)
Keynes, J. M.

and Cambridge tradition 210
on determinism vs. originative choice
    188
Grand Design of 193
on influence of Stock Exchange
    values 58(n.1)
on investment and income 123(n.1)
and marginal efficiency of capital
    170(n.3)
on Marshall 211–12
as a mathematician 206
and monetary theory 138–43, 213,
    215–18
multiplier principle of 124, 150,
    151(n.1), 154(n.1), 155
personal characteristics of 223
on probability 45, 216
on uncertainty 103(n.2), 212, 213,
    216, 217
on unemployment 217–18
Knight, F. H. 103(n.2)

Leibniz, G. W. 45, 216
Leontief, W. 194, 208, 219

Marshall, A.
    on evolutionary change 210–12
    and imperfect competition 218
    marginal principle of 192–3, 212, 235
    as a mathematician 201, 206
Morgenstern, O. 23, 86–7
Musgrave, R. A. 102n
Myrdal, G. 103(n.2)

Pareto, V. 201, 206, 236
Polanyi, M. 14(n.1)
Popper, K. 14(n.1), 23

Quesnay, F. 208

Robertson, D. H. 210
Robinson, J. 219
Rostow, W. 184

Sayers, R. S. 165

Subject Index

absorption, time rate of
  of G-essential resources 126, 127, 131–7
action schemes
  choice of 36–48, 72–81, 104
  sequels of 40–48
anticipation
  distress by 3, 6, 9–11, 18, 55–7, 105–8
  enjoyment by 3, 6, 9–11, 13, 18, 40–41, 55–7, 67–8, 105–8
Anticipations, Uncertainty and Dynamic Planning (Hart) 103(n.3)
ascendancy
  of sequels of action 42–3
  as variable of feeling 47
assimilation
  of events, into expectations 119–20
assumptions
  role of, in economic theories 224, 239

big bang hypothesis
  in cosmology 33
blueprints, investment
  defined 59, 109
  effect of surprises on 69–72, 118–20
  effect of time on 59–69, 79, 110–18, 120
business cycle *see* trade cycle

calendar-axes 30, 38
Cambridge tradition 210
capital
  marginal efficiency of 170–75
  marginal productivity of 146–8
capital-to-output ratio 219
Cartesian systems 30
causation
  choice and 31–3, 182–3
  vs. function 180–82
chance, games of 20
choice
  of action schemes 36–48, 72–81, 104
  between more than two assets 98–102, 109

between two assets 91–8
of blueprints 59–72, 109–20
and causation 31–3, 182–3
desiredness and 39–43, 47, 56, 105, 106
vs. determinism, in decision-making 7–9, 12–13, 18–23, 28–9, 33, 47, 179–94, 240
and free will 7–9, 13, 72
and history 31, 32, 35, 72, 77, 184–5, 207
possibility and 38–43, 187–8
process of, in individual 72–81, 186–7
see also decisions
'Classic and current notions of "measurable utility"' (Ellsberg)
  article in *Economic Journal* 86(n.1)
coefficient of contrast 81
coefficient of money transactions 138, 143, 145, 147
consumer-satisfaction 11–12
consumption
  of economy, defined 123
  form of Keynesian consumption function 227
  multiplier and 125, 137, 150–59
contrast, coefficient of 81
crises, dynamics of 123–37

decision intervals
  and interest rates 11–12
decisions
  determinism vs. originative choice in 7–9, 12–13, 18–23, 28–9, 33, 47, 179–94, 240
  effect of perfect foresight on 20, 23–4, 48, 185, 239
  effect of uncertainty on 6–7, 13, 22, 25, 41, 174
  guided by imagination 13, 18, 20–23, 179, 186, 188, 191
  to invest 58–81, 103–20 *passim*, 123–31, 160–76

'Suggestion for simplifying the theory of money, A' (Hicks)
article in *Economica* 217
suggestions
role of, in decision-making 33–4
supply curves
of instruments expected to yield uniform net returns in perpetuity 164, 175
short-period, of G-essential resources 125, 126–7, 131, 136
surprise, potential
cardinality of 82–90
and decision to invest 58–81, 108–20
in expectational dynamics of individual 53–8, 91, 104–8
for ratios of price changes between more than two assets 98–102
for ratios of price changes between two assets 91–8
as variable of feeling 47
surprises, actual
effect of, on expectations 69–72, 118–20
effect of, on investment 69–72, 119
effect of, on neo-classical value theory 210
effect of, on trade cycle 185
symbol-situations 73–7

Tableau economique (Quesnay) 208
tastes, of individuals 150, 186
taxation
effect of, on investment 166
technological advances
effect on economic theory 207, 210, 211, 230
theories, economic *see* economic theories
'Theory of investment decisions, A' (Shackle)
article in *Oxford Economic Papers* 53(n.1)
Theory of Value and Distribution, The (Euler) 209
thought, economic *see* economic theories
time
concept of, in economics 3–13 *passim*
dynamic 4, 16–17

effect of, on investment 59–67, 110–18, 120
expectational 4, 17
imaginary 4, 16, 17–18
inside view of 14, 15–16, 17, 24
measurement of 88–9
memory 4, 16, 18
and multiplier 151–6
outside view of 14–15, 16, 17, 24–6
as a space 14–15, 29
time-discounting of net returns 161–76 *passim*
as a transient present 15–16, 29–31
trade cycle
and change 185
monetary theories of 138–49
training of economists 235–42
transactions motive
for holding money 213, 215
Treatise on Money (Keynes) 138, 215
Treatise on Probability (Keynes) 216

uncertainty
bounded 22, 25
econometrics and 201–2, 240–41
effect of, on decisions generally 6–7, 13, 103, 174
of entrepreneur, regarding intentions of others 123, 125–6, 131
of focus gains and focus losses 41, 115–16
and frequency tables 84
importance of, in economic theories 239–40
Keynes on 103(n.2), 212, 213, 216, 217
Marshall on 211
of prospective yield of plant 127–37, 154, 160–76 *passim*
see also expectations; foresight, perfect; surprise, potential
'Uncertainty and inducements to invest' (Hart)
article in *Review of Economic Studies* 103(n.3)
unemployment
Keynes on 217–18
Uthwatt Committee 91, 101
utility
cardinality of 86–9